T0289235

The Arches Reader

National Park Readers Series
Edited by David Stanley

The Grand Teton Reader,
edited by Robert W. Righter

The Capitol Reef Reader,
edited by Stephen Trimble

The Glacier Park Reader,
edited by David Stanley

The Rocky Mountain National Park Reader,
edited by James H. Pickering

A Zion Canyon Reader,
edited by Nathan N. Waite and Reid L. Neilson

THE ARCHES READER

EDITED BY JEFFREY D. NICHOLS

The University of Utah Press
Salt Lake City

The Defiance House Man colophon is a registered trademark of the University of Utah Press. It is based on a four-foot-tall Ancient Puebloan pictograph (late PIII) near Glen Canyon, Utah.

Library of Congress Cataloging-in-Publication Data

Names: Nichols, Jeffrey D., editor.
Title: The Arches reader / edited by Jeffrey D. Nichols.
Other titles: National park readers.
Description: Salt Lake City : The University of Utah Press, [2024] | Series: National park readers series | Includes bibliographical references.
Identifiers: LCCN 2023048954 | ISBN 9781647691394 (paperback) | ISBN 9781647691400 (ebook)
Subjects: LCSH: Arches National Park (Utah)--Description and travel. | Canyonlands National Park (Utah)--Description and travel. | Arches National Park (Utah)--History--Literary collections.
Classification: LCC F832.A7 A73 2024 | DDC 979.2/58--dc23/eng/20231101
LC record available at https://lccn.loc.gov/2023048954

Cover artwork: *See America*, silkscreen by Frank S. Nicholson. Courtesy of the Library of Congress.

Errata and further information on this and other titles available at UofUpress.com.
Printed and bound in the United States of America.

CONTENTS

INTRODUCTION

Geology is the star attraction in many national parks, but Arches National Park reveals erosional wonders like no other place on earth. There's something thrilling and slightly unsettling about a big orange rock with a hole in its middle, or a ribbon of stone flung like a spider's thread from one rock face to another. At first your eyes might not accept that they are seeing blue sky or snow-capped mountains framed by stone. There are so many stony holes here of so many shapes and sizes that people spend years "hunting" unrecorded arches, quarreling over measurements and categories, and dreaming up original names. As I write, the official arch count is over two thousand, constituting the greatest concentration of arches on earth, but any exact number will be obsolete by the time you read this. And arches are only part of the story: water and wind over hundreds of millions of years have carved this sandstone desert into towers, fins, bluffs, and petrified sand dunes. As if evocative clouds had turned to stone, Arches formations resemble skyscrapers, gossiping people, marching soldiers, even elephants.

Like many contributors to this book, I am a transplanted easterner (from upstate New York). I fell in love with the high desert at first sight, on a 1972 vacation in the family station wagon. My father had a spontaneous whim to visit Mesa Verde, and the clear, dry air and tough, sparse piñon-juniper forest (not to mention the "lost cities") enchanted twelve-year-old me. But it took me a while to get back to the western desert. When I moved to Salt Lake City in 1989, Arches became a stop on periodic visits to Moab to hike and bike. Eventually, the park became part of my extended backyard. My wife Cheryl and I spent years daydreaming about building a getaway spot somewhere. Whenever I would become infatuated by a place (Bozeman! Point Reyes!), Cheryl would remind me of the Moab area with its embarrassment of beauty: the La Sal Mountains, the Colorado River, the Back of Beyond, and Arches National Park. "Red rocks," for short.

So we built a little straw-bale house at Pack Creek Ranch in 2006 (with neighbors like Ken and Jane Sleight and Edward Abbey's in-laws) and started to learn the land. We've visited Arches in many seasons, mostly on day trips in a car with family and friends (the kind of "windshield tourism" Abbey hated). Like so many others, we drive the familiar route past Park Avenue and out to the Windows, walk around the Wolfe cabin, puzzle at petroglyphs, and visit the world's most beautiful campground with views of the peaks of the La Sals erupting through the sandstone layers.

But the best experiences have come on foot, even sometimes by boat. Cheryl and I inched carefully along former Park Superintendent Bates Wilson's icy trail to Delicate Arch on a full-moon February night. A friend and I walked into the park through the cottonwoods and lush grass of Courthouse Wash from the trailhead near the Colorado River bridge, splashing in deep pools along the way. David Stanley (general editor of the National Park Readers series) and I found a roosting great horned owl in the Fiery Furnace, a heap of mouse bones and furry pellets marking the spot like the mouth of a troll's cave. On long, lazy floats down the Colorado "Daily" (a one-day river trip), we watched great blue herons fish the Arches-side bank and beavers slip into the red waters. In addition to its outrageous, oversized acts of erosion, Arches also offers quiet treasures that surprise as they unfold.

It's a relatively small park; the original national monument designated by President Herbert Hoover in 1929 under the auspices of the Antiquities Act comprised only 4,520 acres. The monument was divided into two noncontiguous sections, what are today called The Windows and Devil's Garden (not to be confused with the area that Alexander Ringhoffer called Devil's Garden, which is today called Klondike Bluffs; see the essay on Devil's Garden later in this volume). Franklin D. Roosevelt enlarged the monument to over thirty-three thousand acres in 1938, incorporating Klondike Bluffs; after a small change by Dwight Eisenhower, Lyndon Johnson more than doubled it in 1969. Congress made Arches a national park in 1971, with just over seventy-three thousand acres. In 1998 the Lost Spring

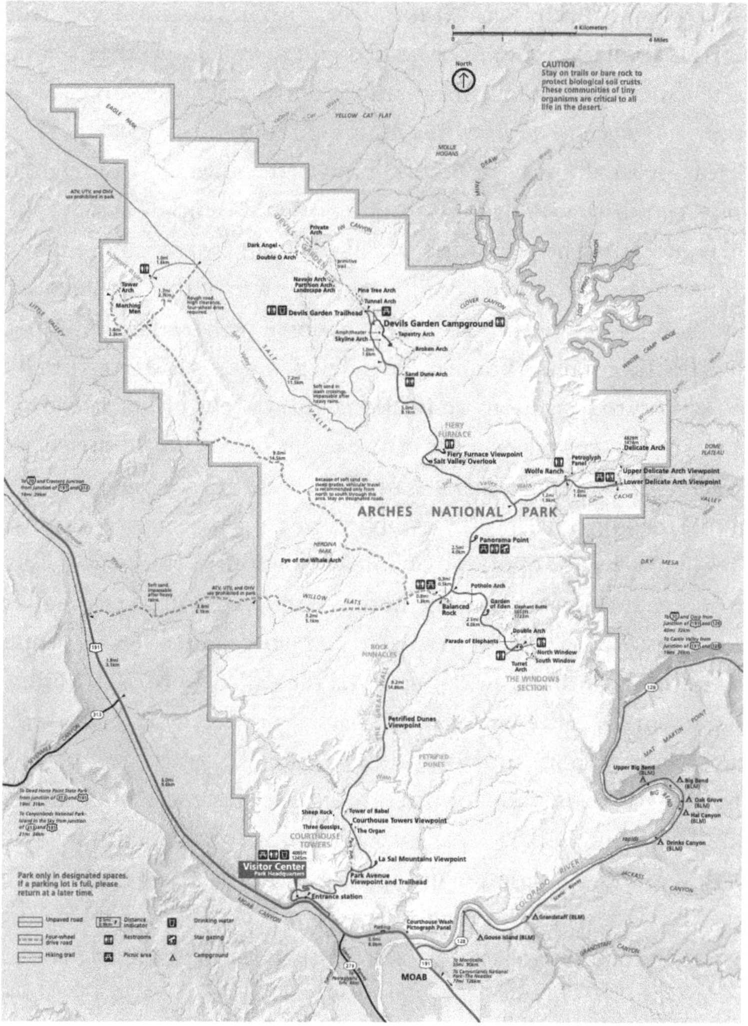

Arches National Park, 2021. Map courtesy of National Park Service.

Canyon addition brought the total to over seventy-six thousand acres, or about 119 square miles. The park today is bisected by a well-designed main road that allows visitors in cars to "do" the most spectacular sites in a day, and the vast majority of visitors don't get more than a few hundred yards from their vehicles.

Others, however, have come to know the park intimately, through years of employment, multiple visits, or residence. Arches has awed, inspired, and sometimes confused millions of people, and many have written about this place that has stirred their imaginations and shaped their lives. Some of their varied voices are represented in this anthology.[1]

The park has always been closely linked to the town of Moab, eight miles south. Arches has never had in-park lodging, and camping is still confined to only one place. The post-World War II uranium industry made the sleepy ranching and orchard town boom, and the growth of the middle class with its automobiles and vacations made the national park road trip an American staple. After the uranium boom collapsed in the 1970s, Moab reinvented itself as an "adventure recreation" destination, with dozens of hotels and restaurants serving hikers, bikers, river runners, and off-road thrill drivers. While many tent campers, trailer haulers, and RVers camp in the park, most people sleep in Moab or other nearby campsites and make day trips into Arches. The result may be one of the most complete identifications between gateway town and national park anywhere in the country. And since before the park was designated, Moabites have explored and worked there. Other people are drawn to the park from far away, either via the Park Service or as visitors, and end up staying. While a visit to Moab doesn't necessarily include a trip into Arches, a visit to Arches usually includes Moab.

This book begins with a piece by the writer most associated with Arches, Edward Abbey. Abbey spent two seasons in Arches as a ranger in the late 1950s, just as the monument's quiet, isolated early years were slipping away in the face of an enormous increase in park visitation, one aspect of America's automobile-obsessed postwar culture. Abbey shaped his journals into a moving, meditative, angry book, *Desert Solitaire,* that celebrates the wild desert but mourns its loss to what Abbey called "industrial tourism." Ironically, Abbey described the Arches he loved so well that the book became a bestseller, and masses of readers since have wanted to see "the most beautiful place on earth" for themselves.

Everyone who has written about Arches since 1968 has had to reckon with *Desert Solitaire*. Amy Irvine, a southern Utah native and environmental activist, answers Abbey chapter by chapter, beginning with his iconic "First Morning." Together, Abbey and Irvine set our stage for the park's wonders and the conundrum of seeking solitude in the face of industrial tourism.

The first main section of this book, "The Place of Rainbows," borrows a Hopi term for the Arches region.[2] This section features writers who focus on the physical landscape and non-human life. The proper scale of time in Arches is geological rather than biological. People have lived in the region for perhaps twelve thousand years, a blip in the hundreds of millions of years of water and wind required to shape the landscape we see today. The geological processes are ongoing, of course. Erosion never sleeps, and some arches have formed and others have collapsed in human time. Wall Arch, for example, fell in 1991, and several enormous pieces have recently split off Landscape Arch. But the extraordinary features we see now are more or less what humans have always seen. The sandstone layers that spawn arches were laid down between one hundred million and three hundred million years ago as sediments in a series of inland seas that filled and receded. Layers of salt between the sandstone flowed and bulged, deforming the sandstone into fractured domes. The Colorado River, which now marks the Park's southern boundary, began slicing through these layers about six million years ago. Millennia of flowing water, freeze-thaw cycles, and to a lesser extent wind, shaped the formations we now see. Most of the park's best-known features, including Delicate Arch, Balanced Rock, and the Fiery Furnace, are the eroded remnants of Entrada sandstone deposits from the Late Jurassic period.

The complicated sandstone stratigraphy around Arches also includes mineral elements with specific and disturbing uses. Pitchblende, later named uraninite, is a uranium-bearing ore that occurs in small amounts in many places throughout the Colorado Plateau. The discovery of these ores had momentous consequences for Moab and the history of the wider world.

Arches is more than rock, of course; it's also natural habitat that has changed enormously over the millennia. In the Mesozoic era, between 63 million and 230 million years ago, dinosaurs lived and died in swamps and shallow seas that once covered parts of the park. We can still see their fossilized bones and footprints.

Over the most recent centuries, the center of the Colorado Plateau where arches form has received about eight to ten inches of annual precipitation; temperatures reach over one hundred degrees Fahrenheit in the summer and can dip below zero in the winter. There is some running water; Salt Wash and Courthouse Wash flood in the spring and maintain trickles through most of the hottest summers. That water supports scattered growths of bunch grasses, flowers, shrubs, piñon pines, and junipers that can feed humans and other animals. Still, much of the terrain is bare rock or sand with scattered patches of soil, perfectly suited for certain reptiles, birds, amphibians, insects, mammals, and dozens of tough plants. Terry Tempest Williams closes this section of the book with a meditation on landscape and love at a place just downriver from the park.

The next section, "Living and Working in Arches," brings people into the story. In the stretch of human time before 1929 CE [common era], when Arches National Monument was established, this land meant other things beyond scenic wonder. The people we call Ancestral Puebloans and others recorded their presence on walls. We don't know for certain what those petroglyphs (images pecked into rock) and pictographs (painted on rock) meant to the artists or their cultures. The Ancestral Puebloans evidently left the area around 1300 CE, perhaps as a result of prolonged drought. Later Numic and Athabascan peoples also carved and painted figures on walls. Generations of Utes, Paiutes, Gosiutes, Shoshones, Diné (Navajo), Hopis, Zunis, and others used trails through the area for trade and travel across the broken Colorado Plateau.

We cannot be certain who was the first European or Euro-American to see the Arches region. Juan María Antonio Rivera came to the south bank of the Colorado at present-day Moab in 1765, but neither he nor any other Spanish explorer described the arches formations. The fur trappers and traders of the early nineteenth century didn't write about them either, even though they used a trail between New Mexico and California, misleadingly called the Old Spanish Trail (it was evidently blazed in the 1820s, after Mexican independence), that used the Moab ford. One French Canadian trapper, Denis Julien, left his name and date (June 9, 1844) on a fin in Devil's Garden, as he did in several other places across the Colorado Plateau.

In 1847, the first of thousands of religious exiles calling themselves members of the Church of Jesus Christ of Latter-day Saints arrived in the Great Salt Lake Valley, about two hundred miles north of Arches. In 1855, their president/prophet Brigham Young "called" a forty-man mission to plant a

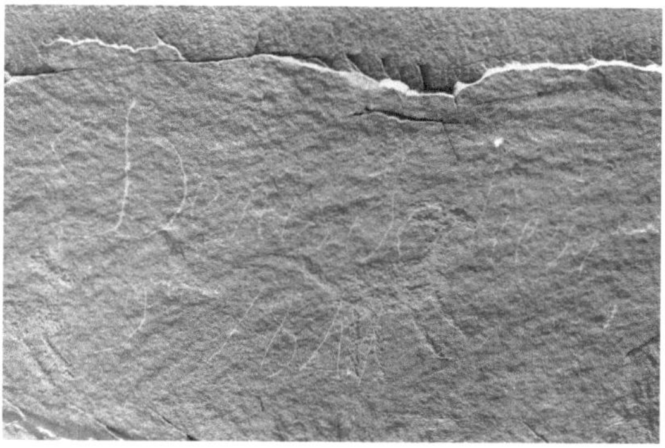

Denis Julien inscription, near Dark Angel arch. Photo courtesy of Arches NP/ Jim Capps, Jim Stiles, 1977.

colony in the valley to the south of Arches, across the Colorado and west of what they called the Elk Mountains (later called the La Sals). Before the first snow flew, Indigenous peoples drove the Mormon settlers out.

Probably the next new peoples to come to the Arches region were cowboys looking for bunch grasses and water for their herds; we don't know if any of them wrote about the striking landscape. One of the earliest ranchers was an African American named William Grandstaff, who may have grazed cattle in a beautiful side canyon on the south side of the Colorado River, just across from Arches, from the 1870s until about 1881. After decades of racist designations, that canyon now bears his last name. Other ranchers introduced cattle and sheep from the north side of the river.

By the 1880s a few dozen ranchers and farmers had settled in what they called "Spanish Valley" and founded the town of Moab at the northern (lower) end of that valley. Most settled on the south side of the river and used Courthouse Wash as part of the long trip to the settlements to the north. They also supplied beef and other commodities to the mining camps of western Colorado, which were easier to reach around the south end of the La Sals.

A few Euro-Americans have lived in what became the park. John Wesley Wolfe staked a homestead in 1898 in Salt Wash near Delicate Arch and lived with his son and, briefly, his daughter and her family, raising hogs, cattle, and vegetables while he prospected for gold. Arches continues to play a

Some visitors to Arches are moved to record their visit on stone. Moises Martinez may have been herding cattle or sheep. Photo courtesy of Arches NP/ Jim Capps, Jim Stiles, 1977

small role in the local grazing economy: ranchers move cattle from the mountains down to the desert in the fall and back again in the spring, sometimes using a historic driveway in Courthouse Wash. When the Denver and Rio Grande Western Railroad (D&RGW) finished an east-west route forty miles north of Moab in 1883, the north-south trail through Arches became a stage and wagon road connecting Moab to the tiny depot of Thompson.

The next section of the reader, "A Wonder for the World," introduces the federal government and the National Park Service as major players in the Arches story. A Hungarian-American prospector named Alexander Ringhoffer wandered into what he named "the Devil's Garden" (today's Klondike Bluffs) in 1922 and promoted its tourist potential, although it took until 1929 for the national monument to be designated. Some of today's Arches National Park was protected on paper but was virtually unmanaged and practically unvisited in the 1930s. The Park Service relied on Frank "Boss" Pinkley, superintendent of the Southwest National Monuments, to supervise Arches and twenty-six other units from his distant post at Casa Grande Ruins in Arizona. Pinkley commissioned Frank A. Beckwith, a polymathic newspaper editor with no formal scientific training, to lead an expedition to Arches in 1933. Beckwith bestowed lasting names on several features that would become famous, like Delicate Arch, Landscape Arch, and Balanced Rock, and called (in classic Western booster fashion) for tourist infrastructure.

Beckwith's message fit the development ethos of the Park Service's early leadership as well as the depression-fighting jobs programs of the New Deal. The year of Beckwith's report, 1934, marked the lowest recorded visitation ever at Arches: 275 people. Development at Arches came slowly, and so did the tourists. In 1937 annual visitors finally topped one thousand, only to fall back to six hundred or so during World War II. For the first few decades of the monument, a "custodian" or "superintendent" with (sometimes) a maintenance worker plus one full-time and a few seasonal rangers, struggled to manage the entire place. The first resident superintendent, Russell Mahan, was not appointed until 1948. Some of the most interesting writing about Arches comes from those sleepy days: the early superintendents' chatty, digressive monthly reports to their superiors. These reports describe a wide range of mundane duties, especially the never-ending maintenance of rough, rocky roads made slick by rain or snow and frequently washed out by floods. During the winter, park personnel might see fewer than a dozen visitors in a month (always meticulously reported). The New Deal brought Civilian Conservation Corps workers to the park, and they helped bridge the washes and pave the first roads. By the late 1940s national magazines had "discovered" the park, and the "adventure tourism" and uranium booms were just around the corner.

Bates Wilson became the best known of Arches' superintendents, and his long tenure (1949–1971) saw big changes: paved roads, a visitor center, a new entrance, and, most significantly, the growth of mass visitation. It seemed that everyone knew Bates and his stories, his Dutch-oven meals, and his parties. He hired Abbey, and Abbey turned his colleagues into characters in *Desert Solitaire.* Wilson helped implement Arches' share in "Mission 66," an ambitious Park Service effort to upgrade the system's infrastructure for its fiftieth anniversary. Meanwhile the state improved the north-south highway, now U.S. Route 191. In 1970, the federal government finished Interstate 70, which parallels the old D&RGW rail line. Arches and Moab had become relatively easy to reach. By the time Wilson retired, annual Arches visitation had topped two hundred thousand. In 2010 over 1 million came, and 2021 saw over 1.8 million visitors.

The rangers and superintendents spend much of their working days dealing with those human visitors. Perhaps their most important duty is safety. On a good day, the tens of thousands of people might suffer any number of ordinary misfortunes, but extreme heat and alluring rocks bring additional threats, as essays here document.

Of course, visitors to the park shape the place and how it is perceived just as do those who work there or write about it. James Swensen analyzes the iconic *Life* magazine cover of April 1953: Josef Muench's photo of Delicate Arch, a shot that has launched millions of imitators. People leave their marks in many ways, including in trail registries and notes of complaint. Every change in the park has brought debate, from those who want more protection for the landscape to ranchers and miners who fear for the loss of their livelihoods.

The Three Gossips, the Marching Men, Balanced Rock, the Fiery Furnace, and the distant La Sal mountains attract plenty of visitor attention. But the arches are obviously the main focus of a park visit. National parks don't just preserve their features and wildlife; often, they actively manage them, like elk or wolves in Yellowstone. Sometimes, visitors and Park Service staff worry about the fragility of Arches' iconic features. There are reasons for their concerns; the very existence of arches, towers, and fins are physical proof of the remarkable powers of erosion on sandstone. Delicate Arch has long been a subject of particular concern, perhaps partly because of the name (did people worry that it might collapse when it was called Schoolmarm's Bloomers?), but mostly because of its beauty and prominence. Delicate has been featured on Utah license plates and on a 2014 quarter-dollar coin. No arch gets more attention than Delicate, and no arch is the subject of more worry.

By the 1970s, it was clear that Arches' quiet days were not coming back. The park was more popular every year, at the same time as contests over Western public lands were heating up. The crowds pose the same problems that plague other beloved parks: litter, air pollution, crime, crowded roads, lack of parking, full campsites; and conversely, demands for limits and pleas for restraint. Hikers trample the fragile biological (formerly called cryptobiotic) soils and scrawl their initials into the rock or across petroglyphs. One of the most striking petroglyphs, known as the Courthouse Wash panel, was badly defaced in 1980. Like parks around the country, Arches closed in March 2020 during the COVID-19 pandemic. When it reopened, the parking lots reached capacity in less than three hours. Park Service officials have repeatedly investigated possible solutions to the dilemma of popularity, including a shuttle system, entrance limits, and expanded parking. Each idea (carefully and expensively researched) has its advocates and virulent opponents. As of this writing, the Park has implemented a system of reservations and timed entry (i.e., a set number of vehicles in a set period) during peak hours of peak seasons. One has only to follow Arches' official Facebook page to see the sometimes-angry responses to this initiative.

The last section of this book, "Imagining Arches," mixes poetry and fiction with narrative. Those are far from all the genres that feature Arches. The park and its surroundings are so dramatic they have furnished settings for many movies and television shows, including 1988's *Indiana Jones and the Last Crusade* and 1990's *Thelma and Louise.*[3] Terry Tempest Williams closes this section, and the volume as a whole, with a reminder of what it means to belong to a place.

Arches National Park is beset by the challenges that face the entire NPS system—and the planet. Climate change, overcrowding, and vandalism may transform this place so beloved by so many. But the holes in rocks, the fins and buttes, and the breathtaking spans endure (and change), and they will continue to awe and inspire. Come explore Arches for yourself.

Notes

1 Documents are reproduced as they originally appeared (with a handful of exceptions), without using [sic].

2 In Hopi, *Pavayoykasi.* Richard Stoffle et al., "Ethnographic Overview and Assessment for Arches National Park" (Tucson: Bureau of Applied Research in Anthropology, University of Arizona, 2016), 114.

3 "Film History," Moab to Monument Valley Film Commission, https://www.filmmoab.com/film-history.

1

The First Morning (1968)

Edward Abbey

Edward Abbey was born in Pennsylvania in 1927 and first saw the Southwest from the open door of a boxcar in 1944. He fell in love with the landscape and spent the rest of his life writing essays and novels, mostly about the desert southwest. In 1956 and 1957 he worked as a seasonal ranger in what was then Arches National Monument. The memoir and essay collection that he wrote about those years, Desert Solitaire, *has come to be considered a classic.*

It seems appropriate to give Abbey the first word. I suspect that he would be pleased.

This is the most beautiful place on earth.

There are many such places. Every man, every woman, carries in heart and mind the image of the ideal place, the right place, the one true home, known or unknown, actual or visionary. A houseboat in Kashmir, a view down Atlantic Avenue in Brooklyn, a gray gothic farmhouse two stories high at the end of a red dog road in the Allegheny Mountains, a cabin on the shore of a blue lake in spruce and fir country, a greasy alley near the Hoboken waterfront, or even, possibly, for those of a less demanding sensibility, the world to be seen from a comfortable apartment high in the tender, velvety smog of Manhattan, Chicago, Paris, Tokyo, Rio or Rome—there's no limit to the human capacity for the homing sentiment. Theologians, sky pilots, astronauts have even felt the appeal of home calling to them from up above, in the cold black outback of interstellar space.

For myself I'll take Moab, Utah. I don't mean the town itself, of course, but the country which surrounds it—the canyonlands. The slickrock desert. The red dust and the burnt cliffs and the lonely sky—all that which lies beyond the end of the roads.

The choice became apparent to me this morning when I stepped out of a Park Service housetrailer—my caravan—to watch for the first time in my life the sun come up over the hoodoo stone of Arches National Monument.

I wasn't able to see much of it last night. After driving all day from Albuquerque—450 miles—I reached Moab after dark in cold, windy, clouded weather. At park headquarters north of town I met the superintendent and the chief ranger, the only permanent employees, except for one maintenance man, in this particular unit of America's national park system. After coffee they gave me a key to the housetrailer and directions on how to reach it; I am required to live and work not at headquarters but at this one-man station some twenty miles back in the interior, on my own. The way I wanted it, naturally, or I'd never have asked for the job.

Leaving the headquarters area and the lights of Moab, I drove twelve miles farther north on the highway until I came to a dirt road on the right, where a small wooden sign pointed the way: Arches National Monument Eight Miles. I left the pavement, turned east into the howling wilderness. Wind roaring out of the northwest, black clouds across the stars—all I could see were clumps of brush and scattered junipers along the roadside. Then another modest signboard:

WARNING: QUICKSAND
DO NOT CROSS WASH
WHEN WATER IS RUNNING

The wash looked perfectly dry in my headlights. I drove down, across, up the other side and on into the night. Glimpses of weird humps of pale rock on either side, like petrified elephants, dinosaurs, stone age hobgoblins. Now and then something alive scurried across the road: kangaroo mice, a jackrabbit, an animal that looked like a cross between a raccoon and a squirrel—the ringtail cat. Farther on a pair of mule deer started from the brush and bounded obliquely through the beams of my lights, raising puffs of dust which the wind, moving faster than my pickup truck, caught and carried ahead of me out of sight into the dark. The road, narrow and rocky, twisted sharply left and right, dipped in and out of tight ravines, climbing by degrees toward a summit which I would see only in the light of the coming day.

Snow was swirling through the air when I crossed the unfenced line and passed the boundary marker of the park. A quarter-mile beyond I found the ranger station—a wide place in the road, an informational display under a lean-to shelter, and fifty yards away the little tin government housetrailer where I would be living for the next six months.

A cold night, a cold wind, the snow falling like confetti. In the lights of the truck I unlocked the housetrailer, got out bedroll and baggage and moved in. By flashlight I found the bed, unrolled my sleeping bag, pulled off my boots and crawled in and went to sleep at once. The last I knew was the shaking of the trailer in the wind and the sound, from inside, of hungry mice scampering around with the good news that their long lean lonesome winter was over—their friend and provider had finally arrived.

This morning I awake before sunrise, stick my head out of the sack, peer through a frosty window at a scene dim and vague with flowing mists, dark fantastic shapes looming beyond. An unlikely landscape.

I get up, moving about in long underwear and socks, stooping carefully under the low ceiling and lower doorways of the housetrailer, a machine for living built so efficiently and compactly there's hardly room for a man to breathe. An iron lung it is, with windows and venetian blinds.

The mice are silent, watching me from their hiding places, but the wind is still blowing and outside the ground is covered with snow. Cold as a tomb, a jail, a cave; I lie down on the dusty floor, on the cold linoleum sprinkled with mouse turds, and light the pilot on the butane heater. Once this thing gets going the place warms up fast, in a dense unhealthy way, with a layer of heat under the ceiling where my head is and nothing but frigid air from the knees down. But we've got all the indispensable conveniences: gas cookstove, gas refrigerator, hot water heater, sink with running water (if the pipes aren't frozen), storage cabinets and shelves, everything within arm's reach of everything else. The gas comes from two steel bottles in a shed outside; the water comes by gravity flow from a tank buried in a hill close by. Quite luxurious for the wilds. There's even a shower stall and a flush toilet with a dead rat in the bowl. Pretty soft. My poor mother raised five children without any of these luxuries and might be doing without them yet if it hadn't been for Hitler, war and general prosperity.

Time to get dressed, get out and have a look at the lay of the land, fix a breakfast. I try to pull on my boots but they're stiff as iron from the cold. I light a burner on the stove and hold the boots upside down above the flame until they are malleable enough to force my feet into. I put on a coat and step outside. Into the center of the world, God's navel, Abbey's country, the red wasteland.

The sun is not yet in sight but signs of the advent are plain to see. Lavender clouds sail like a fleet of ships across the pale green dawn; each cloud, planed flat on the wind, has a base of fiery gold. Southeast, twenty miles by line of sight, stand the peaks of the Sierra La Sal, twelve to thirteen thousand feet above sea level, all covered with snow and rosy in the morning sunlight. The air is dry and clear as well as cold; the last fogbanks left over from last night's storm are scudding away like ghosts, fading into nothing before the wind and the sunrise.

The view is open and perfect in all directions except to the west where the ground rises and the skyline is only a few hundred yards away. Looking toward the mountains I can see the dark gorge of the Colorado River five or six miles away, carved through the sandstone mesa, though nothing of the river itself down inside the gorge. Southward, on the far side of the river, lies the Moab valley between thousand-foot walls of rock, with the town of Moab somewhere on the valley floor, too small to be seen from here. Beyond the Moab valley is more canyon and tableland stretching away to the Blue Mountains fifty miles south. On the north and northwest I see the Roan Cliffs and the Book Cliffs, the two-level face of the Uinta Plateau. Along the foot of those cliffs, maybe thirty miles off, invisible from where I stand, runs U.S. 6–50, a major east-west artery of commerce, traffic and rubbish, and the main line of the Denver–Rio Grande Railroad. To the east, under the spreading sunrise, are more mesas, more canyons, league on league of red cliff and arid tablelands, extending through purple haze over the bulging curve of the planet to the ranges of Colorado—a sea of desert.

Within this vast perimeter, in the middle ground and foreground of the picture, a rather personal demesne, are the 33,000 acres of Arches National

Monument of which I am now sole inhabitant, usufructuary, observer and custodian.

What are the Arches? From my place in front of the housetrailer I can see several of the hundred or more of them which have been discovered in the park. These are natural arches, holes in the rock, windows in stone, no two alike, as varied in form as in dimension. They range in size from holes just big enough to walk through to openings large enough to contain the dome of the Capitol building in Washington, D.C. Some resemble jug handles or flying buttresses, others natural bridges but with this technical distinction: a natural bridge spans a watercourse—a natural arch does not. The arches were formed through hundreds of thousands of years by the weathering of the huge sandstone walls, or fins, in which they are found. Not the work of a cosmic hand, nor sculptured by sand-bearing winds, as many people prefer to believe, the arches came into being and continue to come into being through the modest wedging action of rainwater, melting snow, frost, and ice, aided by gravity. In color they shade from off-white through buff, pink, brown and red, tones which also change with the time of day and the moods of the light, the weather, the sky.

Standing there, gaping at this monstrous and inhuman spectacle of rock and cloud and sky and space, I feel a ridiculous greed and possessiveness come over me. I want to know it all, possess it all, embrace the entire scene intimately, deeply, totally, as a man desires a beautiful woman. An insane wish? Perhaps not—at least there's nothing else, no one human, to dispute possession with me.

The snow-covered ground glimmers with a dull blue light, reflecting the sky and the approaching sunrise. Leading away from me the narrow dirt road, an alluring and primitive track into nowhere, meanders down the slope and toward the heart of the labyrinth of naked stone. Near the first group of arches, looming over a bend in the road, is a balanced rock about fifty feet high, mounted on a pedestal of equal height; it looks like a head from Easter Island, a stone god or a petrified ogre.

Like a god, like an ogre? The personification of the natural is exactly the tendency I wish to suppress in myself, to eliminate for good. I am here not only to evade for a while the clamor and filth and confusion of the cultural apparatus but also to confront, immediately and directly if it's possible, the bare bones of existence, the elemental and fundamental, the bedrock which sustains us. I want to be able to look at and into a juniper tree, a piece of quartz, a vulture, a spider, and see it as it is in itself, devoid of all humanly ascribed qualities, anti-Kantian, even the categories of scientific description. To meet God or Medusa face to face, even if it means risking everything human in myself. I dream of a hard and brutal mysticism in which the naked self merges with a non-human world and yet somehow survives still intact, individual, separate. Paradox and bedrock.

Well—the sun will be up in a few minutes and I haven't even begun to make coffee. I take more baggage from my pickup, the grub box and cooking gear, go back in the trailer and start breakfast. Simply breathing, in a place like this, arouses the appetite. The orange juice is frozen, the milk slushy with ice. Still chilly enough inside the trailer to turn my breath to vapor. When the first rays of the sun strike the cliffs I fill a mug with steaming coffee and sit in the doorway facing the sunrise, hungry for the warmth.

Suddenly it comes, the flaming globe, blazing on the pinnacles and minarets and balanced rocks, on the canyon walls and through the windows in the sandstone fins. We greet each other, sun and I, across the black void of ninety-three million miles. The snow glitters between us, acres of diamonds almost painful to look at. Within an hour all the snow exposed to the sunlight will be gone and the rock will be damp and steaming. Within minutes, even as I watch, melting snow begins to drip from the branches of a juniper nearby; drops of water streak slowly down the side of the trailerhouse.

I am not alone after all. Three ravens are wheeling near the balanced rock, squawking at each other and at the dawn. I'm sure they're as delighted by the return of the sun as I am and I wish I knew the language. I'd sooner exchange ideas with the birds on earth than learn to carry on intergalactic communications with some obscure race of humanoids on a satellite planet from the world of Betelgeuse. First things first. The ravens cry out in husky voices, blue-black wings flapping against the golden sky. Over my shoulder comes the sizzle and smell of frying bacon.

That's the way it was this morning.

2

The First Morning, A Reply (2018)

Amy Irvine

Amy Irvine is a seventh-generation Utahn. A former wildlands firefighter, she has worked for the National Park Service and the Southern Utah Wilderness Alliance while writing for many environmental publications. She is the author of the prize-winning memoir, Trespass: Living at the Edge of the Promised Land.

Hey, Mr. Abbey, can you hear me down there? This yolk of sun has broken on a horizon sawed in two by saguaros and I've hopscotched my way through crypto and cacti, sidestepped a sidewinder, and given two middle fingers to an Air Force jet that buzzed me while my pants were down to pee on the playa. And now I'm squatting graveside in this lower Sonoran desert that is your resting place—a desert that has, thank the horned gods, not succumbed to the *Mad Max* lunacy in Moab.

We should talk. About the redrock country of Utah. *Desert Solitaire* was published fifty years ago this year, and as timeless as that book is, things are changing in ways even your prescient, nimble mind could not have imagined.

I'm going to sit here a minute and take in the surroundings. This is a desert more soft and yielding than those of southern Utah, one less feverish in color, less tortuous in form. It's a bit easier to breathe here, isn't it? This place doesn't excite—not the way canyon country does—the extremes in our nature. And it holds the whole of the borderlands—both sides—denying our tendency toward sharp stark divisions and dumbed-down dualities. So it's interesting, Mr. Abbey, that you chose here to lie *in situ*—given your aversion to immigration. Then again, maybe you wanted to return to Arches for a perennial season—but the park's tumescent popularity dissuaded. After all, you predicted rightly that the solitude you found there once upon a time was a much-diminished resource; if it was going, going, it's now nearly gone. In Arches, your bones could not possibly turn to dust in silence.

And that's why I am here today. To talk to you about solitude. Both the lack of it and the need. You see, it's getting pretty crowded, even in Utah, where public lands once felt infinite. I wonder if we know anymore what your definition of the word even means—the feeling that is not loneliness but "loveliness and a quiet exaltation."

So I hope you'll come up and sit with me. For we must chew on this notion of what solitude was, and now is. I'd suggest a walk—knowing we'd both love to roam under this honeycomb of sky that drips early morning gold onto spindly arms of ocotillo, through the pale pink translucence of jackrabbit ears. But I'm guessing that's a lot to ask at this point, given your twenty-nine-year repose. Why don't we just sit, dig our heels into these still-cool volcanic ball bearings that masquerade as soil. I promise to seek some semblance of restraint. It won't be easy. The questions, the concerns—they threaten to rush from my body like a river freed from a blown-up dam.

Tell you what. Let's start with what is panoramic, and political. How about I rant for a bit, before working down to what is personal. And then we keep going. By nightfall, let's hope we hit bedrock—that naked, common ground.

By the way, I covered my tracks. If word got out, the GPS plot points would be posted on the Internet (long story, that) and you'd never know another moment of posthumous peace. Rest assured I got here by stealth, and now I'm sweaty, squatted, and waiting on the parched, prickly kind of land we both love. The shadows of vultures cut across my skin. They think I'm dead but never have I been so alive! Because despite what seems like increasingly dark times for the planet, these wild places persist. Places that exfoliate our neuroses. That refuse to coddle our compulsions. That remind us, in these times of profound greed, what we really need.

About Moab: you can probably imagine the jacked-up monster trucks, maybe even the Razors—these golf carts on steroids, the least sexy form of transportation known to man. But I bet you can't fathom the BASE jumpers—that's right, people now don shiny, baggy disco suits and leap off the tallest red cliffs like flying squirrels. There are also beefed-up all-terrain bikes that can circle the White Rim in a day, if you've got the quads for the job. And those delicious, hidden swimming holes in Millcreek Canyon? Some days the Bureau of Land Management has to close off access—because several hundred people are already writhing in them amid a thick scrim of sunscreen, Jaeger, and Red Bull. The entire city—plus the surrounding valley, Behind the Rocks, and beyond—emits an ever-present belch of engines. They shine Lycra and sweat caffeine. As for Arches—no matter where you stand in the park, you can hear the steady roar of it all. Everywhere you look there are these hyped-up, tricked-out, uber-fit, machine-like humans that pump, grind, climb, soar, and scramble through the desert so fast they're just a muscled blur. The land's not the thing, it's the buzz.

So there's work to be done. Our public lands—the West's de facto wilderness, its national parks and monuments—they are endangered in ways we never conceived of. Utah is in the worst shape—so many of its incomparable wildlands were protected within two of the nation's newest national monuments but our so-called Commander-in-Chief has filleted each one, leaving only the stark bones in custody. This dismemberment of the Bears Ears and Grand Staircase-Escalante, two places you knew and loved, represents the largest maiming of public lands' protection in the nation's history.[1]

This means the green light is brighter than ever for the usual suspects of industry and motorized yahoo-ism, but the land is threatened by our ilk, the muscle-powered outdoor wanderers, too. Which is to say you, Mr. Abbey, may have developed whole fleets—generations' worth—of desert defenders, but now they're out there en masse, bumping into one another on the very ground on which you taught them to go lightly and alone. They are as much the problem as they are the solution, and it's hard to know how we don't divvy that down the middle, into us and them, right and wrong.

Your headstone says, "No Comment," but I'm hoping to discuss what we do next. You should know up front that I'm admiring, but not starstruck.

You got some things right, but you got other things wrong. Like calling the desert "Abbey's country." Can you imagine, in my own book about Utah, if I had called it "Amy's country"? I could have justified it; my family has been there for seven generations and counting. Yet even with such credentials the clan of my surname doesn't get to call it *ours*—because it's all stolen property: whatever the forefathers didn't snatch from the region's Native Americans on one occasion, they took from Mexico on another. But that's what the white man does. He comes in after the fact and lifts his leg on someone else's turf. You, sir, were no different.

Another thing: there'll be no chumminess today. I won't be calling you Ed, or Cactus Ed—although your fans do. They have good reason for assuming familiarities. When *Desert Solitaire* was published in 1968, you crowbarred open the American consciousness and the red raw desert strode right in. Like a cocklebur caught in a coyote's tail, you went with it—indistinguishable from all the convoluted canyons, scoured-out washes, mesas tiered like wedding cakes, mercurial creeks, rasping whiskers of bunchgrass, and the obsidian objections of ravens. There were also those geologic, gymnastic backbends—your beloved arches.

The New Yorker called your book an "American masterpiece." And sure enough, by the time the ragweed, dust, and scree of those essays settled, all of what you had to say took up some serious psychic real estate. You, Mr. Abbey, still lurk there. Like Hitchcock shuffling through his own film, one might not even notice you. But you're present all right, even as you bask in the director's chair. *Desert Solitaire* framed the American West through your lens, and so we see through the glass brightly: the Utah desert is not just a place to explore, not just a resource to exploit. It is a body—both politic and erotic. In every way it's scandalous.

Your claiming of Utah's desert outback taught an entire nation what it means to be in collective possession of a place. At the same time you taught us that one's interest in national lands is not a given—although the idea of it certainly is. It is only truly ours after we have gotten out of the car and wandered far enough off the trail to get lost and use up our last drop of water. Only after we've been out enough times—to draw blood, fry skin, write eulogies, pull stakes, see ghosts, and duct tape a flapping sole—should we feel in possession of them. But those of us who have done our time out there know this is the mirage, the trick of light on water that is actually scoured sand. It's the rough country, after all, that's in possession of us and not the other way around.

Look, it's early. But I've primed the old Coleman and the coffee is on.

Note

1 President Bill Clinton proclaimed the Grand Staircase–Escalante National Monument in September 1996 under the auspices of the Antiquities Act of 1906. President Barack Obama used the same authority to designate the Bears Ears National Monument (after consultation with and lobbying by a coalition of Tribes with ancestral links to the place) in December 2016. By executive order, President Donald Trump reduced Bears Ears by about 85 percent in December 2017, and Grand Staircase–Escalante by about half. In October 2021, President Joe Biden reinstated the boundaries of both monuments.

PART I

THE PLACE OF RAINBOWS

3

A Natural Bridge in Utah (1898)

Arthur Winslow

The following article appears to be the first scientific notice of the sandstone formations in the Arches region. Like everyone since, Arthur Winslow, state geologist of Kansas, tried to account for what causes these extraordinary holes in rocks. His emphasis on "wind erosion" is exaggerated; as a friend once said during an arch-making argument, "wind don't do shit!"

The remarkable natural bridge[1] illustrated in this article has, so far as I know, never been called attention to before, and is, therefore, entitled to rank as a new discovery among the curiosities of nature. It is an object rivaling the celebrated natural bridge of Virginia in magnitude and even exceeding that classic in interest when one considers its probable origin.

The view was taken in southeastern Utah not far from Moab, on the Grand River, in the midst of the great arid region lying west of the Rocky Mountains and some fifty miles from any railway. It was not my good fortune to be able to visit the locality myself, but the prints were obtained by me from the original photographer in Moab, when on a somewhat hurried return from a mine examination in the Blue Mountains to the south. The dimensions of the bridge, as estimated by the photographer, are about 500 feet in span and about 150 feet in height. A comparison of the bridge with figures shown in the original photograph in the right-hand corner and with the tree growth near by indicates that these dimensions are quite possible.

The bridge is, in all probability, a monstrous product of wind erosion. The rock appears to be one of the friable Mesozoic sandstones which are

Landscape Arch and person (prior to 1991 rockfall). Photo courtesy of Arches NP.

widely exposed in this region. Other examples of wind action...were seen by me while travelling through the country, so located that no other cause could be assigned. Strong and prolonged winds are frequent here, as anyone who has sojourned in that country can testify to his misery. The sands carried by these winds are whirled about in the depressions of the rocks, and excavate wind pot-holes in the friable sandstones with great rapidity. A wall or slab of such rock is by degrees entirely penetrated, giving rise to the so-called window rocks which are frequently seen in isolated buttes high above the surrounding level. Our natural bridge, I conclude, is simply an extreme or abnormal enlargement of such a 'window.' Possibly some water channel may have assisted in the process, but the view does not indicate this, but shows the bridge to be high above the main water course. The dimensions of the bridge, or rather the shape of the space covered by it, are also against this idea, as the ordinary channel cut by a stream through rock is deep and narrow.

Note

1 Accepted convention holds that a "bridge" spans water; Winslow writes about an "arch," one which is today known as Landscape Arch.

4

Geology of Arches (1934)

Joseph C. Anderson

Joseph C. Anderson was an assistant to Frank A. Beckwith in the Arches National Monument Scientific Expedition of 1933–1934. In this excerpt, Anderson describes some geologic processes that created Arches' spectacular geography, as well as some dinosaur fossils.

The Arches National Monument, consisting of three closely related areas, covering approximately 7500 acres of land is located in the south-central part of Grand County, Utah.

Situated as it is in the disturbed area flanking the La Sal Mountains the National Monument is difficult to reach as only low-grade desert roads lead from the main highways into the vicinity, and from the ends of these long hikes or horseback trips are required to reach the attractions in the monument proper. For this reason very few people outside of the nearby settlements are acquainted with the spectacular erosion forms to be seen, which consist of numerous sandstone arches, cliffs, pinnacles, vertical slabs and badland erosion. Moab which is the nearest town, and the County seat of Grand County lies about eight miles south.

The present investigation was begun in December 1933 and completed in April 1934, as a project, with appropriation from the Federal Civil Works Administration, and under the direction of the National Park Service through Zion National Park.

Instructions required reconnaissance investigation in archeology, topography and geology. For the purpose of this report the results of geologic reconnaissance only will be treated.

Previous Work

While there is no published work on the Arches, parts of the region have been covered by several different publications. The most recent reports on the area and those covering the immediate vicinity came as a result of the oil prospecting activity around Moab in recent years....

Physical Conditions

The topography varies radically over different parts of the area, each of the three divisions having distinct characteristics. The section known as The Arches is a northeast-southwest trending string of narrow mesa rock lands dropping off to steep cliffs on all sides, and the tops of the mesas are inaccessible because of the vertical walled cliffs which are in no place cut low enough for ascent. Around the cliff mesa lands are low rolling sandstone hills which on the north side break off and dip moderately toward the main drainage in that direction known as Salt Wash.

Situated along the north rim of the Salt Valley Anticline is the area known as The Devil's Garden, where the massive sandstones have been fractured and eroded into long rib-like slabs which stand closely spaced and at times alone in low sandy flats. These vertical slabs attain heights estimated at 350 feet.

The Yellow-Cat section presents an entirely different aspect. Here high buttes are weathered into typical badland forms. The greatest difference in elevation at this place amounts to more than 500 feet.

The vegetations [*sic*] is in keeping with the climate of the area which is arid. Black brush, junipers and the two-needle pinion represents the most abundant of the vegetation, though there are occasional clumps of cottonwood, scrub oak and willows where conditions are favorable. There is one characteristic and unique tree that deserves special consideration. In the summer it dots the landscape with patches of bright green—it is the Single-leafed ash (Fraxinus anomola). In protected places where over-grazing by sheep has not exterminated them, there are numerous flowering annuals of brilliant and varied hues. And, of course, there is the usual large number of cactus and yucca characteristic of desert regions.

Stratigraphy

Due to the almost total absence of fossils in the rock formations of the Arches National Monument, the stratigraphy has been determined almost entirely on stratigraphic position and lithology. The oldest rock formation in the area is Triassic Chinle, which is exposed in the bottom of Salt Wash in the east end of the Arches area, where it forms a steep slope from the base of vertical Wingate cliffs to the bottom of the canyon. Above the Wingate which was not measured, but estimated at 250 to 300 feet, occurs a series of lavender colored, coarse grained sandstones and some thin shale beds that form a stepping platform up to the base of the Navajo Sandstone. This sandstone has been identified as the Kayenta formation because of its lithologic characteristics and position between two easily identified formations. Its thickness was estimated at 225 feet.

The Navajo Sandstone which forms the gently sloping platform on which the arch-building formations rest is a light cream to buff, heavily cros[s]-bedded formation whose thickness was determined by alidade observations at 390 feet.

The contact between the Navajo and Carmel formations was chosen where the cream-colored sands change definitely to the deep brown-red color, characteristic of the Carmel sediments. This formation while not measured is 60 to 70 feet thick, and exhibits a crinkly condition that as yet has not been explained. The crinkling has distorted the overlying Entrada Sandstone and makes definite contact difficult to define.

It is impossible to measure exactly the thickness of the Entrada Sandstone in the area, but a close calculation from alidade observations indicates that there is 380 feet exposed at the Arches and at the Devil's Garden.

The formation is massive, generally buff cross-bedded sandstone, differing from the Navajo in that it is a darker buff with cross-bedding much less extensive and sweeping in character. Numerous small cavities occur along bedding planes and give a honeycombed effect to the surface of an exposure. The upper 50 or 75 feet of this formation is white, coarser grained, unevenly cemented sandstone.

Resting on the slightly undulating surface of the Entrada Sandstone is the Summerville formation, a thin gritty shale 32 feet thick, composed of alternate layers of red, greenish and white shale and impure sandstone. Measurement of the formation was made with a hand-level some three miles west of Willow Springs in the unsurveyed area of T 24 S, R 21 E. The Summerville occurs as a thin band in the topography below heavy ledges of Salt Wash Sandstone and above long gentle platforms of Entrada Sandstone, or as long snaky ridges on the Entrada which forms the 'slick-rock' bench around Willow Springs and southeast and west of Yellow-Cat Knolls.

The Morrison formation composed of sandstone and shales, is exposed in the Yellow-Cat district to the extent of 500 feet. The lower part, essentially layers of heavy cross-bedded, often conglomeritic sandstone with occasional shale breaks is known as the Salt Wash member of the Morrison. The upper shale beds are variegated gray, green, lavender and pink, eroded into intricately complicated topographic designs. The formations just described of Morrison age contain abundant fossil remains of dinosaur bones. Known bone deposits occur within a hundred feet of the base and range some 300 feet above. Eroded fragments of silicified bone occur widle [*sic*] over the surface and in places are so thickly strewn as to almost completely cover the ground. Embedded bones occur one or two at a place and do not seem to be with a complete skeleton, but there is little doubt that careful search would disclose more or less complete deposits.

The Dakota sandstone and younger formations have not been identified within the boundaries, but occur in close proximity to the north end of the Yellow-Cat section and on the east end of the Devil's Garden where the formations dip steeply and fault, throwing beds of Mancos Shale in contact with the formation.

Structural Relationships

The warping and folding that accompanied the uplifting of the La Sal Mountains is no doubt the cause of the structural relief that made possible the unique erosional forms to be seen in the area. The Arches are located on the north flank of the Courthouse Syncline, on the west side of the Colorado River. The rocks dip gently to the westward and to both sides forming an open anticlinal structure rising toward the nearby mountains.

At the west end the dips abruptly change, reverse their trend and become a part of the Salt Valley Anticline Structure.

The Devil's Garden owes its grotesque erosion forms directly to the fracturing or vertical jointing of the massive Entrada Sandstone in the course of the formation of the Salt Valley uplift. The jointing parallels the long axis of the anticline and gradually disappears down dip [*sic*] toward the synclinal closure. Running water was not a factor in the formation of the arches and natural bridges found in these two areas as was the case in the White Canyon to the south. Wind erosion, aided by the weathering of the rock due to moisture and temperature changes, seems to have been the primary factors in seeking out soft and loosely cemented spots and working them through to large natural arches. In the Devil's Garden a huge hole was bored through a thick massive sandstone slab with the wind, rain and frost as the only apparent tools used in its carving.

The large arches, or windows as they are sometimes called, found in the Arches section are not so hard to explain because of their occurrence in the more easily weathered Carmel formation with the massive Entrada Sandstone capping. A freak of natural erosion forms is found in the formation of a double arch. Rising from a common base, two long delicate arms at right angles to each other reach to the nearby cliff. A short distance away two large windows have been carved through the cliffs—massive and heavy. No less remarkable is the carving of the high rock mesas in which the arches occur. Long fingers of rock, deep gorges and channels with irregularly carved sides.

The Yellow-Cat Knolls composed, as they are, of shale and easily eroded grit are located in a structural depression, and being protected from weathering because of their structural position have persisted and withstood the erosion that is gradually stripping these softer formations from the slickrock bench.

Economic Geology

Though nothing of economic value is being produced from the Arches National Monument or immediate vicinity, a consideration of economic possibilities is important because of the active prospecting in the vicinity for gas and oil. Should a productive oil horizon be found in the Salt Valley

Anticline, a large part or all of the National Monument would become favorable for oil production because of its close relationship to that structure.

The Yellow-Cat district has been actively worked for Vanadium ore which occurs in the Salt Wash Sandstone, but mining operations ceased a few years ago when larger more easily processed deposits made production here unprofitable.

The Paradox formation of Pennsylvanian age, exposed in Salt Valley, is known to contain salt, gypsum, and some potassium salts. The results of core drilling conducted in the valley are not known.

5

Bonanza at Big Indian (2002)

Raye C. Ringholz

The Colorado Plateau contains deposits of a rare and powerful substance in great demand since World War Two: uranium. The uranium mining boom transformed Moab and brought many new jobs, along with much attention and many visitors, to Arches. During the prospecting boom, Arches rangers sometimes had to expel enthusiastic prospectors or remove claim stakes within the park boundaries. But uranium left a toxic legacy that ravaged miners and still threatens the Colorado River with millions of tons of tailings, heaped up in a pile just southwest of Arches that is being slowly moved by rail to a site near Crescent Junction at enormous public expense.

Raye Ringholz worked for the National Park Service at Arches, and later wrote a history of Moab's boom time, Uranium Frenzy, *from which the following story of Charlie Steen's dramatic discovery in 1952 is drawn. The Mi Vida mine that Steen discovered is in Lisbon Valley, southeast of Moab. Steen built his dream home on a bluff overlooking Moab, along with the refining mill on the bank of the Colorado that left all those tailings. He was a popular, civic-minded citizen who threw legendary parties. Today, his home is a restaurant full of prospecting memorabilia.*

A year was enough. A year when every rasp of the saw, each thwack of the hammer drove the dream of uranium deeper. All the time that he worked as a carpenter in Tucson, Charlie thought of nothing but his twelve claims at Big Indian. He tortured himself with newspaper articles and stories in mining magazines.

"More uranium was mined in the Colorado Plateau in 1951 than in any previous year."

"In November 1950, 145 claims were staked; February 1951 tallied 600."

"J. W. Gramlich received the first AEC bonus payment of $9,672 for 2,763 pounds of uranium oxide in .20 percent from his Morning Star and Evening Star claims on Lion Creek."

By April 30, 1952, Charlie Steen could postpone his quest no longer. Selling the trailerhouse for $350, he stuffed the family belongings into a two-wheeled cart hitched to the back of the jeep. Excess baggage rode under a tarp on top of the vehicle.

The Steens said goodbye to Tucson and headed back to the Colorado Plateau. Their destination this time was Cisco, Utah, a desolate whistlestop for the D&R.G. Railroad located a couple of hours west of Grand Junction.

Cisco was a dot in the flat, windy scrubland that stretched from the Book Cliffs on the north to the snowy-peaked La Sal Mountains southward. The town sat like a dry blister on the lip of Highway 50–6. It consisted of a cafe–beer hall, a general store and Buddy Cowger's service station. Little more. The few trailers and lean-to shanties of the local squatters disappeared into the sagebrush and rolling sandhills.

"We arrived looking like 'The Grapes of Wrath,'" Charlie remembered, "but we were in fine spirits and full of hope. We rented a tarpaper shack for $15 a month and stoked the stove with scavengered railroad coal."

But euphoria was short-lived. M. L., exhausted and run down to begin with, developed pneumonia on their first night in Cisco. Worried and deflated, Charlie put her in the hospital at Fruita, Colorado, and faced this latest rout as best he could. His Big Indian claims on the far side of the La Sals seemed farther away than ever.

Somehow, he managed to keep the family going while M. L. regained her health. They learned to cope with kerosene lanterns in lieu of electricity. They hauled water in five-gallon cans from the Cisco railroad tank. They dug holes "behind the nearest hill" for a bathroom.

With few close neighbors, they devised their own entertainment. The children escaped from the confines of the one-room shack to a seemingly endless backyard that invited exploration. There were dinosaur bones and rocks to collect, sequin-sized desert blossoms to admire, snakes, lizards and darting creatures to track.

Charlie kept his dream alive by poring over geological charts and writing letters to friends and acquaintances soliciting their help in financing his search. Meanwhile the wallet emptied, and the grocery bill swelled to over $300.

Then one day much to Charlie's surprise, a check for $100 arrived. Miraculously, another appeared. And another. Even better, his mother came to help. Rose sold her home and furniture in Houston. Now into her fifties and with several marriages behind her, she decided to throw her assets into her son's quest. She gave him the check from her sale and volunteered to join him on the claim to help set up a camp and cook for him. Charlie's spirits rallied. When M. L. had recovered sufficiently to take care of their brood, he and Mama Rose took off for the Big Indian Wash.

The backcountry had changed from the previous year. Tire tracks scratched red trails over sand stretches where no signs of life appeared before. Rustic prospectors' camps squatted among the rocks. Lone wanderers haunted the clifftops with Snooper, Lucky Strike, Vic Tic or Babbel radiation counters clicking encouragement.

A few small tailings piles marked a smattering of "doghole" mines. These were nothing but cramped, unventilated, unsophisticated holes in the ground. They were barely large enough to accommodate the one or two owners who crawled inside and clawed out insignificant deposits of low-grade ore. There was no room or money for the mucking machines, slushers, shovel loaders and ore cars of the larger mines operated by VCA, USV and Climax Uranium. The independent miners sweated over simple jackhammers, compressors, shovels and wheelbarrows. Then they had to truck their diggings to the nearest mill or AEC buying station, sometimes hundreds of miles away.

Charlie's excitement rose when he saw his own claim markers. The forty-eight cornerstones stood just as he had placed them. The tin cans holding location notices remained intact. He walked over the property and showed Rose where he planned to drill. He was eager to get started.

The first task was to bulldoze a four-mile route from the county gravel road up to his claims. He paid miner Wilfred Brunke $500 to do the "cat" work. Rose organized a makeshift cook shack and bunkhouse. Together they hauled food, water and supplies from Moab, over forty miles away.

The next item was a better drilling rig than the little one used for shallow prospecting. He made a deal with his old friend Bill McCormick to borrow a secondhand diamond drill in exchange for forty-nine percent of the action...if any.

He repaired the rickety machine as well as he could. Then he hauled it to the middle of his Mi Vida claim. The locals guffawed.

"The damn fool placed it 1,700 feet back from the rim in a location that didn't have a single indication of surface ore," they said. It was "Steen's Folly" all over again.

But Charlie stuck with his theory. He vowed that uranium deposits existed in anticlinal structures favorable to oil reservoiring. In drilling behind the rim, he violated all proven practices for uranium mining.

He decided to sink his bore hole through the Wingate Formation. The Wingate sandwiched itself several layers below the Morrison Formation and just above the Chinle and Shinarump strata. The AEC had already established that the Morrison was barren in this region. He would bypass this more common uranium-bearing sandstone and target the Shinarump conglomerate. There had been a number of recent discoveries in the layer. By entering through the Wingate he would lessen the drilling distance. There was a better chance to hit carnotite before his patched-up drill collapsed.

Even so, the pump broke. Drill bits wore out. Each breakdown brought more delay, more expense. Merchants at the mining hardware stores cooled when Charlie came in asking for credit.

M. L., stranded in Cisco, kept up a spirited correspondence during Charlie's long absences. "Being an introvert certainly comes in handy in this particular part of the country," she wrote her friend Beverly. "I've learned things about myself that I could have learned in no other place in the world."

She took up painting. She learned to cook the out-of-season venison "5,000 different ways." And, "I've become the darndest rock hound you ever heard of. If we ever have a decent home, I want one room with nothing in it but show cases to display minerals."

M. L.'s one luxury was rolling Bull Durham cigarettes. She compensated for this extravagance by making quilts from the empty tobacco bags. When she couldn't afford to buy tobacco, and that was often, she scrounged for butts along the dirt roads.

"Have found no ore, and have darned near perished, but I have absolutely found it an impossibility to worry," her letters to Beverly stated. "I used to be a chronic worrier, but I'm so happy and as irresponsible as Andy [their third son] when it comes to worrying about what is to become of us. I love it here. I have learned to laugh instead of gripe, and by gosh, enjoy living!"

It was more difficult for Charlie to remain optimistic. There seemed to be one frustration after another. Every time he celebrated some small victory, another misfortune was waiting. It had been so from the beginning.

When he finally got a grubstake and staked his claims on Big Indian, Rose had suffered a heart attack. He had to drop everything and move to Tucson, take up carpentry again. Then, they no sooner saved enough cash to come back to the Plateau when M. L. came down with pneumonia. He had to put the claims on the back burner once more until she got back on her feet. Finally everything started to look better. Some checks arrived from friends to whom he had written. Rose recovered and came to help. McCormick loaned him the drill. But the damn rig broke down again and again. He had to keep shelling out money for repairs and more supplies. Now there were only a few dollars left. Everything hung on this one hole. If it proved to be barren, the tale would be over.

He started drilling on the day before Independence Day, 1952. It was hot, in the nineties. The desert burned. Charlie and Rose stood beside the spindly derrick. It looked like a toy in the vast, empty canyon.

"Well here goes," Charlie said as he fired the motor.

There was a whirring sound. The drill revolved. Grinding, gnawing noises filled the silence as the bit screwed itself into solid rock. The bit, encrusted with diamonds, the hardest mineral known to man, chewed through the petrified detritus. Inch by inch it probed geologic strata seeking the horizon of ore. Smoke and dust spewed from the deflector as it burrowed.

Charlie sweated over the hole. He began pulling up cores. He laid the foot-long cylinders of sandstone in a row according to their order of occurrence. If he hit something, he would know just how deep it was by its position in the line.

He examined the samples for traces of uranium. There wasn't a sign of the bright yellow ore. He would recognize carnotite if he saw it.

On July 6th, the weather changed. Dark thunderheads gathered to cool the temperatures to just under 80 degrees. By the time the afternoon rains came, the bore reached 72 feet. The cores turned dirty grey. He continued eating into the formation until he had pulled out fourteen feet of the stuff. It was foreign to him. He tossed it on the ground with the other rock lengths and continued drilling. His calculations indicated paydirt at about 200 feet. He still had a way to go.

The summer heat returned. One blistering day seemed to meld into another. The old drill started groaning and smoking, but Charlie persisted. He got down to 197 feet. Then it happened. The stem spun free. There was a loud, whirring noise.

"Jesus Christ!" he yelled as he dove to switch off the engine.

He knew by the sound that the pipe had broken and most of it was stuck in the hole. He had no way to retrieve it. No more money.

Charlie and Rose didn't talk much as they broke camp. He prepared to drive the 100 miles to Cisco, dropping his mother off at Moab on the way. Absent-mindedly, he tossed one of the grey cores into the back of the jeep. He would at least satisfy his curiosity about the odd material that he did strike.

It was July 18th when the jeep rattled up to Buddy Cowger's service station in Cisco. Charlie was grimy with red dust and his face well baked by the sun. His toes stuck out from the ends of his boots. The smile was gone. He didn't look much like the exuberant dreamer who had left for the Big Indian only a couple of months before.

Cowger was sitting in his wheelchair near the gas pump. An accident with a cyanide gun had left him paralyzed from the waist down, but his handicap didn't keep him from getting in on the uranium fever. At every opportunity he dragged himself in and out of his jeep and crawled around on his hands and knees to scout promising terrain. A brand new Lucky Strike Geiger counter was his pride and joy. Uranium talk was his passion.

"Any luck?" he asked Charlie.

"Lost 160 feet of drill stem."

Cowger shook his head sympathetically.

"Spun off the drill pipe 30 feet from the top."

Cowger knew that Charlie hoped to hit ore at about 200 feet. He felt sorry for the persistent string bean of a guy who couldn't even afford a Geiger counter.

"I've been testing some cores the kids brought in," he said, trying to cheer his friend. "Don't look too bad."

He put one under the counter and the needle registered slightly.

Charlie reached into the jeep and pulled out his ugly grey rock.

"Hell I've got better stuff than that," he joked.

"Well put her under," Cowger laughed.

Charlie jabbed the sample under the counter. The instrument swung clear off the scale.

The men stopped laughing.

"Try it again," Cowger said.

The needle pegged. The counter chattered like static.

"My God!" he shouted. "You've hit it!"

Charlie hadn't recognized the unimpressive grey stone as pitchblende.

M. L. pinned the last diaper on the line. She detested washday. Cold water. Little soap. Four rambunctious boys who thrived on dirt. She hurried back into the house out of the heat.

The sound was faint, at first. Someone yelling. Whooping. She peeked out of the window to see who it was just as Charlie loped across the field, shrieking, "We've found it! It's a million dollar lick!" and ran straight into the clothesline. Her freshly washed diapers hit the dirt with him.

"My wash," she moaned.

"We've hit it, M. L," Charlie sobbed. "It's a million dollars!"

It took her a minute to believe him. Then all she could do was cry.

The kids didn't quite understand, but their parents' antics convinced them that they should be happy. M. L. insisted on a family picture to commemorate "the day." Charlie slicked up into some clean suntans and she put on a fresh white blouse, calf length skirt, ankle socks and "penny loafers." They walked back to the service station and piled the kids on the hood of the jeep for the photo. Then they sped down the rutted road to share their good fortune with the neighbors.

Charlie decided to get control of the area surrounding his strike before

The Steen Family on the Day of Discovery. Photo courtesy of the Moab Museum (Southeastern Utah Society of Arts and Sciences).

releasing the news to the press. He spent the next two months staking almost forty claims along the flank of the Lisbon anticline and adjacent to the Mi Vida. In thanks for their help during the bad times, he invited several friends to get in on the action. Bob Barnett staked some claims, as did their Cisco neighbors Holly Seeley and Buddy Cowger. Only after firmly establishing "the Steen line" did Charlie announce his find. The story broke in the *Denver Post* on August 30, 1952.

The following week a brief notice appeared in the Moab, Utah, *Times-Independent*:

> Charles A. Steen, field geologist of Cisco, reported last week that he had discovered the mineral pitchblende in the Big Indian mining district, which is nine miles south of La Sal.... The pitchblende was found in the first diamond core hole drilled by Steen on the Linda Mujer group of claims which he staked in 1951.

In another story in the same edition, the reporter reported:

> By listening to the radio these days it is difficult to determine whether we are enjoying a wave of prosperity or if we are on our last gasp. It's comforting to look up at those old red rocks and know that there will be very little happening to them in the next four years.

Moab, the dusty little farming community, slept on, unaware of an approaching boom. The Mormon farmers, as industrious and ultra-conservative as their pioneer forefathers, paid little attention to the flurry of fortune-hunting outsiders (they called them "Gentiles") who parked trailers and pitched tents along the town's dirt roads. To them, heading out in the "toolies" for a weekend "go" at prospecting was a normal form of innocent recreation. They'd been doing this since the radium days. Therefore, they were unimpressed with the feisty little Texan who claimed a bonanza.

Despite the fact that Charlie's sample cores proved to be primary pitchblende, people didn't believe him. The strike occurred in a much shallower horizon than expected. It was in the Chinle, a formation virtually unknown as a uranium producer. The AEC even said the Big Indian region was barren. Rumors circulated that Charlie had salted his claim.

"Nobody would believe I really had something," he later said. "They accused me of salting the hole with pitchblende so I could sell stock. But it seemed to me the point was, if I salted it, where did I get the pitchblende to salt it with? Canada?"

Popular disbelief in the authenticity of the strike made it difficult to raise money to mine the ore. Charlie insisted on splitting his 51 percent interest in the venture with Rose. After all, her grubstakes kept food on the table those many years. But they were broke. They had nothing to put back in the operation.

To make matters worse, Bill McCormick revealed that he had a silent partner in his 49 percent interest. The partner claimed the discovery was worthless. He didn't want to sink any more money into further drilling and expensive exploration. He wanted out.

Charlie started looking for investors in Salt Lake City, Grand Junction and Denver. To no avail. Then one day in early September he received a letter from William T. Hudson, of Casper, Wyoming. Hudson, his former boss at Chicago Bridge and Iron in Houston, had read the story in the

Denver Post. He sent his congratulations to the young man whom he had helped through college.

"Well, you surely fooled me when you went off prospecting," he wrote. "Somehow I had always sort of guessed that you would wind up a lawyer, possibly a patent lawyer because of your engineering background."

He asked if there was any way he could help.

Two weeks later Charlie called Hudson. He told him that McCormick's percentage was for sale. He wondered if Hudson might be interested. Hudson said he couldn't invest more than about $5,000. Possibly Dan O'Laurie, another former Chicago Bridge and Iron colleague, would be a prospect. The next day O'Laurie flew down to Moab to talk things over. He liked the proposition. The two men bought out McCormick's partnership for $15,000. And O'Laurie loaned the corporation about $30,000 to start work.

Now Charlie had capital. But not enough, he figured, to sink a number of additional drill holes to prove the field. He decided to put his money into a shaft. He knew it was a gamble, but one he had to take. Once again, everyone thought he was crazy.

The recognized practice in uranium mining was to core a number of samples in promising areas and examine the cuttings for evidence of mineralization. In this way a claim was blocked out and the tonnage of an ore body was estimated. This procedure was important as ore usually occurred in sporadic rolls or pods with unpredictable continuity. It was possible for a deposit to pinch out or disappear entirely.

Moab resident Howard Balsley, who was nicknamed "Mr. Uranium" and was active in the uranium industry from the early radium days, explained the phenomenon in a speech before the American Mining Congress on September 23, 1952:

> Uranium ore is just about the most erratic and inconsistent mineral I know of. Unless a uranium property has been drilled and the ore bodies proved and delimited, one may have a wonderful face of ore today and witness its complete disappearance tomorrow. There is no assurance whatever, so far as I know, of the continuity of a uranium ore pocket or roll.

Phil Leahy, the first manager of the AEC Raw Materials Division at Grand Junction, concurred. Collie Small quoted him in *Collier's*, September 10, 1949:

> Spread a layer of white beans over the bottom of the tub. Toss in one or two blue beans. Cover the layers with a newspaper and repeat the operation until the tub is full. (The layers represent the formations where ore is found.) Now take a long hatpin, poke it down through the layers, and see how many blue beans you can hit. That's drilling for uranium.

"It was bad geology, but good economics," Charlie admitted. If he had drilled more exploratory holes, he would have been out of money. He gambled on sinking the shaft on a single hole and finding enough ore as he went along to pay the costs.

On October 4th, he started a six-by-eight-foot timbered shaft thirty feet southeast of the borehole. Three weeks later, he went to Moab to find a lawyer. He went to form a corporation.

Mitch Melich was the only attorney in the town of approximately 1,200 people. He practiced out of a one-room office on the mezzanine of the bank. A handsome forty-year-old, his appearance hinted at his Serbian ancestry—a thick crop of straight, black hair, dark, heavy-browed eyes, olive complexion. He was responsive to the tattered fellow with worn-out boots and patches in his pants who showed up in his office unannounced. He knew poverty firsthand.

Mitch grew up in the copper mining town of Bingham Canyon, Utah. His father, a grocer, died when he was ten. His mother couldn't read or write English. The youngster worked his way through high school. Then, in order to attend the University of Utah, he put in eleven hour shifts during the summers on Kennecott's track gang for $4.25 a day.

As a sophomore in college, Mitch decided to toss his education in favor of a full-time job at the mine. Fortunately, Lou Buchman, his foreman, recognized the boy's potential. He fired him, gave him his check and sent him back to school. Three years later, Mitch had a law degree.

Diploma in hand, it didn't take him long to discover that the legal fraternity wasn't waiting for his talents. There were no openings in Salt Lake City's law firms. A friend talked Mitch into going to Moab.

"What the hell is there in Moab?" he asked. The town then boasted a population of 850.

He decided little was better than nothing. He borrowed $300 from the First Security Bank in Salt Lake and headed south in the fall of 1934. For $100 a year he became city attorney and received a $50 retainer as legal counsel for the bank. His first year's earnings totaled $950.

As the community's only lawyer, Mitch had a stepping-stone into politics. In 1942, he was the first Republican in the district in 25 years to be elected to the state senate. Four years later, his popularity earned him a second term. He ran a third time in 1950, but lost.

"Maybe it was a good thing because that was when the uranium boom started," he later said. "Had I been in the state senate, I might not have become active in the uranium business."

Perhaps it was this recent political defeat that honed his interest in Charlie's proposal.

"I've found a uranium mine and I want to form a corporation," Charlie said. "The mine's in Utah and I'm from Texas, so I think we'll call it Utex—Utex Exploration Company."

Mitch was intrigued by Charlie's self-confidence. He agreed to draw up the papers in exchange for a small amount of stock. Suddenly, the struggling lawyer found himself a partner in an unproven uranium company.

With his corporation formally launched there was nothing for Charlie to do but sweat out the shaft. He oversaw the operation as head geologist. O'Laurie handled finances. Bob Barrett signed on as job foreman in return for 4,800 shares of O'Laurie's stock. They moved a secondhand building to the site and set up a bunkhouse for a small crew. Rose cooked.

It was slow work. Drilling through layers and layers of rock. Blasting the hole with explosives. Mucking out debris with electric shovels. Timbering the sides to keep them from caving in. Foot by foot the gap widened and deepened. Foot by foot the tailings pile grew. Day by day the knot in Charlie's stomach tightened. What if the hole proved barren? What if the rich deposit of his borehole was a fluke? What if the AEC and all the others were right?

October passed. Thanksgiving approached. The mine inched closer to the depth of his original discovery. Still no ore. Charlie knew the miners working for him considered it lunacy to sink a shaft without coring a grid. He prayed that he would prove them wrong.

December first marked his thirty-first birthday, but it was work as usual for Charlie, with no planned celebration. Then the drills reached 68 feet and he got the birthday present of a lifetime. The hole bottomed into heavy, grey ore measuring over fourteen feet of primary pitchblende. A later radiometric assay indicated a staggering 0.34 to 5.0 percent of U_3O_8.

Charlie knew he had the biggest strike in the history of the Colorado Plateau. He had proved his theory beyond a doubt. There was primary ore in the district, and it lay in formations other than the Morrison and Shinarump.

"I can remember that night," he recalled. "My mother and I went down to Moab. It was about 10 o'clock and I had a quart of whiskey. We went to a hotdog stand where the bus station used to be. We were the only ones there. The whole town was locked up. That was the night of the discovery of the shaft and that was the last time that Moab went to sleep at 10 o'clock for a long time."

6

17-Year-Old Youth Finds Dinosaur Bones While Herding Cows (1934)

Frank A. Beckwith

The Moab Times-Independent *has reported on Arches since Justus Corbin founded a predecessor newspaper in 1896. Corbin, an indefatigable booster of his adopted hometown, was constantly searching for a resource that would make Moab flourish. Loren "Bish" Taylor, another great advocate for tourism development, eventually took over the paper, and his descendants still publish the weekly. In this* Times-Independent *article, Frank Beckwith (leader of a scientific expedition described later) narrates the discovery of dinosaur fossils in 1934. The current whereabouts of these fossils is unknown, as is their species, but they may have been from a sauropod.*[1]

[K]eith Wright 17-year old boy working at Wolf[e] cabin for Custodian J. M. Turnbow last week discovered a valuable deposit of dinosaur bones while pursuing his duties of herding cows, this deposit yielded three sections of vertebrae which are larger than a goodsized dinner plate the largest one being over a foot in diameter and about six inches thick. The bones are placed in the charge of Custodian Turnbow and will be cleaned and cemented and then (as government property) be placed in The Times-Independent office that all may see. This display will be a very valuable contribution to the publicity of the region.

While I was working the territory around Mr. Turnbow's cabin he mentioned to me a deposit of large dinosaur bones, which he had seen several years before but could not call to memory the location. On Wednesday Keith

Wright was sent out for some cattle and by the greatest good luck ran fairly into this deposit so elated was he that he changed his course to where I was working and informed me of the find. That afternoon I visited the spot dug out and assembled the surface finds of bones and from the assortment got the three vertebrae which are so good a display that they merit being placed on permanent display in Moab to advertise the region.

The deposit was found a scant half mile east of Mr. Turnbow's cabin a former find was a half mile west so that now discoveries have been made on both sides of his ranch house. In fact that territory begins to vie with Yellow Cat in its prolific yields of dinosaur bones. These are in a fairly good state of preservation but the deposits are peculiar in that they were found in a very shallow depth of loose, soft blue and dim red earth which is not over two to three feet deep lying on some tilted sandstone. All that is left of the original greater depth of this dinosaur bearing strata of soft earth is this small depth which each successive rain wears to a narrower stratum. Ordinarily, dinosaur remains are found in soft earth however (as in this case) if that earth erodes away the bones are left stranded on the rock surface or else in what little remains of the former earth covering.

Keith was so elated over this find that it bothered him in his sleep and one night Turnbow heard him talking in his sleep and Keith yelled

Head that dinosaur he's getting away from me

Turnbow listened to what would follow when he was convulsed with laughter when Keith next yelled

Heck he's bit me!

Turnbow jostled him roughly in the ribs and said Wottinell are you talking about?

Keith replied sleepily A feller has peculiar dreams don't he and nestled off to sleep again.

The Thrill of Finding Them

Stop to think a moment of the various lucky conditions which must coordinate to make all conditions for the successful finding of a dinosaur bone.

1. A very good theory is this recapitulated. The dinosaur fed upon or near a slow moving stream, rich in semi tropical vegetation. He died from any cause either natural or accidental.

2. Before the bones disintegrated, there must be a freshet or any moving of a large deposit of sand or mud upon those bones to preserve them from further decay and from bacteria.
3. That occurred let us say fifteen to thirty million years ago when coal was in the making. The land received many more depositions of material piled upon it some water laid and some may have been wind blown lodges of rock may even cap over the softer earth.
4. Successive erosions as mother earth's surface shrank or was upturned in varying alternations may give evidence of partial wearing away of capping rock and various throes of nature elevating (as is the case in this district) until
5. After the lapse of 15,000,000 to 30,000,000 years the cap rock is worn and tumbles the covering it gave protecting the soft earth disappears the soft earth begins rapidly to wear and man (who was non existent at the time the dinosaurs lived) now roams the desert waste, and
6. That particular deposit containing the self-same dead dinosaur becomes enough bared to reveal a bone.

Think of these six conditions which must be fulfilled had the dinosaur disintegrated soon after death of course no bones remain of that one to be found. Doubtless countless numbers of them met death and passed back to the elements. But some one or dozens did get covered it went through all the convulsions of mother earth's crust upheavals successive alternations above and below the sea's surface and some one or many survived to today.

Hence the thrill of finding that particular one which survived all the conditions. It is no wonder that bone diggers (and they are a crazy lot of knutts) get unwound when they run across one for it bridges thirty million years in one huge stride.

When Carbon county coal was being made in a warm semi tropical area in this region the dinosaur lived and ate that rich and lush growth huge unwieldy reptiles they ate fought and died some one out of countless others got quickly covered all conditions were favorable for preservation and today, we who use that coal for our warmth find the intellectual pleasure of again reconstructing in the mind's eye the head in the Moab postoffice across the street asking for its mail!

Eighty two feet long is the length of one mounted specimen in the Carnegie Museum at Pittsburgh Pennsylvania and higher at the hips than any two auto trucks that ever delivered their tonnage on the streets of Moab.

So the thrill to a paleontologist upon finding a dinosaur bone is reviewing instantly all those series of conditions which must have coordinated perfectly, through thirty million years—a bridging of the time from then to now in the moment of the find. No wonder they go knutts. Or that a boy talks about them in his sleep.

Note

1 The paleontologist Dr. John Foster, former curator of the Museum of Moab, confirms that the National Park Service has no record of fossils from a 1934 site. Foster suspects that the 1934 specimen may be related to sites worked in 1967 and 2003 where sauropods were excavated. John Foster, personal communication with editor, July, 13, 20, and 30, 2020.

7

Biology on Horseback (1947)

D. Elden Beck

The zoologist and entomologist D. Elden Beck taught at Brigham Young University for years and led annual expeditions into the Arches region. In the following excerpt, Beck describes a 1947 trip with several other scholars and lists some of the specimens he collected.

Itinerary

Provo, Utah
April 24, 1947

Left Provo at 2 P.M. enroute to Moab and Arches National Monument headquarters, arriving at the headquarters at seven o'clock. It was a most enjoyable ride, non-tiring and made pleasant by the association we all had in conversation.

Dr. George H. Hansen and Dr. Bertrand Harrison continually remarked about the geological and botanical features of the landscape as we rode along. This made the tour most interesting and valuable to all of us.

Near Moab (about 10 miles North) we stopped to take some photographs. The distant LaSal Mountains with their snow-capped peaks were quite picturesque in the evening sunlight.

Arriving at the Monument headquarters, we made our arrival known to Mr. Mahan, Custodian of Arches National Monument, and then we went on to Moab for supper. Subsequent to supper a visit was made to Mr. Roy

Holyoak's residence and there we completed arrangements for our pack and saddle horses. This done, we returned to headquarters where a visit was enjoyed with Mr. Mahan. He showed some Kodachrome slides of areas in and around the Monument which we would see the following day. At 9:30 P.M. all members retired making their beds in all directions on Mr. Mahan's lawn—sky clear and cool

Moab–Freshwater
April 25, 1947

With the dawn the sleeping bags began to move, come sunup and a few (meaning Reed Biddulph, Roman Andrus and Beck) unsacked to do pictures. Beck and Biddulph to photo and Roman to pen and chalk sketch. Two hours were spent climbing the hills back of headquarters. Many dramatic scenes in sunrise mode were presented and some 'shot.'

Breakfast was taken at Moab after which we returned to 'Monument' headquarters where our supplies and equipment were placed on waiting pack horses. This completed, we climbed on our saddle ponies ready to enter the Monument.

At 10:30 A.M. the cavalcade of seventeen horses bearing men and equipment started up the cliff face, north of the headquarters building. It was quite an enthusiastic crowd which took off. However, it wasn't long until the proverbial professorial stiff legs and sore posterior extremities became apparent. The spectacular scenery kept everyone interested sufficiently in the aesthetic to take some of the discomfort away for at least part of the time.

'Each to his own' was characteristic of the members of the party. Dr. Harrison to his plants, Reed Biddulph to his photos, Roman Andrus to his sketching, Dr. Hansen to his geological observations, etcetera. This separateness however was not completely one of independence, for the activities of each person contributed much to the edification and the total enjoyment of the group.

It was only a few moments' climb up the face of the escarpment above the 'Monument' headquarters. Our trail carried us about half way up the cliff face and then turned eastward, bringing us out on relatively level bench land which stretched away eastward to the Colorado River some six or seven miles away. Following a northward course at the base of towering sandstone cliffs it was almost with breathtaking suddenness that we descended into Courthouse Towers Valley.

Out of Courthouse Towers Valley, into a desert wash (Courthouse Wash), with a gradual climb and still northward in course we attained the same general level of land we were on when we descended into Courthouse Towers Valley. In the distance, northeastward, was dimly outlined the 'Windows' section of the monument.

The area traversed was a mixture of many areas I have visited in various parts of southern Utah. The similarity was both physical and biological.

Part of the survey group separated at the road to the 'Windows' section of the Monument. Four of us went over to the 'Windows,' about four miles to the east. The other members went on to make camp at Freshwater in Freshwater Canyon. This camp is two miles west of abandoned Wolf[e] Ranch. Biddulph and I did some photographic work of the arches and windows at the 'Windows' area. Dr. Harrison collected plants and made notes on observations. Andrus busied himself sketching the 'arches.'

As evening came to a close our small party which went to the 'Windows' section was afraid of being lost. Before we separated from our party earlier in the afternoon, we were directed by the guide to follow the trail. Wild horses and cattle had created many trails where there should have been one but we just guessed at our route and our assistant guide was sure we were to go a certain direction. Just as we had about decided that our night would be spent somewhere in the desert, Roy Holyoak, our guide, came down a trail over what looked like impossible terrain and said, "Just about gave you fellows up—camp is just a little further on." Brother, did that camp look good! The broad valley we had traversed between the Windows and Freshwater we were told was Salt Valley.

Freshwater
April 26, 1947

Breakfast and camp duties done, some of the survey party prepared to make a day's tour of country west of Freshwater. This tour carried us to the Landscape Arch. Mr. Holyoak, our guide, said it was only a distance of about three miles away. But the way my rear end felt at the day's end, it seemed as though we had traveled three times that distance. Actual map figures indicate the distance as about 13 miles.

The route we took to the Landscape Arch was by way of the Devil's Garden. The latter region is a fantastic geological formation, more than equally as interesting as the several arches we saw and photographed during the day. The Devil's Garden in the locale of the Fiery Furnace is made up of a series of stone buttresses, fins and buttes arranged in many forms, representing various stages of erosion. The upper reaches of each individual structure was rounded and saucer-like with the bases elongated and fin-like, having an east-west alignment, yet some were at right angles with each other.

At the Landscape Arch we were rewarded for our arduous travel, by the sight of this beautiful and remarkable bridge. The narrow dimensions of the arch and its length of the span makes one wonder what unseen force is holding the bridge in place. We were met with a most unfortunate situation however in that poor sunlight prevented making a good photographic story of the bridge.

After spending a couple of hours at the Landscape Arch, our group traveled southeast. Finding a trail down the escarpment which marks the northern rim of Salt Valley, we descended into the valley. Reaching the desert wash at the bottom of the valley, we traveled eastward to our camp at Freshwater. Upon arrival at camp we found that Dr. Hayward and James Bee had done a fine day's work with their collecting and observational studies with the birds and mammals.

Freshwater,
Wolf Ranch, Moab,
Provo
April 27, 1947

At 9:00 A.M. we packed our horses preparatory to departing on our return trip to 'Monument' headquarters. The tour took us by way of Delicate Arch, thence to the 'Windows Section,' the Courthouse Towers and to Monument headquarters.

All of us agreed that the stay at Freshwater had been much too brief. Each of us had a sampling however of our respective interests.

The tour to Delicate Arch was much more worthwhile than expected. First of all the trip took but a very short time to make. We went over the hill from Freshwater Spring to Wolf Ranch, a ride of about 20 minutes. The view north from the top of the hill above Wolf Ranch is most picturesque. From Wolf Ranch to Delicate Arch one climbs out of the canyon bottom up over "slick rock," a Navajo sandstone exposure on a bare rock trail to the Arch, a distance of about 45 minutes horse travel. The spectacular setting for Delicate Arch is impressive. Approaching the arch directly from the front (west), one does not see the opening to the arch. It appears as a column of rock, each side of which is a giant whirlpool, bowl-like depression, flanked above and to the east with a wall of sandstone. The upper wall of sandstone is sculptured into many interesting and weird forms.

We spent quite some time in photographing the 'arch' from all angles. The sun came out from the clouds at the right time and we had perfect photo weather.

We did not like to leave the place but had to return to headquarters by night fall, and then the drive on home to Provo, so we reluctantly departed from the Delicate Arch.

At 6:15 we arrived at headquarters near Mahan's home. After unpacking from horses and repacking in the bus, paying our guides, and bidding good-bye until another day, we climbed into old Betsy and struck out for home. All of us were tired and stiffened muscles added to our physical discomfort, but it was universal that none of us would have missed the trip.

Soldier's Summit was covered with snow and slush which made us thankful for the pleasant weather we had enjoyed the past few days but apprehensive of what would be our status at home in Provo.

Our fears were unfounded, for rain had hit Utah Valley which only made the Valley greener and my garden in better condition. We arrived at 10:30 P.M. and went our separate ways to our homes.

Field Collection Records

Numbered Collection Notes & Observations
D. Elden Beck

No. 1, Frogs — 26 April 1947
Freshwater Springs — D. E. Beck

Collected three specimens of this frog but saw nine; they would dive down into the deep pools of water. Above camp are several pools varying from the largest approximately 25 feet across and 5 feet deep to those a foot or so across and a few inches deep. These are seep pools and the plant growth is lush. In the living condition the frogs are brownish with the lateral surface pale green. Under-surface whitish to pink.

No. 2, Insects — 26 April 1947
Freshwater Springs — D. E. Beck

The water beetle faunae is very abundant as to numbers but poor in species. They were taken on and in the water pools.

No. 3, Insects — 26 April 1947
Freshwater Springs — D. E. Beck

Collected in same situations as in No. 2.

No. 4, Spider — 26 April 1947
Freshwater Springs — D. E. Beck

Collected on my sleeping log as I arose.

No. 5, Insects — 25 April 1947
Courthouse Towers Environs — D. E. Beck

These were collected in a side pool in a desert wash a few miles north of Courthouse Towers section of the Monument.

No. 6, Ants — 26 April 1947
Freshwater Springs — D. E. Beck

Near the seep pool at the head of the canyon above camp I turned rocks over a few feet away from the pools and stream. These ants were very common in many places.

No. 7, Cricket 26 April 1947
Freshwater Springs D. E. Beck
Collected under overturned rock near seep pool.

No. 8, Crane Fly 26 April 1947
Freshwater Springs D. E. Beck
Collected from sweeps made over Solomons Seal plants near seep pool.

8

The Colorado
Archetypal River (2014)

Brooke Williams

Brooke Williams is a writer, outdoor guide, and environmental advocate who has lived with his wife, Terry Tempest Williams, in Castle Valley, across the river from Arches. All streams in the park drain into the Colorado River.

It became clear to me that cold day that I'd neglected most of what the Colorado River had to teach me. Sandy Ass Beach was beneath two feet of hard snow, flawless but for marks left by the sharp tips of dog claws and recent wind.

The winter of 2013 was mythically cold in the high desert, and weeks of sinking temperatures had frozen the Colorado River. Two or three times a week we drove the river's edge for fifteen miles between the turn off to Castle Valley, where our home is, and Moab, where we buy books and food and gas. I use a large boulder near Big Bend to gauge the river's flow. Great Blue Herons fish at one of two particular turns in the river. Just out of town, Canada Geese are often wading in the shallows—along with mallards or mergansers, depending on the season. The color of the river changes daily based on the weather (from dark green to khaki to the color of persimmons moments after a flash flood in a side canyon.) Winter hid all this. By mid-February I missed that river.

I worry about that river. The same climate changes that are causing monster storms and rising seas, famine, and fire, are drying up the Colorado Plateau by starving the river that feeds it, and I needed to see it strong. I wanted it full.

Most of the year I take the dogs down to a small sandy cove we call Sandy Ass Beach. Five years ago my friend Chris and I spotted the pure glowing sand of this Shangri-la from downstream and forced our way along the river's edge through dense willow and tamarisk. We knew we'd found a small paradise. Although occasionally we see signs that people boating the Daily (a popular stretch of river that commercial companies turn into a playground and locals use for regular pilgrimage) might take lunch breaks on our beach, we treat it as if it's ours. Somehow we own that beach. Some days the only tracks we find are those we left the week before.

I'd never seen Sandy Ass Beach during such a hard winter. While the dogs tested the ice and checked their familiar willows and rocks, I squatted there chuckling about how in June I would dig a shallow hole and lie there naked. But the same cliff-shade that makes my beach bearable as the summer swelters and throbs had trapped and cooled the sharp, slow air, against which my down parka and wool hat were powerless that winter day.

Downstream there was no sign of the river, only a perfect surface like a white floor troweled smooth by a craftsman. Upstream the current compressed into a narrow channel had forced a black part of the river to the surface, where it curved between sensuous white snow banks as in a fairy tale. Directly in front of me lay total chaos. Foot-thick ice freed by the upstream current, meeting the immovable, had buckled and climbed and frozen into a disaster.

The Colorado River is the lifeblood of 30 million people. It waters 3 million acres of farmland and produces 1,800 megawatts of hydropower. It drains a quarter-million square miles in seven western states. For the Paiutes, Hopis, Utes, Navajos, Apaches, Ourays, Uintahs, Havasupais, and a dozen other tribes, the Colorado River is part of their historical legacy and continues to provide both spiritual and economic benefit. The river supports thousands of wild species, many endemic. Lifeblood, life force, this river is the archetype for this region, the Colorado Plateau, which for many is America's true heart.

Carl Jung, one of the great thinkers of all time, believed that archetypes are universal symbols shared by every human who ever lived, passed from generation to generation in a way similar to the way genes are inherited. The hero, the wise old man, the fool, the trickster, the Great mother and sky father, the devil, the scapegoat, the warrior, the lover. All are archetypes present in the human psyche since we first appeared. Stones, caves, mountains, and rivers are also archetypes and are often transformational in nature. A cave appearing in a dream could mean death and rebirth, illumination; a stone could symbolize the simplest, deepest experience. Mountains are places of great insight. Rivers represent the passing of time or the boundary between one thing and another, between now and then. When archetypes appear in literature, they often elicit a deep, emotional response.

Rivers are often characters in literature—such as the stages of life that the River Styx represents in the *Odyssey* or the freedom from captivity and child abuse and slavery that Huck Finn's mighty Mississippi represents. In *Siddhartha,* Hesse's river is a constant, foundational: "the river is everywhere at once, at the source and at the mouth, at the waterfall, at the ferry, at the rapids, in the sea, in the mountains, everywhere at once, and...there is only the present time for it, not the shadow of the past, not the shadow of the future."[1]

Jung suggested that archetypes are instinctual images, the symbols that represent the language of the collective unconscious, that *"layer where man is no longer a distinct individual, but where his mind widens out and merges into the mind of mankind...where we are all the same."*[2] According to others, the collective unconscious contains the entire evolutionary history of our species, including all the tools we've ever needed to save ourselves.

Jung again:

> Besides the intellect [we each have] symbols, which are older than the historical man, which... still make up the groundwork of the human psyche. It is only possible to live the fullest life when we are in harmony with these symbols. *Wisdom is a return to them.*[3]

As modern humans, we steer clear of this inner world. We've been seduced into thinking that all our technology and information and beliefs have made obsolete the vast amounts of evolutionary material existing beneath the conscious surface, beyond the ability of our science to explain and describe. We believe in a "God species,"[4] and that we are it. For most of our history this inner world was the source of our survival. And we've done very well. Could ignoring this "evolutionary material" be closing off most of the library in which our complete knowledge is contained? Due to the warming climate (the "super" storms, rising seas, and mass extinctions), the next decade may be the most important in the entire history of our species. The solutions we have available to deal with our problems seem inadequate. Wouldn't this be a good time to use that old, deep part of the library (the places with dark wood, long tables with those iconic lamps, books without bar codes)? What do we have to lose? How do we enter that part of the library? Why is it closed? What are we afraid of?

Wisdom.

If wisdom is a return to our deep old symbols, we have forsaken it, selling it off to corporate interests who seem to have planned its obsolescence.

When we first moved to Castle Valley, I thought I had a deep relationship with the Colorado. I'd floated much of it on numerous river trips, both commercial and private. I was an above-average swamper—one of the people on most commercial trips who ties up the boat, coils ropes, deals with the groover (what river runners call the toilet) and serves as the sous-chef/dishwasher at meals. I'd hiked along its banks and explored many of its side canyons. Everything changed for me when I met the love of my life and abandoned my career path (I'd been hired to row the back-oar on a triple-rig in Cataract Canyon). Something shifted when this river became a regular part of our lives—daily we drive along it, swim in it, or stack its stones into art. Before, every trip to the Colorado required scheduling, planning—methodical thinking, conscious effort. Since moving close next to the river, the planning and thinking and effort associated with it have all evaporated, along with any expectation. Now we just go. Like primitive hunters, we only know one thing: that we do not know what will happen next.

Something always happens.

Years ago Terry, Rio, and I were at the river late one hot summer day. We were floating in an eddy watching light drop and colors deepen, and just when the cliffs turned purple we saw the Hatch. A massive cloud of just-born mayflies suddenly engulfed us—mayflies in our eyes, hanging from our brows, mating in our hair. We breathed in mayflies and rinsed their nymph-skins off of our skin. Then it was over. I was of two minds. I wondered if it was just the situation or if they were a bit larger and lighter in color and perhaps of a different species than those with which I'd grown familiar. At the same time I thought about what this moment meant—how short life is, how fleeting, much of it taking place beneath all surfaces. Later my two minds joined on discovering the Latin name of the mayflies, *Ephemeroptera*, from the root "ephemera," meaning "all things that exist or are used or enjoyed for a short period of time."

Something always happens. Will I notice?

While I can count on one hand the number of mayflies I've seen since the millions I saw that summer evening, I've become obsessed with dragonflies and damselflies.[5] One bright spring day at Sandy Ass Beach I decided to learn some specifics about damselflies. I can pin it down to one individual—a damsel with a red spot as if its metal wings were being welded to its body by a glowing torch. It was perched in a dead tamarisk. Years ago damselflies had become my totem animal when I was visited by one in a daydream (by this I mean the generosity with which they inhabit my life, the value and significance they bring to it). So powerful was this experience that it led me to consider the role these creatures have played in the lives of people throughout history. In many cultures dragonflies and damselflies are the messengers between the inner and outer worlds and represent the souls of the dead. Since that moment the appearance of a dragonfly or damselfly has triggered a heightened awareness of what is going on around me. Either a dead relative is trying to communicate with me or I am receiving a message from the inner world. Or both.

The wild world has always fascinated me, and I consider myself a good amateur naturalist. I knew there must be many dragonfly species, but the best I could do was put them into one of two categories. The larger dragonflies (usually metallic blue or green in color) hold their wings out perpendicular to their bodies when perched, while the smaller, blue damselflies lay their wings parallel along their back. That all changed the day the bright red damsel, with its wings glowing red, perched in that tamarisk.

Back home that evening, I searched the Internet for clues about that damsel, wings afire. Part of me hoped that I'd seen magic, the only being of its kind, a gift from the gods, a message. Part of me wanted to be exact, to learn its range, its habits, its long Latin name. No dragonfly had ever mystified me as this one did.

American rubyspot (Hetaerina Americana): even its photo was glorious.[6] I have eight books now—mainly field guides—on dragonflies and damselflies. I find that their metaphorical/archetypal significance deepens with my scientific knowledge, such as that gleaned from a recent article in the *New York Times*.[7]

I once spent fifteen minutes with a variegated meadowhawk dragonfly. I saw him from a distance and lay down in the water, inching closer and closer until I was within one foot of the tall blade of dried grass where he perched. I watched as he flew off eight times and returned seven times to chew and swallow the same species of small gnat.

Late that same summer I watched seventy-four pairs of powdered dancers (*Argia moesta*) on short logs floating in the shallow eddy. Males, attached to the back of the females' heads, hovered, watching, ready to pull their mates to safety should a predator approach while she releases her eggs into the river. I sank into the mud while trying to photograph them and could barely pull myself out.

What happened to the mayflies, herons and geese, damsel eggs and nymphs in June 2011, when for a week the Colorado River flowed deeper and wider than I'd ever seen? Sandy Ass Beach was drowned.[8] Huge logs and live uprooted cottonwoods moved downstream like small islands, their limbs vertical with lime-colored spring leaves waving like flags. A massive late season snowstorm high in the headwaters was followed by weeks of sun and warmth that flooded the river to 90,000 cubic feet per second. Would the giant creature this river had become, as it has done only rarely in the recent past, once again force its way across its desiccated delta to the sea?

While some river water may have trickled temporarily into the Gulf of California that summer, most of it was stolen by diversion canals or trapped by one of the many dams, though these lake levels have dropped dramatically in recent years. In 1922, when the Colorado River was divvied up, the region was experiencing an unusually wet period: the river's flow totaled 17.5 million acre-feet. Today the annual average of 14.7 million acre-feet must be allocated among seven states and Mexico, all of which are experiencing exploding urban populations and climate change. Recent studies suggest that a warming climate will affect the Colorado Plateau more than the rest of the country. Hotter, drier weather could reduce river flows by 10 to 30 percent. This host of challenges led to the American Rivers listing of the Colorado as America's Most Endangered River in 2013.[9]

The bigger question for me was what will happen to the mayflies and the dragonflies and damselflies when drought diminishes the river? What will happen to the willows and the willow flycatchers and the fish and the ospreys that hunt them? What will happen to the evening light with less to reflect it?

The next year, one of the last autumn days, the river seemed low enough to walk across. I thought of a recent photograph of the riverless Colorado River delta, littered with old tires and plastic bottles and oozing with brown foaming muck. For tens of thousands of years those were healthy wetlands, loud with the songs of birds and the chatter of insects, a place soothed by the soft sounds of reeds and marsh grasses rubbing against one another. Before dams and droughts, dolphins could be seen catching the fish that they'd chased sixty miles up the river. They say the incoming tide racing up the river made "a noise like a train."[10]

The newly exposed slime at the base of Sandy Ass Beach gave off fetid, organic smells. Imagining the fumes rising from what the Colorado River Delta has become frightened me. The river was so low that a new island appeared upstream from Sandy Ass beach. The air temperature was so perfect that it disappeared. The dogs lay in the sand next to me, watching the river flow past. I too became a resting dog—just watching. An autumn leaf fell from an oak on the bank above us. They watched it. I watched it. A small fish rose in the eddy. We all watched it. Then above that new grassy island something began to happen. Hundreds of damselflies—I could only see them when low light from the setting sun came in at the perfect angle—were feeding on some invisible late season hatch.

What happens to us when our archetypes lose their source? What happens when we dream of an animal that has gone extinct or the passing time symbolized by a river that now quits before it ends? Will the changing climate and the drought associated with it force us to create new archetypes? (I would have missed those feeding damselflies had the river not dropped to that depth.)

Then came this cold winter and the only sunny days in the past week. As we always do, we pull off the road. The dogs are crazy to get out. The moment the door opens, they're down the trail, now buried beneath snow. As I grab my pack and close the door, they have already disappeared. Theirs are the only tracks in the snow, barely softened by the afternoon sun. I follow them, turning east and passing by the large, turtle-shaped boulder (long ago we pioneered a new way to Sandy Ass Beach, completely avoiding the river's complex edge) then into and out of the wash and up the hill where they've just passed the three giant cottonwoods standing like statesmen below. Although the trail is invisible, the dog track follows it perfectly between the willows and the squawbush. I've forgotten which of the three tunnels through the tamarisk leads to Sandy Ass Beach, and that old pull-top beer can that usually guides me has disappeared in the snow. No matter, the dogs know the way.

Half an hour later, sitting hunched in the snow on that cold day, stiff but not quite paralyzed, I watch the river blossom into its archetype.

Downstream the frozen white floor of river ice covered by soft snow—I was there once, oblivious to the life force flowing beneath me. Everything I thought I needed was on that surface. Anything beneath it seemed old, antiquated, at best inconsequential and at worst distracting. That was the past. Now, in the present, with the ice directly in front of me, I know the river is down below, inside, flowing strong and purposeful, deep and green and muscular and filled with stories and clues. On top the ice chunks buckling and bending and twisting before breaking loose become my own chaotic transformation as the deep river forces its way through the surface from below. Upstream, tomorrow or next month or next year, the river's strongest current will move quietly, part of the surface. The inner and outer rivers (my inner and outer worlds) will soon join into one.

Notes

1 Hermann Hesse, *Siddhartha*, 1172–74.
2 Quoted in Edward Hoffman, *The Wisdom of Carl Jung*, 60 (emphasis added).
3 Edward Hoffman, *The Wisdom of Carl Jung*, 22 (emphasis added).
4 Mark Lynas, *The God Species: How the Planet Can Survive the Age of Humans*.
5 Dragonflies have front wings that are broader than their hind wings and hold their

wings out at rest; damselflies have front and back wings that are the same size and are held over their body (parallel to the body axis) at rest.

6 See http://www.cirrusimage.com/damselfly.htm for an image.

7 Natalie Angier, "Nature's Drone, Pretty and Deadly," *New York Times*, April 1, 2013, https://www.nytimes.com/2013/04/02/science/dragonflies-natures-deadly-drone-but-prettier.html.

8 See http://www.youtube.com/watch?v=Z2At_vLhq5s to view a video I made of that day.

9 American Rivers, http://www.americanrivers.org/.

10 Henry Fountain, "Relief for a Parched Delta," *New York Times*, April 16, 2013, https://www.nytimes.com/2013/04/16/science/earth/optimism-builds-for-effort-to-relieve-a-parched-delta-in-mexico.html.

9

Cliffrose and Bayonets (1968)

Edward Abbey

Abbey didn't like to be called a nature writer (or a regional writer, or a Western writer, as he tells Bruce Hamilton in a later piece in this reader). But he was a careful observer and eloquent chronicler of the world around him, including plants, animals, and the land itself.

May Day.

A crimson sunrise streaked with gold flares out beyond Balanced Rock, beyond the arches and windows, beyond Grand Mesa in Colorado. Dawn winds are driving streamers of snow off the peaks of the Sierra La Sal and old man Tukuhnikivats, mightiest of mountains in the land of Moab, will soon be stripped bare to the granite if this wind doesn't stop. Blue scarves of snow flying in the wind twenty miles away—you wouldn't want to be up there now, as they say out here, 13,000 feet above the sea, with only your spurs on.

In honor of the occasion I tack a scarlet bandanna to the ridgepole of the ramada, where my Chinese windbells also hang, jingling and jangling in the breeze. The red rag flutters brightly over the bells—poetry and revolution before breakfast. Afterwards I hoist the Stars and Stripes to the top of the flagpole up at the entrance station. Impartial and neutralist, taking no chances, I wish good fortune to both sides, good swill for all. Or conversely, depending on my mood of the moment, damn both houses and *pox vobiscum*. Swinish politics, our ball and chain.

The gopher snake has deserted me, taking with him most of my mice, and the government trailerhouse is a lonely place this morning. Leaving the

The National Park Service says this is "probably" seasonal ranger Edward Abbey in the Fiery Furnace. Photo courtesy of Arches NP/Lloyd Pierson, 1957.

coffee to percolate slowly over the lowest possible flame, I take my cherrywood and go for a walk before breakfast. The wind blows sand in my teeth but also brings the scent of flowering cliffrose and a hint of mountain snow, more than adequate compensation.

Time to inspect the garden. I refer to the garden which lies all around me, extending from here to the mountains, from here to the Book Cliffs, from here to Robbers' Roost and Land's End—an area about the size of the Negev and, excepting me and the huddled Moabites, uninhabited.

Inventory. Great big yellow mule-ear sunflowers are blooming along the dirt road, where the drainage from the road provides an extra margin of water, a slight but significant difference. Growing among the sunflowers and scattered more thinly over the rest of the desert are the others: yellow borage, Indian paintbrush, scarlet penstemon, skyrocket gilia, prickly pear, hedgehog cactus, purple locoweed, the coral-red globemallow, dockweed, sand verbena. Loveliest of all, however, gay and sweet as a pretty girl, with a fragrance like that of orange blossoms, is the cliffrose, *Cowania stansburiana*, also known—by the anesthetic—as buckbrush or quinine bush.

The cliffrose is a sturdy shrub with gnarled trunk and twisting branches, growing sometimes to twice a man's height. When not in bloom it might not catch your eye; but after the winter snows and a trace of rain in the spring it comes on suddenly and gloriously like a swan, like a maiden, and the shaggy limbs go out of sight behind dense clusters of flowers creamy white or pale yellow, like wild roses, each with its five perfect petals and a golden center.

There's a cliffrose standing near the shed behind the trailer, shaking in the wind, a dazzling mass of blossoms, and another coming up out of solid sandstone beside the ramada, ten feet tall and clothed in a fire of flowers. If Housman were here he'd alter those lines to

> Loveliest of shrubs the cliffrose now
> Is hung with bloom along the bough...

The word "shrub" presents a challenge, at least to such verse as this; but poetry is nothing if not exact. The poets lie too much, said Jeffers. Exactly. We insist on precision around here, though it bend the poesy a little out of shape.

The cliffrose is practical as well as pretty. Concealed by the flowers at this time are the leaves, small, tough, wax-coated, bitter on the tongue—thus the name quinine bush—but popular just the same among the deer as browse when nothing better is available—buckbrush. The Indians too, a practical people, once used the bark of this plant for sandals, mats and rope, and the Hopi medicine man is said, even today, to mash and cook the leaves as an emetic for his patients.

Because of its clouds of flowers the cliffrose is the showiest plant in the canyon country, but the most beautiful individual flower, most people would agree, is that of the cacti: the prickly pear, the hedgehog, the fishhook. Merely opinion, of course. But the various cactus flowers have earned the distinction claimed for them on the basis of their large size, their delicacy, their brilliance, and their transience—they bloom, many of them, for one day only in each year. Is that a fair criterion of beauty? I don't know. For myself I hold no preference among flowers, so long as they are wild, free, spontaneous. (Bricks to all greenhouses! Black thumb and cut-worm to the potted plant!)

The cactus flowers are all much alike, varying only in color within and among the different species. The prickly pear, for example, produces a flower that may be violet, saffron, or red. It is cup-shaped, filled with golden stamens that respond with sensitive, one might almost say sensual, tenderness to the entrance of a bee. This flower is indeed irresistibly attractive to insects; I have yet to look into one and not find a honeybee or bumblebee wallowing drunkenly inside, powdered with pollen, glutting itself on what must be a marvelous nectar. You can't get them out of there—they won't go home. I've done my best to annoy them, poking and prodding with a stem of grass, but a bee in a cactus bloom will not be provoked; it stays until the flower wilts. Until closing time.

The true distinction of these flowers, I feel, is found in the contrast between the blossom and the plant which produces it. The cactus of the high desert is a small, grubby, obscure and humble vegetable associated with cattle dung and overgrazing, interesting only when you tangle with it in the wrong way. Yet from this nest of thorns, this snare of hooks and fiery spines, is born once each year a splendid flower. It is unpluckable and except to an insect almost unapproachable, yet soft, lovely, sweet, desirable, exemplifying better than the rose among thorns the unity of opposites.

Stepping carefully around the straggling prickly pear I come after a few paces over bare sandstone to a plant whose defensive weaponry makes the cactus seem relatively benign. This one is formed of a cluster of bayonetlike leaves pointing up and outward, each stiff green blade tipped with a point as intense and penetrating as a needle. Out of the core of this untouchable dagger's-nest rises a slender stalk, waist-high, gracefully curved, which supports a heavy cluster of bell-shaped, cream-colored, wax-coated, exquisitely perfumed flowers. This plant, not a cactus but a member of the lily family, is a type of yucca called Spanish bayonet.

Despite its fierce defenses, or perhaps because of them, the yucca is as beautiful as it is strange, perfect in its place wherever that place may be—on the Dagger Flats of Big Bend, the high grasslands of southern New Mexico, the rim and interior of Grand Canyon or here in the Arches country, growing wide-spaced and solitaire from the red sands of Utah.

The yucca is bizarre not only in appearance but in its mode of reproduction. The flowers are pollinated not by bees or hummingbirds but exclusively by a moth of the genus *Pronuba* with which the yucca, aided by a liberal allowance of time, has worked out a symbiotic relationship beneficial and necessary to both. The moth lays its eggs at the proper time in the ovary of the yucca flower where the larvae, as they develop, feed on the growing seeds, eating enough of them to reach maturity but leaving enough in the pod to allow the plant, assisted by the desert winds, to sow next year's yucca crop. In return for this nursery care the moth performs an essential service for the yucca: in the process of entering the flower the moth—almost accidentally it might seem to us—transfers the flower's pollen from anther to pistil, thus accomplishing pollination. No more; but it is sufficient.

The wind will not stop. Gusts of sand swirl before me, stinging my face. But there is still too much to see and marvel at, the world very much alive in the bright light and wind, exultant with the fever of spring, the delight of morning. Strolling on, it seems to me that the strangeness and wonder of existence are emphasized here, in the desert, by the comparative sparsity of the flora and fauna: life not crowded upon life as in other places but scattered abroad in spareness and simplicity, with a generous gift of space for each herb and bush and tree, each stem of grass, so that the living organism stands out bold and brave and vivid against the lifeless sand and barren rock. The extreme clarity of the desert light is equaled by the extreme individuation of desert life-forms. Love flowers best in openness and freedom.

Patterns in the sand, tracks of tiger lizards, birds, kangaroo rats, beetles. Circles and semicircles on the red dune where the wind whips the compliant stems of the wild ricegrass back and forth, halfway around and back again. On the crest of the dune is a curving cornice from which flies a constant spray of fine sand. Crescent-shaped, the dune shelters on its leeward side a growth of sunflowers and scarlet penstemon. I lie on my belly on the edge of the dune, back to the wind, and study the world of the flowers from ground level, as a snake might see it. From below the flowers of the penstemon look like flying pennants; the sunflowers shake and creak from thick green hairy stalks that look, from a snake's viewpoint, like the trunks of trees.

I get up and start back to the trailer. A smell of burning coffee on the wind. On the way I pass a large anthill, the domed city of the harvester ants. Omniverous red devils with a vicious bite, they have denuded the ground surrounding their hill, destroying everything green and living within a radius of ten feet. I cannot resist the impulse to shove my walking stick into the bowels of their hive and rowel things up. Don't actually care for ants. Neurotic little pismires. Compared to ants the hairy scorpion is a beast of charm, dignity and tenderness.

My favorite juniper stands before me glittering shaggily in the sunrise, ragged roots clutching at the rock on which it feeds, rough dark boughs bedecked with a rash, with a shower of turquoise-colored berries. A female, this ancient grandmother of a tree may be three hundred years old; growing very slowly, the juniper seldom attains a height greater than fifteen or twenty feet even in favorable locations. My juniper, though still fruitful and full of vigor, is at the same time partly dead: one half of the divided trunk holds skyward a sapless claw, a branch without leaf or bark, baked by the sun and scoured by the wind to a silver finish, where magpies and ravens like to roost when I am not too close.

I've had this tree under surveillance ever since my arrival at Arches, hoping to learn something from it, to discover the significance in its form, to make a connection through its life with whatever falls beyond. Have failed. The essence of the juniper continues to elude me unless, as I presently suspect, its surface is also the essence. Two living things on the same earth, respiring in a common medium, we contact one another but without direct communication. Intuition, sympathy, empathy, all fail to guide me into the heart of this being—if it has a heart.

At times I am exasperated by the juniper's static pose; something in its stylized gesture of appeal, that dead claw against the sky, suggests catalepsy. Perhaps the tree is mad. The dull, painful creaking of the branches in the wind indicates, however, an internal effort at liberation.

The wind flows around us from the yellow haze in the east, a morning wind, a solar wind. We're in for a storm today, dust and sand and filthy air.

Without flowers as yet but bright and fresh, with leaves of a startling, living green in contrast to the usual desert olive drab, is a shrub known as singleleaf ash, one of the few true deciduous plants in the pinyon-juniper community. Most desert plants have only rudimentary leaves, or no leaves at all, the better to conserve moisture, and the singleleaf ash seems out of place here, anomalous, foredoomed to wither and die. (*Fraxinus anomala* is the botanical name). But touch the leaves of this plant and you find them dry as paper, leathery in texture and therefore desert-resistant. The singleleaf ash in my garden stands alone along the path, a dwarf tree only three feet high but tough and enduring, clenched to the stone.

Sand sage or old man sage, a lustrous windblown blend of silver and blue and aquamarine, gleams in the distance, the feathery sterns flowing like hair. Purple flowers no bigger than your fingernail are half-revealed, half-concealed by the shining leaves. *Purple* sage: crush the leaves between thumb and finger and you release that characteristic odor, pungent and bittersweet, which *means* canyon country, high lonesome mesaland, the winds that blow from far away.

Also worthy of praise is the local pinyon pine, growing hereabouts at isolated points, for its edible nuts that appear in good years, for its ragged raunchy piney good looks, for the superior qualities of its wood as fuel—burns clean and slow, little soot, little ash, and smells almost as good as juniper. Unfortunately, most of the pinyon pines in the area are dead or dying, victims of another kind of pine—the porcupine. This situation came about through the conscientious efforts of a federal agency known formerly as the Wildlife Service, which keeps its people busy in trapping, shooting and poisoning wildlife, particularly coyotes and mountain lions. Having nearly exterminated their natural enemies, the wildlife experts made it possible for the porcupines to multiply so fast and so far that they—the porcupines—have taken to gnawing the bark from pinyon pines in order to survive.

What else? Still within sight of the housetrailer, I can see the princess plume with its tall golden racemes; the green ephedra or Mormon tea, from which Indians and pioneers extracted a medicinal drink (contains ephedrine), the obnoxious Russian thistle, better known as tumbleweed, an exotic; pepperweed, bladderweed, snakeweed, matchweed, skeleton weed—the last-named so delicately formed as to be almost invisible; the scrubby little wavyleaf oak, stabilizer of sand dunes; the Apache plume, poor cousin of the cliffrose; gray blackbrush, most ubiquitous and humble of desert plants, which will grow where all else has given up; more annuals—primrose, sourdock, yellow and purple beeplant, rockcress, wild buckwheat, grama grass, and five miles north across the floor of Salt Valley, acres and acres of the coral-colored globemallow.

Not quite within eyeshot but close by, in a shady dampish secret place, the sacred datura—moonflower, moonlily, thornapple—blooms in the night, soft white trumpet-shaped flowers that open only in darkness and close with the coming of the heat. The datura is sacred (to certain cultists) because of its content of atropine, a powerful narcotic of the alkaloid group capable of inducing visionary hallucinations, as the Indians discovered long before the psychedelic craze began. How they could have made such a discovery without poisoning themselves to death nobody knows; but then nobody knows how so-called primitive man made his many other discoveries. We must concede that science is nothing new, that research, empirical logic, the courage to experiment are as old as humanity.

Most of the plants I have named so far belong to what ecologists call the pinyon pine-juniper community, typical of the high, dry, sandy soils of the tablelands. Descend to the alkali flats of Salt Valley and you find an entirely different grouping: shadscale, four-winged saltbush, greasewood, spiny horsebrush, asters, milk vetch, budsage, galletagrass. Along the washes and the rare perennial streams you'll find a third community: the Fremont poplar or cottonwood tree, willow, tamarisk, rabbitbrush or *chamisa*, and a variety of sedges, tules, rushes, reeds, cattails. The fourth plant community, in the Arches area, is found by the springs and around the seeps on the canyon walls—the hanging gardens of fern, monkey-flower, death camas, columbine, helleborine orchid, bracken, panicgrass, bluestem, poison ivy, squawbush, and the endemic primrose *Primula specuiola*, found nowhere but in the canyonlands.

So much for the inventory. After such a lengthy listing of plant life the reader may now be visualizing Arches National Monument as more a jungle than a desert. Be reassured, it is not so. I have called it a garden, and it is—a *rock* garden. Despite the great variety of living things to be found here, most of the surface of the land, at least three-quarters of it, is sand or sandstone, naked, monolithic, austere and unadorned as the sculpture of the moon. It is undoubtedly a desert place, clean, pure, totally useless, quite unprofitable.

The sun is rising through a yellow, howling wind. Time for breakfast. Inside the trailer now, broiling bacon and frying eggs with good appetite, I hear the sand patter like rain against the metal walls and brush across the windowpanes. A fine silt accumulates beneath the door and on the window ledge. The trailer shakes in a sudden gust. All one to me—sandstorm or sunshine I am content, so long as I have something to eat, good health, the earth to take my stand on, and light behind the eyes to see by.

At eight o'clock I put on badge and ranger hat and go to work, checking in at headquarters by radio and taking my post at the entrance station to greet and orient whatever tourists may appear. None show. After an hour of waiting I climb in the government pickup and begin a patrol of the park, taking lunch and coffee with me. So far as I know there's no one camping in the park at this time, but it won't hurt to make sure.

The wind is coming from the north, much colder than before—we may have sleet or rain or snow or possibly all three before nightfall. Bad weather means that the park entrance road will be impassable; it is part of my job to inform campers and visitors of this danger so that they will have a chance to get out before it's too late.

Taking the Windows road first, I drive beneath the overhanging Balanced Rock, 3500 tons of seamless Entrada sandstone perched on a ridiculous, inadequate pedestal of the Carmel formation, soft and rotten stone eaten away by the wind, deformed by the weight above. One of these days that rock is going to fall—in ten, fifty, or five hundred years. I drive past more free-standing pinnacles, around the edge of outthrust ledges, in and out of the ravines that corrade the rolling terrain—wind-deposited, cross-bedded sand dunes laid down eons ago in the Mesozoic era and since compressed and petrified by overlying sediments. Everywhere the cliffrose is blooming, the yellow flowers shivering in the wind.

The heart-shaped prints of deer are plain in the dust of the road and I wonder where the deer are now and how they're doing and if they've got enough to eat. Like the porcupine the deer too become victims of human meddling with the natural scheme of things—not enough coyotes around and the mountain lions close to extinction, the deer have multiplied like rabbits and are eating themselves out of house and home, which means that many each year are condemned to a slow death by starvation. The deerslayers come by the thousands every autumn out of Salt Lake and California to harvest, as they like to say, the surplus deer. But they are not adequate for the task.

The road ends at the Double Arch campground. No one here. I check the garbage can for trapped chipmunks, pick up a few bottlecaps, and inspect the "sanitary facilities," where all appears to be in good order: roll of paper, can of lime, black widow spiders dangling in their usual strategic corners. On the inside of the door someone has written a cautionary note:

> Attention: Watch out for rattlesnakes, coral snakes, whip snakes, vinegaroons, centipedes, millipedes, ticks, mites, black widows, cone-nosed kissing bugs, solpugids, tarantulas, horned toads, Gila monsters, red ants, fire ants, Jerusalem crickets, chinch bugs and Giant Hairy Desert Scorpions before being seated.

I walk out the foot trail to Double Arch and the Windows. The wind moans a dreary tune under the overhanging coves, among the holes in the rock, and through the dead pinyon pines. The sky is obscure and yellow but the air in this relatively sheltered place among the rocks is still clear. A few birds dart about: black-throated sparrows, the cliff swallows, squawking magpies in their handsome academic dress of black and white. In the dust and on the sand dunes I can read the passage of other creatures, from the big track of a buck to the tiny prints of birds, mice, lizards, and insects. Hopefully I look for sign of bobcat or coyote but find none.

We need more predators. The sheepmen complain, it is true, that the coyotes eat some of their lambs. This is true, but do they eat enough? I mean, enough lambs to keep the coyotes sleek, healthy and well fed. That is my concern. As for the sacrifice of an occasional lamb, that seems to me a small price to pay for the support of the coyote population. The lambs, accustomed by tradition to their role, do not complain; and the sheepmen, who run their hooved locusts on the public lands and are heavily subsidized, most of them as hog-rich as they are pigheaded, can easily afford these trifling losses.

We need more coyotes, more mountain lions, more wolves and foxes and wildcats, more owls, hawks and eagles. The livestock interests and their hired mercenaries from the Predator Control Agency have pursued all of these animals with unremitting ferocity and astonishing cruelty for nearly a century, utilizing in this campaign of extermination everything from the gun and trap to the airplane and the most ingenious devices of chemical and biological warfare. Not content with shooting coyotes from airplanes and hunting lions with dogs, these bounty hunters, self-styled sportsmen, and government agents like to plant poisoned meat all over the landscape, distribute tons of poisoned tallow balls by air, and hide baited cyanide guns in the ground and brush—a threat to humans as well as animals. Still not satisfied, they have developed and begun to use a biochemical compound which makes sterile any animal foolish enough to take the bait.

Absorbed in these thoughts, wind in my eyes, I round a corner of the cliff and there's a doe and her fawn not ten yards away, browsing on the cliffrose. Eating flowers. While she could not have heard or scented me, the doe sees me almost at once. But since I stopped abruptly and froze, she isn't sure that I am dangerous. Puzzled and suspicious, she and the fawn at her side, Madonna and child, stare at me for several long seconds. I breathe out, making the slightest of movements, and the doe springs up and away as if bounced from a trampoline, followed by the fawn. Their sharp hooves clatter on the rock.

"Come back here!" I shout. "I want to talk to you."

But they're not talking and in another moment have vanished into the wind. I could follow if I wanted to, track them down across the dunes and through the open parks of juniper and cliffrose. But why should I disturb them further? Even if I found them and somehow succeeded in demonstrating my friendship and good will, why should I lead them to believe that anything man-like can be trusted? That is no office for a friend.

I come to the North Window, a great opening fifty feet high in a wall of rock, through which I see the clouded sky and the hazy mountains and feel the funneled rush of the wind. I climb up to it, walk through—like an ant crawling through the eye socket of a skull—and down the other side a half-mile to a little spring at the head of a seldom-visited canyon. I am out of the wind for a change, can light up my pipe and look around without getting dust in my eyes; I can hear myself think.

Here I find the track of a coyote superimposed on the path of many deer. So, there is at least one remaining in the area, perhaps the same coyote I heard two weeks ago wailing at the evening moon. His trail comes down off the sandstone from the west, passes over the sand under a juniper and up to the seep of dark green water in its circle of reeds. Under the juniper he has left two gray-green droppings knitted together with rabbit hair. With fingertip I write my own signature in the sand to let him know, to tip him off; I take a drink of water and leave.

Down below is Salt Creek Canyon, corraded through an anticline to the bed of the Colorado. If I were lucky I might find the trail of bighorn sheep, rumored still to lurk in these rimrock hideaways. In all these years of prowling on foot through the canyons and desert mountains of the Southwest I have yet to see, free and alive in the wild, either a lion or a bighorn. In part I can blame only my ignorance and incompetence, for I know they are out there, somewhere; I have seen their scat and their tracks.

As I am returning to the campground and the truck I see a young cottontail jump from the brush, scamper across the trail and freeze under a second bush. The rabbit huddles there, panting, ears back, one bright eye on me.

I am taken by the notion to experiment—on the rabbit. Suppose, I say to myself, you were out here hungry, starving, no weapon but your bare hands. What would you do? What *could* you do?

There are a few stones scattered along the trail. I pick up one that fits well in the hand, that seems to have the optimum feel and heft. I stare at the cottontail hunched in his illusory shelter under the bush. Blackbrush, I observe, the common variety, sprinkled with tightly rolled little green buds, ready to burst into bloom on short notice. Should I give the rabbit a sporting chance, that is, jump it again, try to hit it on the run? Or brain the little bastard where he is?

Notice the terminology. A sportsman is one who gives his quarry a chance to escape with its life. This is known as fair play, or sportsmanship. Animals have no sense of sportsmanship. Some, like the mountain lion, are vicious—if attacked they defend themselves. Others, like the rabbit, run away, which is cowardly.

Well, I'm a scientist not a sportsman and we've got an important experiment under way here, for which the rabbit has been volunteered. I rear back and throw the stone with all I've got straight at his furry head.

To my amazement the stone flies true (as if guided by a Higher Power) and knocks the cottontail head over tincups, clear out from under the budding blackbush. He crumples, there's the usual gushing of blood, etc., a brief spasm, and then no more. The wicked rabbit is dead.

For a moment I am shocked by my deed; I stare at the quiet rabbit, his glazed eyes, his blood drying in the dust. Something vital is lacking. But shock is succeeded by a mild elation. Leaving my victim to the vultures and maggots, who will appreciate him more than I could—the flesh is probably infected with tularemia—I continue my walk with a new, augmented cheerfulness which is hard to understand but unmistakable. What the rabbit has lost in energy and spirit seems added, by processes too subtle to fathom, to my own soul. I try but cannot feel any sense of guilt. I examine my soul: white as snow. Check my hands: not a trace of blood. No longer do I feel so isolated from the sparse and furtive life around me, a stranger from another world. I have entered into this one. We are kindred all of us, killer and victim, predator and prey, me and the sly coyote, the soaring buzzard, the elegant gopher snake, the trembling cottontail, the foul worms that feed on our entrails, all of them, all of us. Long live diversity, long live the earth!

Rejoicing in my innocence and power I stride down the trail beneath the elephantine forms of melting sandstone, past the stark shadows of Double Arch. The experiment was a complete success; it will never be necessary to perform it again.

Back in the warm pickup I enjoy a well-earned sandwich and drink my coffee before driving on another six miles, through clouds of wind-driven dust and sand, to the old Turnbow Cabin and the beginning of the trail to Delicate Arch.

Once there was a man named Turnbow who lived in the grimy wastelands of an eastern city which we will not mention here—the name, though familiar to all the world, is not important. This Turnbow had consumption. His doctors gave him six months. Mr. Turnbow in his despair fled to the arid wilds, to this very spot, built the cabin, lived on and on for many years and died, many years ago.

The cabin stands on the banks of the unpotable waters of Salt Creek, a shallow stream on a bed of quicksand. Drinking water is available half a mile upstream at a tributary spring. Turnbow Cabin itself is a well-preserved ruin (nothing decays around here) made of juniper, pinyon and cottonwood logs, no two alike in shape or size. The crudity of the construction followed from the scarcity of wood, not lack of skill. The cracks between the unhewn logs were chinked with adobe; a few fragments still remain. The walls have a morbid greenish hue that matches the coloration of the nearby hills; this is dust from the Morrison formation, a loose friable shale containing copper oxides, agate, chert, and traces of vanadium and uranium. There is a doorway but no door, a single window and no glass. The floor consists of warped, odd-size planks. In one corner is a manger for horses, an addition made long after the death of Mr. Turnbow. Cobwebs complete with black widow spiders adorn the darker corners under the ceiling. In the center of the room is a massive post of juniper shoring up the ancient, sagging roof, which is a thatchwork affair of poles, mud and rock, very leaky. As shelter, the cabin cannot be recommended, except for its shade on a hot day.

Back of the cabin are the lonesome Morrison hills, utterly lifeless piles of clay and shale and broken rock, a dismal scene. In front are the walls of Dry Mesa and Salt Creek Canyon. It is a hot, sunken, desolate place, closed in and still, lacking even a view. As Genghis Khan said of India, "The water is bad and the heat makes men sick." A haunted place, in my opinion, haunted by the ghost of the lonely man who died here. Except for myself no one lives within thirty miles of Turnbow Cabin.

With relief I turn my back on this melancholy ruin and take the golden trail up the long ledge of Navajo sandstone which leads to Delicate Arch. I cross the swinging footbridge over Salt Creek, pestered on the way by a couple of yellow cowflies (cattlemen call them deerflies). The cowfly, or deerfly if you prefer, loves blood. Human blood especially. Persistent as a mosquito, it will keep attacking until either it samples your blood or you succeed in killing it, or both. The most artful among them like to land in your hair and attach themselves to the scalp, where they will not be noticed until too late. But they are home-loving insects; once over the bridge and away from the slimy little creek you leave them behind.

Many have made the climb to Delicate Arch, so many that the erosion of human feet is visible on the soft sandstone, a dim meandering path leading upward for a mile and a half into a queer region of knobs, domes, turrets and coves, all sculptured from a single solid mass of rock. What do the pilgrims see? The trail climbs and winds past isolate pinyons and solitary junipers to a vale of stone where nothing has happened for a thousand years, to judge from the quietude of the place, the sense of waiting that seems to hover in the air. From this vale you climb a second ledge blasted across the face of a cliff, round a corner at the end of the trail and Delicate Arch stands before you, a fragile ring of stone on the far side of a natural Amphitheatre, set on its edge at the brink of a five hundred foot drop-off. Looking through the ring you see the rim of Dry Mesa and far beyond that the peaks of the La Sal Mountains.

There are several ways of looking at Delicate Arch. Depending on your preconceptions you may see the eroded remnant of a sandstone fin, a giant engagement ring cemented in rock, a bow-legged pair of petrified cowboy chaps, a triumphal arch for a procession of angels, an illogical geologic freak, a happening—a something that happened and will never happen quite that way again, a frame more significant than its picture, a simple monolith eaten away by weather and time and soon to disintegrate into a chaos of falling rock (not surprisingly there have been some, even in the Park Service, who advocate spraying Delicate Arch with a fixative of some sort—Elmer's Glue perhaps or Lady Clairol Spray-Net). There are the inevitable pious Midwesterners who climb a mile and a half under the desert sun to view Delicate Arch and find only God ("Gol-dangit Katherine where's my light meter, this glare is turrible"), and the equally inevitable students of geology who look at the arch and see only Lyell and the uniformity of nature. You may therefore find proof for or against His existence. Suit yourself. You may see a symbol, a sign, a fact, a thing without meaning or a meaning which includes all things.

Much the same could be said of the tamarisk down in the canyon, of the blue-black raven croaking on the cliff, of your own body. The beauty of Delicate Arch explains nothing, for each thing in its way, when true to its own character, is equally beautiful. (There is no beauty in nature, said Baudelaire. A place to throw empty beer cans on Sunday, said Mencken.) If Delicate Arch has any significance it lies, I will venture, in the power of the odd and unexpected to startle the senses and surprise the mind out of their ruts of habit, to compel us into a reawakened awareness of the wonderful—that which is full of wonder.

A weird, lovely, fantastic object out of nature like Delicate Arch has the curious ability to remind us—like rock and sunlight and wind and wilderness—that *out there* is a different world, older and greater and deeper by far than ours, a world which surrounds and sustains the little world of men as sea and sky surround and sustain a ship. The shock of the real. For a little while we are again able to see, as the child sees, a world of marvels. For a few moments we discover that nothing can be taken for granted, for if this ring of stone is marvelous then all which shaped it is marvelous, and our journey here on earth, able to see and touch and hear in the midst of tangible and mysterious things-in-themselves, is the most strange and daring of all adventures.

After Delicate Arch the others are anticlimactic but I go on to inspect them, as I'm paid to do. From Turnbow Cabin I drive northwesterly on a twisting road above Salt Valley past a labyrinth of fins and pinnacles toward the Devil's Garden. On the way I pass Skyline Arch, a big hole in the wall where something took place a few years ago which seems to bear out the hypotheses of geology: one November night in 1940 when no one was around to watch, a big chunk of rock fell out of this arch, enlarging the opening by half again its former size. The photographs, "Before & After," prove it. The event had doubtless been in preparation for hundreds maybe thousands of years—snow falling, melting, trickling into minute fissures, dissolving the cements which knit sandstone particles together, freezing and expanding, wedging apart the tiny cracks, undermining the base—but the cumulative result was a matter, probably, of only a few noisy and dusty minutes in which the mighty slabs cracked and grumbled, shook loose, dropped and slid and smashed upon the older slabs below, shattering the peace of ages. But none were there to see and hear except the local lizards, mice and ground squirrels, and perhaps a pair of outraged, astonished ravens.

I reach the end of the road and walk the deserted trail to Landscape Arch and Double-O Arch, picking up a few candy wrappers left from the weekend, straightening a trail sign which somebody had tried to remove, noting another girdled and bleeding pinyon pine, obliterating from a sandstone wall the pathetic scratchings of some imbeciles who had attempted to write their names across the face of the Mesozoic. (Where are you now, J. Soderlund? Alva T. Sarvis? John De Bris? Bill Hoy? Malcom Brown?)

The wind blows, unrelenting, and flights of little gray birds whirl up and away like handfuls of confetti tossed in the air. The temperature is still falling, presaging snow. I am glad to return, several hours later, to the shelter and warmth of the housetrailer. I have not seen a soul anywhere in Arches National Monument today.

In the evening the wind stops. A low gray ceiling of clouds hangs over the desert from horizon to horizon, silent and still. One small opening remains in the west. The sun peers through as it goes down. For a few minutes the voodoo monuments burn with a golden light, then fade to rose and blue and violet as the sun winks out and drops. My private juniper stands alone, one dead claw reaching at the sky. The blossoms on the cliffrose are folding up, the scarlet penstemon and the bayonets of the yucca turn dull and vague in the twilight.

Something strange in the air. I go to the weather station and check the instruments—nothing much, actually, but a rain gauge, an anemometer or wind gauge, and a set of thermometers which record the lows and highs for the day. The little cups on the wind gauge are barely turning, but this breath of air, such as it is, comes from the southwest. The temperature is fifty-five or so, after a low this morning of thirty-eight. It is not going to snow after all. Balanced on a point of equilibrium, hesitating, the world of the high desert turns toward summer.

10

Almost Like Dancing (1998)

Gerald Callahan

Gerald Callahan holds faculty positions at Colorado State University in biology and English. His book River Odyssey: A Story of the Colorado Plateau *combines deeply personal reminiscence with close natural observation.*

I only do it with birds. I'm not sure why. Maybe it's that birds are the most nearly perfect things I know. Or maybe it's because birds are things I'm not—graceful, self-reliant, certain. It makes no difference. And I'd like to tell you I'm proud of what I do. I'm not. I just can't help myself.

I can't, anymore, leave birds—especially birds of prey—crumpled like Coors cans in the middle of a greasy highway.

So this morning, on my way toward Moab, at about seventy-five miles per hour, an owl—a big owl—face down in the far left lane, snares me. "Leave it lie," someone inside of me says. "It's the freeway for God's sake, and who knows when you'll get a chance to turn around again. Besides, it's dead!" But someone else inside has already moved the truck into the left lane, turned on the flashers, and started looking for a place to cross over. I find the next crossover only a couple of miles back.

And then I'm out of the truck, standing on the gritty shoulder of westbound I-70, a breeze full of river water searching in the bunchgrass. It's a great horned owl, the biggest one I've seen. And because even its eyes haven't yet been worked over by the magpies and ravens, it hasn't been dead for long. I nudge him with the toe of my right boot, not caring to go finger-first after an owl only partially dead. He doesn't move. I turn him over onto his back. Only once before have I had the opportunity to look at a big great-horned up close, and that one was already full of maggots. This one is like new. No blood, no broken feathers, no obvious injury at all. Good as the day God made him—except, of course, he's dead.

Dead or alive, though, this is a remarkable machine. One polished over millions of years by the steady hand of evolution, honed, near perfectly, for the sole purpose of killing. And by the size of this guy, he must have been pretty damned good at it. Toes tipped with hooks, big as my fingers—shining, this morning, like fire-polished onyx. A wrinkled palm, almost human-leathery, punctate, skin the color of hunger and death. And square in the center of his serious face a jet-black beak, big as half my fist—a goblet for skin and scale, for flesh and bone. Covered over with feathers—like a blizzard of chocolate and sienna, cinnamon and teak, ivory and sea salt, moonlight and sunrise—no two alike. I spread one stiff wing to its full length—nearly a yard.

I imagine the owl in flight—slow hushed arcs beneath the darkness, eyes full of torchlight. I imagine the terror of shadowed field mice and cottontails, collared lizards, red racers, freshly born coyotes. I imagine a mouthful of warm blood and the sweet pop of gristle.

It's a good morning to still be breathing. I lift the bird into my arms and climb the near embankment. Above the roadway the land opens out to a warm sea of sage and pygmy juniper. Magpies are reading their morning matins, and in the distance the dark canyon of the Colorado splits the low ridge of the horizon. I walk for thirty yards or so, toward a low, thick-limbed juniper tree. The bird is heavy and warm in my arms. The other owl—the one full of maggots—weighed nothing, felt like an armload of winter evening. This bird has the heft of summer.

I lay the owl beneath the tree and prop its head so it faces southeast—where the sun will rise tomorrow. And then, I pull three of his primary flight feathers—long as my forearm—from the end of his left wing and slip them inside my shirt. It is essential. I try to think of something to say, a prayer maybe, something to say out loud. Nothing comes. I wish the owl good hunting and Godspeed.

I walk back to my car. The sun's breath is warm and dry against the skin of my neck, on the backs of my arms. My heart pulses steadily within its sheath. The sky is fat with promise.

Quickly, the pavement is again rattling by underfoot. Again, an odd sense of remorse has settled inside me. And again, I have Interstate 70 mostly to myself. I draw one breath, then another, and then one more. Twenty miles later I've nearly forgotten the owl. Instead of hooks and beaks and bones like flutes, my mind is filled up with old fears and budding uncertainties.

About five years ago something happened, something big. A star in Cassiopeia collapsed, or didn't, as it should have; a flower failed to bloom, or blossomed a string of passionate red petals; a stone, pushed by spring floods, left the spot where it had rested for 3,000 years, or didn't; a river leaped from its bed or failed to—something big. And at that moment, everything, I mean *everything*, changed. Five or so years ago that happened. I hardly noticed then. But I can't ignore the evidence any longer.

I've been a biologist most of my life—specifically, an immunologist, but I like the term biologist better. Maybe because it doesn't seem so closely linked to human medicine, maybe not. Maybe it just sounds earthier. But from about the time I was twelve, a biologist was what I wanted to be. I still want, sometimes desperately, to be a biologist, I'm just not certain anymore what that means.

And it's not that I'm leaving science, exactly. No, it's a whole lot more like science is leaving me—more like the universe one day just said, "That's enough of that shit." And biology, having never been particularly pleased with the job I was doing anyway, slipped out the side door.

Off the road to the right a golden eagle is hanging in a morning thermal, watching the land below—waiting, almost indifferently, for a single lapse, an instant of forgetfulness, a moment of courage. And the eagle knows—no matter how many times before everybody noticed him, no matter how many times before no one mistook him for a cloud or a raven or a swarm of bees—there will be mistakes, soon. The eagle waits, in the shaft of sun-warmed air, and circles.

This section of I-70—after you've left the cities and the river behind and climbed up onto the eastern edge of the Colorado Plateau—to the extent twin ribbons of concrete can, soothes me. The Manti La Sal, snowcapped this January, pierce the sky to the south, tattered old turbans still clinging to their heads this morning. The north is rimmed by the Book Cliffs, laid out here like some new attorney's collection of *The Law Review*. All else is sagebrush and sand punctured by an occasional juniper, but otherwise unmarked, in large part, by man or beast. And of course, there is sky—lots and lots of sky.

Biology taught me my first serious way of looking at things, a deep way. A little like the way the first older woman or man you sleep with shows you how something you've hardly even noticed for most of your life can give you unimagined pleasure when touched very softly, when squeezed a little too hard, or when brushed by human lips. And that's probably good. But after an experience like that it's easy to become obsessed and try to build walls around things, try to isolate a thing—tear it down, build it up, come to know it apart from every other thing in the universe. And then there comes that time in the middle of the night when you wonder, no matter how you try to suppress it, wonder—just for an instant—if it's enough; wonder if maybe you're cheating yourself somehow. Or at least I did. And that's all science was waiting for, that's when science tossed her ring on the bed and stepped out the door.

Now, I don't think she's coming back, and in the 3:00 A.M. darkness of winter mornings, that sometimes scares me.

The turnoff to Cisco interrupts my thinking. Good. I pull to the right, loop south under the freeway, then head west on a narrow little road that ultimately leads to Cisco, Utah. That's a lie, of course—all roads, like rivers, *ultimately* lead to the sea. But in this neck of the woods this road's primary purpose is to transport people from points east into the Cisco metroplex—in the middle of nothing but sagebrush and, for no apparent reason, a collection of ten or fifteen wooden buildings in various states of disrepair and habitation. Some are posted with sternly worded signs that read redly NO TRESPASSING! I can't imagine why anyone would trespass here anyway—in one of these ramshackle wooden buildings, likely full of kangaroo rats and garter snakes, black widows, scorpions, and bats—in the midst of more public land than you or I can even imagine, and every square meter of it just begging for a footfall. But Moab attracts a different kind of crowd these days, and much of that crowd, evidently too much, gets to Moab via Cisco. So who knows.

Before those signs went up I thought this would be a nearly ideal place to live. Middle of nowhere—no telephones, shopping malls, stoplights, school boards, or chambers of commerce. That may have changed. Seems unlikely these men and women would go to the trouble of putting up signs without cause.

A quick left and I'm on the road to Moab. The road from Cisco to Moab is a fine one, full of odd twists and turns, narrow spots, overhangs, washouts, abrupt ups, sudden downs, unexpected lefts, unanticipated rights, and lots of river. The powers that be will probably widen and straighten it any day now. For the moment, I just drive as fast as I can, honk my horn a lot, and imagine how it would be to end my life in this here river.

The road winds past some truly unbelievable places—Dewey—with its inspirational messages, Proudfoot Bend, the Fisher Towers, the Professor Valley. At the end, though, the road just settles into a slow waltz with river and winds through a deep trench of Entrada and Navajo sandstone—twin spirals of petrified earth, their dark red reflection bleeding into the green riffles of the Colorado River. Easier to see here how the river got its name. A wonderful spot. Then, all too abruptly, you're spit out onto State Highway 163, down from Crescent Junction. Sic transit gloria mundi.

I hang a right and pick up the road toward Crescent Junction. Only briefly though—a quick left and I'm onto the Potash Road. There's a little canyon up here I noticed on an earlier trip, and today I'm going back to see if I can find a way in—and out, of course. That's important too.

Past the Moab slough and beyond red-rock walls bristling with bolt ladders, about twenty minutes down the road I locate the spot I'm looking for—a little neck of stone, a bend in the road. I pull off to park. Rain and maybe snow were in the forecast I caught on the radio this morning. But this December day appears to have something else in mind. It's a bit overcast, true. But according to the little thermometer on my pack it's nearly fifty-five, and my feet are anxious for sandstone. I change into my boots, stow the keys under the seat, and fill my water bottle.

As a mixture of Cache la Poudre and Colorado River water trickles into my bottle, I can't help but think how glad I am to be here. The air smells of river and stone, of blue sky and wet willows. My skin feels like someone else's. And I just know something remarkable is about to happen. Not because of omens or auguries, though there've been plenty. I just know this place. Something is always happening.

Much of my time in science was spent trying to make something happen—animals get sick or better, data fit or not my preconceptions, nucleic acids rearrange or not. It isn't like that here. I never know what's coming, true. But I know for sure something is already in the pipeline. I just know it. I know, too, that it's for me and me alone, for certain, every time. I shudder—a victim's spasm of anticipation—shoulder my pack, and head out.

The trip in goes up a little wash that quickly spirals into a cleft between two high walls of Entrada sandstone. The bottom of the cleft is filled with deep red sand. Delightful to look at, a pain in the ass to walk in. Walking in sand is almost like dancing—almost, that is, like waltzing, waltzing with someone you don't much care for to the music of a band that only knows tangos. As soon as I can I work my way up onto a shelf on the west wall and traverse past dry falls. The canyon widens then, opens out to a broad stone hogback littered with black rocks—about twice the size of my fist—pockets of sand, and a handful of mint-green junipers. I stop for water.

The sky's a cirrus custard, and there's a little breeze blowing up from the river. You can smell the water, and something else—something perhaps not as old as water, but near as old as these rocks. It is a fine day, I mean a *fine* goddamn day, for a walk.

Across from where I sit (two canyons away actually, a thing I will learn later) there's an enormous jug-handle arch. Hard to say from this distance, but the arch must be a couple hundred feet high and forty feet thick. The sort of handle that you might find on Thor's jug of mead or Godzilla's jug of fire-breath fuel. I think of water shaving away at that sandstone, trickling in in September, blowing its hydraulic jacks in January, then pulling up stakes and slipping away in the springtime—year after year. One precious millimeter at a time. Water is a powerful mentor.

I shoulder my pack again and head off toward the rim of the near canyon. Between here and the stone ledges above the canyon there's a minefield of cryptogams, little mixtures of algae, fungi, mosses, lichens and what have you, that set the stony soil up for the entrance of bigger things—grasses, trees, and Howard Johnsons, for example. Without them, what little soil there is up here just blows away. Because it takes about a hundred years for these little guys to become sufficiently established to hold back a tablespoonful of soil, it seems...insensitive to crush them underfoot simply because they lie between me and my goal. So I try to avoid them. Walking in sand may be a little like a waltz to tango music, but walking across cryptobiotic soil is a lot more like trying to dance a samba to polka music. Hard to find a good rhythm. From a distance I imagine my gait must look like I've some sort of neurodegenerative disorder. Like there's something not wired quite right, or soldered securely, between spine and brain. Which is true, of course, but not the reason for my stride.

Finally, I'm out onto sandstone again. Here, the Entrada formation rolls over toward the canyon like the crust on a loaf of rock bread, then the sandstone gives up any pretense of horizontal and drops straight into the canyon below—fifty or a hundred feet. I drop my pack. When I was here before I never could find a route into this canyon that looked any better than the one in front of me.

I rig a rappel anchor, then uncoil my rope and toss it into the canyon. I clip the rope to the anchor, pull on my harness, and work my way down the vertical stone wall into the canyon.

Rappelling always makes me mildly sick to my stomach. No matter what my mind is doing, my ass knows that it should not be in the lead when together we are about to step off a cliff. My ass knows this is wrong, deeply wrong, and it reminds me of that. But my mind is attentively occupied elsewhere—noticing each of the grains in the sandstone, its size and texture; noticing the scrub juniper, seemingly growing out of solid rock; feeling each of the movements of my legs, the pressure of the harness, the heat of the rope slipping through my hands, my anal sphincter, the grate of my boots against the rock, the wind across my face; and underneath it all, the odd sense that I might—for no reason at all—just let go. But once again, I don't.

And then I'm down.

Maybe awareness is the answer, the answer to the riddle of life, that is. Untarnished awareness.

Because at this point I'm not sure there's another way out of this canyon, I leave the rope in place, stow my gear, and start up-canyon. This canyon is remarkably water-rich, especially for December—willows and tamarisk, reeds and junipers, and a thin stream of windowpane-clear water grinding at the stones and curling its way to the sea. Again, I feel the Artist's brush along my arms and up my spine. A fine day, a truly fine day.

As it rises, the canyon cuts more deeply into the stone, now five hundred, maybe a thousand feet below the sky-capped rim. Huge red slabs, streaked with black, rise like Lazarus, spattered with water and maidenhair fern, dry and gray this winter.

A raven screams somewhere.

I cross the stream for the last time, and I notice two sets of prints in the sandy soil—one deer, one human. So there is another way into the canyon. The human might have come in as I did, but I doubt that person carried the deer in on his or her back. So I suspect the bottom end of this canyon can be breached. And though both sets of tracks are old, they annoy me. I mean, after all the trouble I've gone to, I still have to share this canyon with the image of another human being. The clouds thicken a little, the wind blows a little colder, and my left foot begins to throb slightly in my boot as I work my way through the undergrowth toward the upper end of the canyon. Why can't other people leave well enough alone, dammit? I think of turning back.

But only a mile or so farther the canyon comes to a dead end a thousand feet below the earth's surface in an alcove of vertical stone. There's a pool, and more maidenhair fern—but unlike those lower down, many of the ferns here are green, hard into December. It's been months since I've seen anything but browns and grays at home. This verdant green rolls around inside my eyes like pearls on an oyster's tongue, and inside my eyes this color of a faraway spring stirs something deep down and very old.

I unshoulder my pack and sit. A long sigh slips from my mouth. Above me the stone rises thirty feet, underhung, thick with ferns, then ledges off, back to the real wall. There the sandstone spires vertically to a frosting of dark caprock, and then to the sky, a sky you can hardly even imagine from so far below. And at the center of it all the pool, black-green, rippled by the wind—deep water that tugs at my eyes and strains my imagination.

I wish Gina were here. She has been as long as I without green. But it is different for her. At times, for her, being without green is like being without air, without sight, without the touch of a human hand. To bridge the brown ditch between autumn and spring, she fills the sills of our winter kitchen with colored bottles sprouting paper-whites and clay crocks with amaryllis rising to crimson spears. And that sustains her, but only just, until we plant pepper and tomato seeds in February and fill the bedrooms with fresh green sprouts. She would like these December ferns, she would like them in her eyes.

Knowing things. Knowing things that no one else has ever known. That's what science was for me. Even a little thing—the location of a bit of sugar along the spiraled shaft of an important protein—known only to you sets you apart, apart from all who came before you, apart from all who surround you. Knowledge, and the power to create it. That's a calling. Hell, that's a sacrament.

But what about the rest of it? What about the power to see what all the others have seen, and to know in that instant what they knew? What about the power to remember—to hold in your cup knowledge deep as these rocks, and to recall who we have been? What about that?

Overhead, the sky has cleared and sunlight is seeping through. Shafts of light work the ripples in the pond. Bits of blue appear in the shredded fabric above. I wonder how long this pond has lain here. A million years, 10 million years? I wonder how these ferns can be this green, deep into this December.

As I sit, the sun on my back, the water at my feet, a snake of contentment uncoils inside of me—an odd sense that, for this moment, it doesn't matter, any of it. I lie there, an hour, maybe an hour and a half, listening to the clouds slide past, to the wind in the pond, the steady seep of dark water through slits and notches in the ancient stone. Then it slithers out again, the snake—back into the red soil, the malachite-green water, the sunbaked, brick-colored walls. I reach for it, but it's gone.

I stretch and rise to leave.

I think then to give something to the pond. Something in return. But I've left the owl's feathers in the truck, and I have nothing else today, nothing a pond would want anyway, nothing of mine that would interest old water.

I think of the stones in the bag hanging on my pack. I pull out a pebble of basalt, a smooth black fingernail-sized chunk I've carried for a long time, and I toss it into the pond. There's a satisfying sploop of water, and then the pebble is gone. Ripples move out in widening arcs until they strike the pond's banks, reflect back on themselves, and slowly die. I start down-canyon.

On the way in I noticed no other exit from this canyon. And though, as I said, there must be one, I head instead for my rope. I intend to drive to Blanding this afternoon, and the light is beginning to fade. I find my rope where I left it, a thing that always relieves me. You wouldn't think anyone would move a rope left like this one, but people do the damnedest things.

However, because I hadn't anticipated using it to get back out of here, there's another dance I have to do to "rescue" myself. I tie the bottom of one end of the rope to a stout little juniper. Then I slip into my harness and tie on my ascender. I clip onto the rope, work my way up the cliff face, over the edge, and onto the top. There, I tie a quick figure-eight knot into the doubled rope at the top, clip it back into the rappel anchor, slip the doubled rope into my descender, and rappel down again. At the bottom for the third time, I untie the end of the rope from the juniper, clip into my ascender, and climb the sandstone face once more. Saved, I sit for a drink of water and a breath or two.

But I don't really think the secret of life is locked up somewhere inside of knowing something no one else has ever known, or even inside the sacred crate of common knowledge, not really. Maybe it's buried instead among the things, like this rope, that tie us to all the rest of it. Things that bind it all into a single thing—one fact, a solitary process, a lone event—the sagebrush beside me, the juniper that held me, the sky that warmed me, the stone I'm sitting on, the view just beyond the next hill, and the fibers that run between them all.

And maybe that ain't it either.

But I don't think science offers any deeper insights than poetry. And that's probably why science packed her bags. Equivocation can sometimes lessen a lady's enthusiasm for an obsessive-compulsive lover like me.

Regardless, it's a hell of a day for a walk. I coil and stow my rope, my harness, the hardware. I shoulder my pack and start back toward the lower canyon. As I'm walking, for no reason I can imagine I recall a baseball game—St. Olaf's versus St. Patrick's, Catholic Youth Organization league championship. I struck out twelve batters that day. We still lost, of course. But I was brilliant!

The breeze is at my back now.

11

Mountain Lion (2011)

Sam Webster

Sam Webster grew up in a ranger's house in Arches National Park. His father, Jim Webster, was chief ranger (Jim contributed a story to this volume) and his archivist mother, Vicki, cataloged many of the National Park Service sources used herein. Sam graduated from Westminster College, where he took one of my classes (and did very well). He began the following story in a creative non-fiction class we both took with Stephen Trimble, editor of The Capitol Reef National Park Reader. *Sam is currently a backcountry ranger at Kings Canyon National Park.*

Contour lines wind across Arches National Park, stretching out across empty plateaus and wide valleys, crowding together around steep cliffs and tight canyons. On a map in a back office of the visitor center, I scan the tight lines forming Courthouse towers, falling to the empty spaces approaching Courthouse Wash, tracing the intricate concentric ovals of the Windows area towards the long, delicate outlines of Salt Valley. Contours trace the fingers of the Fiery Furnace and sketch lines like a seismograph across the fins of Devil's Garden.

Only a few of those lines flow back to the Park Service house I grew up in, outlining the wash I wandered on cool fall evenings and flowing past small canyons and sandstone benches that proved unconquerable to me as a child. They circumscribe the graves of childhood pets, hiding places from my older sister, battle arenas for my toys—landscapes of my childhood imagination, filling in the blank spaces left between the contours of the park.

One dark line wraps around my old home and rises into the park, rippling along the sharp edges of the Courthouse Towers and then carving out the edge of a plateau I have never been on. The contours tug my imagination and curiosity towards a different kind of blank space on the map, one I need to know for myself through these lines. Back now after only a few years away, I clip my radio out of its charger, tuck my uniform shirt into my green jeans, and head out the door.

The main road cuts its own path through the park, undulating slightly with the curves of cliff-faces and moving gently through Courthouse Towers, past the thin towers that dot the valley. As I roll along the pavement, RVs dot the roadside as well, leaning haphazardly off the sloped sides while foreign tourists step on the blackbrush to scan the landscape through a viewfinder. The sun glares off the parking lot full of Chevy Suburbans and rented Impalas at the base of The Organ—the sandstone tower that loomed over Thelma and Louise as they locked a cop in his trunk, that stands in the background of countless family vacation Christmas card photos. Cars and tourists and digital cameras ring the tower's curving lines.

Courthouse Wash is empty, as usual—no one comes to the world famous home of Delicate Arch to see a dry, sandy wash. The crunch of my boots through the rocky wash bed gradually overrides the distant rush of cars and the white noise of tourists as I turn up a drainage embraced by a sloping sandstone fin. Eyes down, I follow the narrowing wash and the few boot prints ahead of me begin to turn back until they melt into the natural ripples in the sand. No cairns dot the field of car-sized boulders covering the first few sandstone benches; no evidence of a footprint on the sandstone or a mangled sagebrush betrays the presence of the last person here.

Hopping from boulder to boulder between the narrowing lines of this drainage, my mind traces the thread of memory back to afternoons of my childhood spent wandering other overlooked places in Arches. On small adventures with a little water bottle and my imagination, I would return at twilight to empty sand out of my sneakers into little dunes on our front porch. Then, I had followed the path of my own curiosity, no marked trails or boot prints defining a true route. I drew my own lines to familiar places and unexplored canyons, reaching new places through routes I knew or chose by instinct, not planning. Now, I knowingly transect those careful contours of the mesa, feeling myself cross a path with each sandstone bench I hoist myself over until I reach the top of the mesa.

But atop the mesa, the lines of the Arches road and the distant highway reorient me. I look instead at the grain of the sandstone beneath my feet. It pulls me to the edge, tracing the contour line my eyes had followed on a now distant map. Miniature basins and canyons cut into the cliff edge, patterned with dark winding, parallel lines as well. I keep my eyes down, watching these details and avoiding the park road hundreds of feet below.

As I walk, the sandstone slopes so gently into the edge of a massive pothole that I almost tumble the twenty feet into its sandy bottom. Before me: a small oasis, green grasses rising high from damp, sandy soil, a small juniper twisting up the far side, trying to work its way out of the shade of the hole. Small, faded-blue berries dotted the sand beneath it. Yucca and sagebrush had found their way to the refuge, crowding in front of the juniper almost ornamentally. A whiptail lizard darts across the entire scene in a flash. Its tail carves faint arcs out of the red sandy soil.

And there in the middle, flattening the tall grass, rests the stiff body of a dead mountain lion.

Eyes still intact, staring up with a posthumous fierceness, her form looks caricaturized, like a drawing in a field guide. Her body is on display in the bottom of this bizarre oasis, a hole carved out of a barren mesa top so full of life it refuses to let any out. Her fur is matted from the last rain, tail curved like a question mark, paws kinked lazily like a sleeping puppy. Each rib ripples her sallow hide and a fraction of her pink tongue pokes from her mouth. I had found her even before the ravens had.

The sight throws me off balance. I fall heavily to the sandstone. The sweat on the back of my uniform chills my nerves, raises bumps along my arms. I pull my knees to my chest. Snippets of stories of sublime encounters with predators flash through my mind—grizzly showdowns and mountain lion stalkings that slam the person with an unsettling reminder of our not-so-dominant place in the food chain. Encountering a mountain lion cruising down a trail heightens one's awareness of life—coming across one starved in the pit of a National Park freezes me with an awful awareness of death. The top of this plateau, sinuous and textured when I first climbed up, now feels a few shades darker. Shadows across small dips and rises in the landscape now hide uncertainty instead of possibility.

The liberating solitude which had bolstered me up to the top of this plateau pushes me back down the drainage as a numbing sense of loneliness. I rumble back towards the visitor center in my work truck, the radio silent, the road empty. The towers in the Courthouse valley seem to reach higher than before, stretching beyond the frame of my windshield. The plateau above Park Avenue looks as pitted and desolate as the one I had just descended, shifting a shade darker as a cloud slides in front of the sun.

I click my radio back onto its charger and hang the keys to my work truck back on their peg in the temp office. My eyes flick to the wall map on my way out the door, landing immediately on a tiny circle on top of the Great Wall—it limns the image of the mountain lion's deep black eye.

12

Winter Solstice at the Moab Slough (1993)

Terry Tempest Williams

Terry Tempest Williams is trained as a biologist. Through a series of distinctive and moving books and essays, she has become one of the most influential voices in the environmental movement. She has lived in Castle Valley for years, upstream from Moab and across the river from Arches. In this piece she contemplates the small, precious wetland reserve on the south bank of the Colorado River, across the river and just downstream of the tailings pile left by the Atlas uranium refining mill Charlie Steen built.

It is the shortest day of the year. It is also the darkest. Winter Solstice at the Moab Slough is serene. I am here as an act of faith, believing the sun has completed the southern end of its journey and is now contemplating its return toward light.

A few hundred miles south, the Hopi celebrate Soyalangwul, "the time to establish life anew for all the world."

At dawn, they will take their prayer sticks, pahos, to a shrine on the edge of the mesa and plant them securely in the earth. The pahos, decorated with feathers, will make prayers to the sun, the moon, the fields, and the orchards. These prayer feathers will call forth blessings of health and love and a fullness of life for human beings and animals.

And for four days, the Hopi will return to their shrine and repeat the prayers of their hearts.

My heart finds openings in these wetlands, particularly in winter. It is quiet and cold. The heat of the summer has been absorbed into the core of the redrocks. Most of the 150 species of birds that frequent these marshes have migrated. Snowy egrets and avocets have followed their instincts south. The cattails and bulrushes are brittle and brown. Sheets of ice become windowpanes to another world below. And I find myself being mentored by the land once again, as two great blue herons fly over me. Their wingbeats are slow, so slow they remind me that, all around, energy is being conserved. I too can bring my breath down to dwell in a deeper place where my bloodsoul restores to my body what society has drained and dredged away.

Even in winter, these wetlands nourish me.

I recall the last time I stood here near the Solstice—June 1991. The Moab Slough was christened the Scott M. Matheson Wetland Preserve. The Nature Conservancy set aside over eight hundred acres in the name of wildness.

A community gathered beneath blue skies in celebration of this oasis in the desert, this oxbow of diversity alongside the Colorado River. A yellow and white tent was erected for shade as we listened to our elders.

"A place of renewal..." Mrs. Norma Matheson proclaimed as she honored her husband, our governor of Utah, whose death and life will be remembered here, his name a touchstone for a conservation ethic in the American West.

"A geography of hope..." Wallace Stegner echoed. "That these delicate lands have survived the people who exploited this community is a miracle in itself." We stood strong and resolute as neighbors, friends, and family witnessed the release of a red-tailed hawk. Wounded, now healed, we caught a glimpse of our own wild nature soaring above willows. The hawk flew west with strong, rapid wingbeats, heartbeats, and I squinted in the afternoon sun, following her with my eyes until she disappeared against the sandstone cliffs.

Later, I found a small striated feather lying on the ground and carried it home, a reminder of who we live among.

D. H. Lawrence writes, "In every living thing there is a desire for love, for the relationship of unison with the rest of things."

I think of my own stream of desires, how cautious I have become with love. It is a vulnerable enterprise to feel deeply and I may not survive my affections. Andre Breton says, "Hardly anyone dares to face with open eyes the great delights of love." If I choose not to become attached to nouns—a person, place, or thing—then when I refuse an intimate's love or hoard my spirit, when a known landscape is bought, sold, and developed, chained or grazed to a stubble, or a hawk is shot and hung by its feet on a barbed wire fence, my heart cannot be broken because I never risked giving it away.

But what kind of impoverishment is this to withhold emotion, to restrain our passionate nature in the face of a generous life just to appease our fears? A man or woman whose mind reins in the heart when the body sings desperately for connection can only expect more isolation and greater ecological disease. Our lack of intimacy with each other is in direct proportion to our lack of intimacy with the land. We have taken our love inside and abandoned the wild.

Audre Lorde tells us, "We have been raised to fear the yes within ourselves...our deepest cravings. And the fear of our deepest cravings keeps them suspect, keeps us docile and loyal and obedient, and leads us to settle for or accept many facets of our own oppression."

The two herons who flew over me have now landed downriver. I do not believe they are fearful of love. I do not believe their decisions are based on a terror of loss. They are not docile, loyal, or obedient. They are engaged in a rich, biological context, completely present. They are feathered Buddhas casting blue shadows on the snow, fishing on the shortest day of the year.

Pahos. Prayer feathers. Darkness, now light. The Winter Solstice turns in us, turns in me. Let me plant my own prayer stick firmly in the mud of this marsh. Eight hundred acres of wetlands. It is nothing. It is everything. We are a tribe of fractured individuals who can now only celebrate remnants of wildness. One redtailed hawk. Two great blue herons.

Wildlands' and wildlives' oppression lies in our desire to control and our desire to control has robbed us of feeling. Our rib cages have been broken and our hearts cut out. The knives of our priests are bloody. We, the people. Our own hands are bloody.

"Blood knowledge," says D. H. Lawrence. "Oh, what a catastrophe for man when he cut himself off from the rhythm of the year, from his unison with the sun and the earth. Oh, what a catastrophe, what a maiming of love when it was made a personal, merely personal feeling, taken away from the rising and setting of the sun, and cut off from the magical connection of the solstice and equinox. This is what is wrong with us. We are bleeding at the roots..."

The land is love. Love is what we fear. To disengage from the earth is our own oppression. I stand on the edge of these wetlands, a place of renewal, an oasis in the desert, as an act of faith, believing the sun has completed the southern end of its journey and is now contemplating its return toward light.

PART II

LIVING AND WORKING IN ARCHES

A boy's size arch, Frank A. Beckwith. Photo courtesy of Jane Beckwith.

13

Descendants of Arches' First Peoples (2016)

Indigenous peoples lived in and passed through the Arches region since time immemorial. They especially used the north-south corridor along Salt Wash and Courthouse Wash to access the easy crossing of the Colorado River, the best such crossing between Grand Junction upriver and what became known as Crossing of the Fathers downstream (under Lake Powell, for now).

Archaeologists (including Lloyd Pierson, the versatile sometime park ranger whose writing appears elsewhere in this volume) have identified dozens of sites within park boundaries that indicate Indigenous presence and use. These range from lithic scatters (places where stone tools were made) to petroglyph panels (pecked rock writing). The park doesn't appear to be a place where large numbers of Indigenous people lived, probably because of its relative aridity, poor soil, and scarce animal life. There's considerably more evidence of habitation in the better-watered Moab and Spanish valleys and La Sal Mountains to the south and southeast. Scholars have found evidence of Indigenous use in Arches during periods they label Paleo-Indian, Archaic, and Irrigated-Farming, the latter of which lasted until drought forced a return to transhumant lifeways with irrigation continuing along the bigger water sources.

In 2016, the Bureau of Applied Research in Anthropology (BARA) at the University of Arizona conducted a lengthy "ethnographic overview and assessment" (EOA) of Arches in cooperation with the National Park Service. The EOA included field visits with the following participating peoples: "the Pueblo of Zuni (or A:shiwi, a term which some prefer), the Hopi Tribe, the Southern Ute Indian Tribe, Ute Indian Tribe-Uintah and Ouray, the Paiute

Sheep petroglyphs near Dark Angel. Photo courtesy of Arches NP/Lloyd Pierson, 1958.

Indian Tribe of Utah, and the Kaibab Band of Paiute Indians."[1] (This is certainly not an exhaustive list of the present-day descendants of those who used the place; the EOA notes there are twenty-six "culturally associated tribes and pueblos" with Arches).[2] In a series of informal conversations and written responses, representatives of the Indigenous peoples talked about what several sites in Arches meant to them and their ancestors.

Members of the Zuni Cultural Resource Advisory Team (ZCRAT) discussed the landscape from an overlook in the park.

When the earth was raw, we were told that spirits were roaming the earth, and as well as our ancestors coming out from the fourth world looking for the middle place, and I think these arches, these windows were there for a purpose, for a reason, to look for the middle place, as well as the hoodoos, that there is a place of cultural significance from our village where we are now. Therefore this is a wondrous land which we came out to, and like my

Moab pictograph panel. Photo courtesy of Arches NP/Jim Capps, 1976.

brother said as well as the medicine clans that came through here doing gatherings and their ceremonies as well as looking for the middle place, it has been told from our history that it is still carried on as of this day, so it is a nice view as well as a good way of knowing our history, that our people roamed these parts of these lands.

All the Indigenous representatives recognized useful plants in Arches, including medicinal purple sage. A large stand of purple sage near the park's entrance is a designated Traditional Cultural Property (TCP) where Indigenous people gather plants. Here, Hopi representatives talked about using plant life found near the Wolfe Ranch.

When it's long and straight you can get a whole bunch of the prayer feather sticks out of one [greasewood], but now they are like this where they are shorter and they are getting branches. There, there is one that is long and pretty straight by itself. Those are the ones that you try to look for. When they are wet, this will just peel right off, this first skin and it gets down to the white part and then you dry it again and you get them all tied up so they will stay straight, of course some of them will bend and stuff but you try to keep them straight.

We saw some of willows growing on the road. Dark green ones. Those are good. The young ones, straight ones like that, are what you get for the prayer feathers. As they receive them, and other feathers, you put them on that too. So there are a whole bunch of feathers on one. You try to find them longer, like these, straight with no branches coming out yet.

Ute representatives described the creation of the Windows region.

One day this earth was round and flat. It did not have all of these rock formations or mountains or the hills or the hillsides or anything like that. He said that he was told one day that our Creator was saying that it looked too plain, you know, it was too flat. And so he asked his brother, asked him to take a quiver, I think that is what he said a quiver. Told him to put it way over there where he going to do some target practicing. But he said that the Creator was going to shoot his bow and arrow through that, but somehow it hit a certain part of that and it bounced off and that traveled all over the world. And it went this way, that way, all direction of this whole world, and made these hills, made these mountains, made these rivers, made these streams. You know that was their interpretation of part of their creation story on how different things were formed. And so finally that arrow came to a rest when it went through all of that motion of creating the valleys and the hills and the mountains. That was his story that he was told at one time. So when you hear that and look at it, you kind of think well yeah it fits together.

Southern Paiute representatives described the Windows landscape.

The Paiutes believe that the rocks, at one time, could talk. At one time the rocks could speak and the birds could talk, the four legged, the insects and bugs could talk, the rabbits, coyotes, wolves. There are people that can talk to the rocks, but you have to be in tune, especially with the plants, and animals, and with the earth. All this stuff, the water, and even the clouds

Ute Petroglyphs near Turnbow (Wolfe) Cabin. Photo courtesy of Arches NP/ Wayne B. Alcorn, 1959.

in the sky, have something to do with these arches. And the hoodoos. It is all there, it is a mythical thing, but it is all there. The stars, the sky, and the moon. Those have something to do with this whole place here. It is so close to the Colorado River, they could go down to the Colorado River and get some water there, or follow these washes that go into the river.

Notes

1 Richard Stoffle et al., "Ethnographic Overview and Assessment for Arches National Park" Final Report (June 2016), 1.

2 Stoffle et al., 37.

14

Quit-Sub-Soc-Its (2017)

Tom McCourt and Wade Allinson

The Elk Mountain Mission had several purposes. Brigham Young wanted the Latter-day Saints to control points of access to Utah Territory, like the ford on the Colorado at today's Moab. Young also wanted to establish Mormon presence throughout the territory, convert Indigenous peoples, raise crops, and extract other needed resources. The Elk Mountain Mission was one of several sent out in the 1850s to the north, south, and west of Salt Lake City. Like several other missions, this one came to grief, as Utes and probably some Indigenous allies drove the Mormons out within months after the events recorded here. Although the mission failed, white settlers had come to the territory to stay. The authors of this excerpt describe the wary contact before Mormons and Indigenous peoples clashed in the fall. The "Elk Mountains" are now called the La Sals, a name that the Dominguez-Escalante Expedition bestowed when they saw them from a distance in 1776.

June 30, 1855. On this day, for the first time, Chief Quit-sub-soc-its, headman of the Elk Mountain Sheberetch Utes, arrived at the Mormon camp with four of his men. He was the savior and recently christened "St. John" of the previous year's scouting expedition. John McEwan wrote admirably in his journal, "He is the same that rescued brother Metcalf from being killed by the natives." Then he added, "The corn at the head of this valley is his."

We are not told where St. John and his people had been during the three weeks the Mormons had occupied his valley, but we are told that he was not happy to find the Mormons planting crops there. According to William Pace, St. John said he didn't know anyone was there until he saw "a great smoke" in the lower valley and came to investigate. When he arrived he was dismayed to find white men planting crops on his land, diverting water from his creek and burning sagebrush to clear more farmland, as if they owned the place.

Fortunately, the interpreter on the scene was Gregory Metcalf, the man St. John had rescued from the Navajos the previous December. The prior relationship between the two surely made the meeting a little more cordial than it might have been. Even so, the aggrieved St. John told Metcalf that never before had he allowed any man, red or white, to live in his valley without his permission. His righteous resentment and implied threat surely set the tone for the rest of the meeting.

To try to appease St. John, a humbled Alfred Billings explained his reasons for being there and apologized for not waiting for the great chief to return before planting his crops. Billings surely told the chief that the missionaries had made every effort to find him and secure his permission before plowing Ute ground, but the growing season was near half over and the farming could not wait.

Fearing the worst, Alfred Billings and his men were astonished when St. John freely forgave them, welcomed them to his valley, and said he had been expecting them. William Pace recorded what happened in his journal.

> He [St. John] said I had a dream the other night and I saw the Mormons coming here to live on my land and I got my men and went to drive them off, but the Great Spirit told me to let the Mormons alone, that we must be good friends and not fight anymore. From that he said he knew it was good for us to be there, that he wanted us to learn his boys how to plow, raise grain and work like we do.

The Mormons must have been truly impressed by this perceived son of Israel who freely recounted his dreams and visions of the Great Spirit. Accustomed to following a prophet of their own, they could easily accept that other men might talk with God. They just didn't expect God to be so open and intimate with a non-Christian Indian.

As a consequence of the Great Spirit's counsel, St. John told the Mormons they could share a portion of his land, but he was a poor man and he wanted to be paid. It was a proper and reasonable request. President Billings was quick to comply. The official record of the meeting is very brief and matter-of-fact: "Quilsossocket came today. Had a talk with him. He said the land is his, that he likes it, that he has but little and wants something for it. We gave him a blanket and 2 shirts and he seemed well satisfied."

As clerk and scribe for the mission, Oliver Huntington probably wrote the account in the president's journal. But 40 years later (1895) he wrote an article for *The Juvenile Instructor Magazine* where he told a very different story about what happened that day.

> Quit-sub-sockets was a small man, about five feet six inches, not given to much talk, and was pleased to see us that we had come to stay and teach them how to live and work. He was willing to divide with us the little good land that he had, but he wanted some nice presents as a token of our friendship, which would also show that we appreciated his surrender of a portion of his land. The president told the interpreter [Gregory Metcalf] to give as such he had to spare of clothing, tools, etc. The interpreter offered some partly worn shirts, butcher knives, small round looking glasses, all of which the chief refused to accept, and sat down on a log in sulky silence. The president was deeply concerned and inquired the cause of his dissatisfaction. The chief got angry and said we had come to rob them of their land and run off their game, that the first thing we did was to lie to him, that he wanted new shirts and the interpreter told him he had none. He knew we had new shirts because he had seen a box full of new ones. The interpreter tried to talk friendly but the chief would not listen and became more angry and boisterous, and finally began to threaten to drive us off his land. The president asked Allen Huntington to try to appease the Big-little chief. He [Huntington] was a natural diplomat as well as a warrior. After much conversation, Allen called for presents and they were forthcoming. A pair of new, white blankets were spread upon the ground and on them were piled for each Indian a good new shirt, lots of tobacco, red paint, a butcher knife for each, and I can't tell all. The chief was

brought a powder horn with a looking glass in the bottom. When the chief looked in the bottom he laughed. Besides that, the chief was given a pound or two of powder, lead and caps to go with it. That mended matters with the Indians for a time.

None of the other missionaries tell the story Oliver relates here. The story is probably heavily embellished to fit Oliver's 1895 agenda. At the time he wrote this account, Oliver was attempting to justify his own actions of going against the will of the mission president. His writings also show a strong dislike for Gregory Metcalf, the mission's official Indian interpreter at the time.

John McEwan recorded another opinion of how things went that day and his account differs from Oliver's. McEwan said nothing about negotiations for the price of the land, but his journal tells that St. John slept at the mission camp that night, something the Ute chief would not have done had there been any bad feelings. The next morning McEwan wrote, "The chief acknowledged this morning that he had dreamed several times of our coming and being on the road. And it was impressed upon him to live and be at peace with us. Thus we see the fulfillment of the sayings and [blessings?] of the servants of God verified unto us, which they told us previous to our departure on our mission." After breakfast that morning, four of the missionaries, including William Pace and Joseph Rawlins, accompanied St. John back to his farm where they helped him irrigate his gardens.

On 2 July, the Mormons moved to their new location on the east side of the valley. All but Oliver Huntington's mess. The "wildest of the flock" boys showed their independence by taking their time and showing up a day late.

Over the previous week a stock corral had been constructed at the new site for the fort. With a large number of natives around the men were feeling the need to keep their livestock secure at night. The corral was made like a stockade, by cutting nine-foot poles and placing them upright and side-by-side in a three-foot-deep trench. The inside dimensions were 100-feet by 60-feet. Near the stockade corral, the missionaries again circled their wagons and made a semi-permanent camp. Their fort would be made of stone, an eternal edifice worthy of their missionary efforts.

For the next week the missionaries built sheds and "shades" using the stock corral as a supporting wall. They also began to quarry stone and haul it by ox teams to where the foundations for the fort were being dug. The men said the rocks were close at hand and easy to quarry. Throughout that week the Indians came in droves, some to trade, some to take advantage of the mission's hospitality, others just to see the white men and their wagons, plows and tools. It was obvious that some of the Indians had never seen a white man before. Living in the cultural vacuum of a huge expanse of desert, the Sheberetch had been isolated like few other tribes.

The Mormons were as eager as the natives to trade, and by Sunday, July 8, trading with the Indians was taking so much time that President Billings called William Holden to assist Gregory Metcalf as a trader. Brigham Young had authorized the missionaries to make personal trades with the Indians, but experience and wisdom dictated that all trading be conducted through authorized traders. Consequently, each man would entrust any article he wished to trade with the trader, and the trader would negotiate a deal with the natives. This policy ensured a measure of uniformity in the value of trade goods as well as helping to prevent misunderstandings and conflicts between the cultures. All traders, by necessity, were bi-lingual.

Over the next several weeks the journal-keepers recorded several passages like, "large bands of Indians keep coming in from all directions." Word had spread that the Mormons were building a trading post in the Elk Mountain Valley. Indians came from as far away as Taos, Santa Fe, and the Pueblo lands of Arizona. Utes came from all over. The various Ute bands of western Colorado and northeast Utah had few trading posts available to them at the time and they were eager to acquire manufactured goods.

The Mormons were excited to trade for horses. They had come to the valley with only a few horses, and horses represented wealth back in the settled valleys of the Wasatch Front. The missionaries didn't have the saddles and bridles needed for the large numbers of horses they were acquiring, but William Pace was a saddle maker. Over the next several weeks his journal is filled with references to the large number of saddletrees he was making to fill the need.

Another commodity the Mormons coveted was dressed buckskin. Oliver Huntington wrote:

> During this time of working and watching, trading with the Indians went on with increasing zeal, as they had great quantities of deer, antelope and mountain sheep skins, which made more serviceable clothing than our cotton or even woolen goods, and they were very cheap skins. The spirit of trading increased until some were ready to sell their bread and weapons of defense for skins, but a good barrier against this extreme was set up by having a committee through which all the trading should be done. Metcalf and Holden were the traders, and if any man wanted to sell a knife, shirt, blanket, or any other article that he could spare, the article was put in the trade wagon and instructions given for what to trade it.

Then, Oliver just couldn't refrain from throwing another pen and ink punch at the Indian traders: "Through this method many complained that when the trader could not sell his own goods, then he will sell mine." In spite of what he said, in all of the journals and records of the mission, Oliver is the only man to ever complain about unfair trading. For their part, the Indians wanted guns and ammunition more than anything else. With 100 pounds of black powder and 38,000 gun caps, the Mormons had ammunition to spare and most of it was traded.

It is surprising that nowhere in the journals does anyone tell of Indians bringing captured women or children to sell as slaves. It might have happened. In fact it probably did happen, but the missionaries simply failed to record it. How they would have dealt with such a thing is not known. Without women to shoulder the burden of caring for redeemed slave children, it is doubtful they would have, or could have, accepted the responsibility of rescuing captives.

With "Indians coming in every day and camping close by us," and "Indians coming and going all the time," it didn't take long for the mission to be overwhelmed. Trading, guarding their livestock, meeting with important native dignitaries and being good hosts consumed a lot of valuable time and resources. As per native and frontier custom, a host was expected to feed his [g]uests, even if they were legion. Then, not because of the trade, but in spite of it, some of the local Sheberetch Utes were becoming quarrelsome.

July 10 was the one-month anniversary of the Mormon presence in the valley and [i]t had been 11 days since St. John and his men had arrived to confront the trespassers. John McEwan wrote in his journal, "Hauled hay. One of the natives told us he wanted us to leave here and quit cutting hay." That same day, Oliver Huntington tells that as the men began l[a]ying the stone foundations for their fort, "the chief" intervened and offered a strong rebuke. Oliver implies that this chief was St. John, but William Pace wrote that he was "Old Nicholas," a chief the Mormons had never mentioned before. Ethan Pettit said, "The chiefs brother [St. John's brother—Old Nicholas] says that we must not build a fort and that we must stay without a fort until our grain is ripe and then we must leave." Oliver elaborated more in his 1895 *Juvenile Instructor Magazine* article:

> We had but fairly started the wall of the fort when the chief came again to know what we were doing, and when he was informed that we were building a place of defense, a fort, which we could occupy in safety, he put in a remonstrance, and strongly denounced the erection of such a structure in his land. He said that we must live in a way that would show that we did not expect to take advantage of them. A long parley was gone through with and the matter left unsettled for that day with a promise from the chief that he would come back next day and finish the talk.

The next day, July 11, began with more Indian antagonism. John McEwan recounted, "Arose early and went to quarry stone. Another Indian rode up on his horse and told us to leave." Later that day St. John came and offered the mission president an olive branch—with a warning.

Apparently there had been some contention among the Utes about the Mormon presence in the valley. In spite of the good trade relations between the two cultures, one faction of St. John's people wanted to drive the Mormons out. They were probably aware of how the Mormons had taken over the Wasatch valleys and the Paiute lands along the Virgin River, and they were wary, as they should have been. Mormons planting crops in the valley was a bad omen. The fort represented a threat. White men cutting wild grass signaled the loss of a valuable natural resource.

It seems that St. John had won the argument for the time being and was imposing his will on the malcontents. However, being a wise and capable leader, he spoke with the mission leadership about some of the concerns his critics were putting forth. He told the missionaries they could continue to live in his valley and teach his people, but he didn't want any more white men to come there. He said there were plenty of white men sharing his land already. To punctuate his sincerity regarding this latter point, St. John reminded the Mormons that the Elk Mountain Valley still belonged to him, and he told them he had a thousand warriors at his command. The mission president either misunderstood the threat or ignored it. His journal says the Sheberetch chief, "manifest a good spirit."

Surely St. John didn't have a thousand warriors. But he could probably recruit a few hundred, judging from the high volume of Indian traffic in the valley at the time. As a conciliatory measure, St. John told the mission president he didn't need to feed the Indians every time they came to his camp. He also "reproved some of his people for their conduct." It is obvious that the Sheberetch chief was walking a tightrope between his given word to the missionaries and his obligation to meet the needs and concerns of his people.

15

William Grandstaff, African-American Frontiersman (2022)

Mary Langworthy

William Grandstaff was one of the first non-Indigenous settlers of what became known as the Moab/Spanish Valley. Gerald Elias and Nick Sheedy helped Mary Langworthy of the Moab Museum piece together some of the details of his life. The difficulty pinning down basic facts and the uncertainties that remain highlight the holes in the "official" records that document past lives. Those research challenges are especially large for people of color, and even more especially for those formerly enslaved. This essay is adapted from a blog post of March 31, 2021, which can be found at: https://moabmuseum.org/william-grandstaff/.

The story of William Grandstaff, a Black frontiersman who once called Moab home, has long held a prominent place in our region's history, and the incomplete record of his life in the Moab Valley has long invited question and controversy. Records recently uncovered by musician and writer Gerald Elias (formerly of Utah) and Nick Sheedy, Lead Genealogist of PBS's "Finding Your Roots" with Henry Louis Gates, Jr., have helped paint a fuller picture of Grandstaff's life, adding rich detail to what we know about him before arriving in Moab. The Museum is grateful for the research efforts of Sheedy and Elias, whose work has added depth and rigor to the known history of Grandstaff's life.

Where was Grandstaff born? This simple question has taken patience and significant sleuthing to answer. A thorough review of census records yields a patchwork of accounts about William Grandstaff's origins, including inconsistent records of his birthplace and birth year. However, according to Sheedy, this is not uncommon for Black Americans, both during the years of slavery and in the decades after. Thanks to Sheedy's thorough records review and interpretations, we now have documentation that allows us to conclude that William Grandstaff was *likely* born into and held in slavery by George Grandstaff in Shenandoah County, Virginia. Based on available records, it is likely that Grandstaff escaped or was released from slavery sometime in the 1850s.

Census records include a wide variety of spellings of Grandstaff's name, as well as differing designations of skin color, birthplace, and parents' birthplaces. Despite these discrepancies, it is considered likely that these records all document the same person: the William Grandstaff who once lived in Moab and later moved to Glenwood Springs, Colorado. The correct spelling of his surname is assumed to be "Grandstaff," as that is how it is most commonly found in records, and because that is the most common variation of this surname.

A Life of the Times

The westward movement of the 1880s and 1890s encouraged the adventurous—and those seeking new opportunity, including many people of color—to pursue a better life in a largely undeveloped region. A variety of historical evidence suggests that Grandstaff joined that movement. A marriage record indicates that William "Dranstaff" and Isabella Bond married in 1857 in Hamilton County, Ohio. By 1868, this William Grandstaff appeared to no longer be living with his wife in Cincinnati, since a "Bell" Grandstaff is listed as a widow in directories. According to Sheedy, "women who had been abandoned or divorced often reported that they were widowed to avoid a stigma when asked by census enumerators or persons who compiled city directories. As such, we might take the 'widowed' status with a grain of salt."

Records also list William Grandstaff as a member of Cincinnati's Black Brigade during the 1860s. The Brigade was composed of local Black men organized to defend Cincinnati from an anticipated Confederate attack in 1862. The men of Cincinnati's Black Brigade were among the first recognized Black volunteers in the Union Army during the Civil War, and

William Grandstaff was listed among the 44 men mustered into the Brigade's Company A.

William Grandstaff ceases to appear in Cincinnati records in the late 1860s. One W. "Granstaaff" or "Gransdorff," aged 30, appears in the 1870 census in Omaha, Nebraska. He was listed as Black and born in Missouri (a clear discrepancy with other birth records), worked as a house servant, and lived with other roomers (both white and Black) in a hotel. Again, Sheedy notes that people who lived in hotels often did not self-report their statistics directly to a census enumerator, and so the information may be less reliable. Despite the birthplace discrepancy, this man is a viable (and the only) candidate from the entire 1870 US Census considered plausibly to be the William Grandstaff who showed up in Utah within the decade.

Grandstaff in Moab

William Grandstaff reportedly arrived in Utah around 1877 and briefly occupied the abandoned Elk Mountain Mission fort along with a Canadian fur trapper nicknamed "Frenchie." The Mission, established in 1855, was a short-lived attempt by The Church of Jesus Christ of Latter-day Saints to colonize the Moab Valley, which failed after a few months due to violent conflict between LDS missionaries and the local Ute people.[1] Settlers reported noticing a small garden at the fort, suggesting that Grandstaff and Frenchie grew food there. Grandstaff was one of the very first non-Native residents to settle in this region, which began to see settlement by prospectors, frontiersmen, misfits, and explorers of all sorts who were venturing west in the 1880s.

After living in the mission's remains and then in a building that he reportedly constructed at what is now Moab Springs Guest Ranch, Grandstaff ran cattle in the canyon a few miles upriver of Moab on the south (left) bank that now bears his name. Grandstaff's canyon is one of the few in the Moab area that has year-round running water, making it highly desirable "real estate" at a time when the region began to see an influx of ranchers and settlers vying for water and food for their stock.

Grandstaff's time in Utah was brief: he reportedly fled Moab in 1881 when tensions between white settlers and local Native Americans turned violent. Rumors circulated that Grandstaff had supplied the Native Americans with alcohol, which angered the settlers, though the truth of these allegations and the backlash Grandstaff faced are hard to substantiate. Grandstaff reportedly left Moab so quickly that he left behind his cattle.[2]

Grandstaff Moves to Colorado

After leaving Moab, Grandstaff moved to Salida, then to Glenwood Springs, both in Colorado. There he married a woman named Rebecca (a marriage certificate has not been located, but she appears as co-owner on properties), operated the Grandstaff Landing Saloon, prospected, and owned a hot spring. He lived in a small cabin on Red Mountain on the outskirts of town. Land sales records and multiple newspaper articles chronicle his land dealings and affairs in and around Glenwood Springs.

Rebecca likely died around 1895 (she ceases to appear in records), after which Grandstaff lived alone. Though his cabin was remote and his lifestyle therefore somewhat solitary, Grandstaff appeared to have had a circle of friends and was civically engaged, even running for Constable in Leadville, Colorado in 1889. Glenwood Springs residents reportedly referred to Grandstaff as "Old Portugee," a nickname that may have indicated a mixed racial background. That identity is supported by multiple census records that record his race as "mulatto" or even, in one instance, as white.

When Grandstaff died in the summer of 1901, an obituary published in the local *Avalanche Echo* supplied perhaps the most human snapshot into his life available in historical records. Community members had noticed Grandstaff's absence in town for several weeks and sent a young boy to check on him. The child found Grandstaff's body; he had evidently been dead for some weeks.

Community members buried Grandstaff on the mountain near his home, reportedly under a tree fashioned into the shape of a cross, and his cabin was burned as a health precaution. The *Avalanche Echo* reported a sobering account of Grandstaff's death and a touching account of his burial:

> The old man lived a solitary life on the top of the mountain where he had several mining claims which he has been working for the past six or seven years. He was accustomed to making regular trips to this town for the purpose of obtaining fresh provisions and visiting his friends, and when his absence became prolonged, they became alarmed.... Old

> Deacon Jones...quietly wandered away from the balance of the party and just as Mr. Bullis was about to begin the burial service, Jones reappeared in a very unobtrusive manner and gently placed a [bouquet] of beautiful wild flowers. This little act of esteem was so in contrast to the other unfortunate conditions that it brought the tears to eyes of the onlookers, who mutely completed the burial and returned home impressed with the beauty of this touching evidence of brotherly affection.
>
> —Avalanche Echo, August 22, 1901.

From slave schedules to census records, from land deeds to newspaper articles, this account of Grandstaff's death provides perhaps the best, most intimate window into his personal life as a valued member of his small community.

Moab, meanwhile, has experienced some friction dealing with Grandstaff's legacy. The canyon that today carries his name was referred to both colloquially and on official maps of the region by an unprintable racial slur well into the 1940s or 1950s, when it became Negro Bill Canyon. The name caused much debate over many years, and the president of the Tri-State NAACP branch, Jeanetta Williams, advocated that the canyon should remain 'Negro Bill Canyon' so as to avoid erasing Grandstaff's racial identity. A renewed effort led by Moab resident Louis Williams and Mary McGann, the then-vice chairperson of the Grand County Council (now Commission), convinced the U.S. Board on Geographic Names to change the canyon's designation in 2017.[3] Today, an interpretive plaque at the popular Grandstaff Canyon hiking trail managed by the Bureau of Land Management provides visitors with a brief history of Grandstaff's life. Every year, thousands of people walk the beautiful trail along the perennial stream through a designated Wilderness Study Area to Morning Glory Arch at the head of the canyon.

Interpreting Grandstaff's History Today

As is always the case with history, many details of William Grandstaff's life remain a mystery. While Elias' and Sheedy's research has added significantly to what the Moab community knows about him, many questions remain about the first Black resident of what we now know as Moab: What was life like for Grandstaff? What were his day-to-day interactions like, as a Black rancher, prospector, and citizen in the Western US in the late 1800s following the tumultuous and painful years of enslavement, the Civil War, and Reconstruction? Were the rumors of his alleged misdeeds in Moab credible? Did racism or (as some have suggested) jealousy over his possession of the finest, wettest canyon near Moab fuel his quick departure?

Beyond the canyon that bears his name, traces of Grandstaff's story live on tangibly in Grand County. An ice house that Grandstaff reportedly constructed survives on the property of the Moab Springs Ranch, and interpretive signage on the property celebrates his legacy. Old charcoal graffiti at a cowboy camp in the Needles District of Canyonlands National Park also makes reference to Grandstaff: a crude sketch depicts a face, and a proclamation that Grandstaff was "wanted dead or alive" and derogatory comments and unprintable racial slurs appear on the cliff walls. It is unknown whether these drawings are contemporaneous with Grandstaff's presence in Utah, but they evidence strong hostility toward him.

While research can illuminate some truths about Grandstaff's life, much of what we do know invites questions that may never be answered. His story is remembered in both Moab and Glenwood Springs. What does Grandstaff's story contribute to the expansive history of race in America?

Gerald Elias commemorated Grandstaff's life in an operatic composition that was performed for the first time at the Moab Music Festival in 2014. The words imagine Grandstaff's deliberation about the decision to leave Moab or stay, wondering if the angry settlers who forced him to leave were motivated by access to his canyon's water rather than any claims that he was bootlegging liquor.[4]

We'll never know all the details of Grandstaff's life, let alone who he was as a human being or the stories he could tell about a formative time in Moab's early days. However, rich new insights into Grandstaff's origins and how his different communities experienced his presence invite us to explore a range of questions that are relevant to our past, our present, and our future.[5]

Notes

1 See "Quit-Sub-Soc-Its" in this volume.

2 For a fuller account, see Rusty Salmon and Robert S. McPherson, "Cowboys, Indians, and Conflict: The Pinhook Draw Fight, 1881," *Utah Historical Quarterly* 69, no. 1 (Winter 2001): 4–28.

3 Among those who previously tried to get the canyon's name changed was the ubiquitous Lloyd Pierson; his files on his unsuccessful effort are at the Moab Museum. Louis Williams drew on Pierson's files and petitioned the U.S. Board on Geographic Names to make the change. Williams gives most of the credit to Mary McGann for leading the successful effort. Louis Williams, telephone call with the editor, October 7, 2020.

4 Elias's "William Grandstaff" can be found at: https://www.youtube.com/watch?v=C4dk8VV50Ns.

5 The Moab Museum extends tremendous thanks to Nick Sheedy and Gerald Elias. The Moab Museum also extends a special thanks to Sharon Haller of the Frontier Historical Museum in Glenwood Springs for generous assistance and a thorough records review. Gerald Elias shared extensive Grandstaff documentation with the editor; personal communication, June 9, 14, 2018. Jedediah Rogers, acquisitions editor at the University of Utah Press, also shared valuable documentation.

16

Wolfe Ranch Memories (ca. 1977)

Esther Stanley Rison

People who see the tiny Wolfe cabin near Delicate Arch may think about how desolate life there would have been. But Esther Rison, who lived there for two years, remembers it differently in this story. Later ranchers used the place, which constituted a private inholding within the monument. Marvin Turnbow owned the cabin and was hired as the first custodian of the monument; he may be the last to have lived there. The cabin (sometimes called the Turnbow cabin) is carefully maintained by the Park Service and listed on the National Register of Historic Places. Maxine Newell, a longtime Park Service employee, turned Esther's story into a children's book, A Story of Life at Wolfe Ranch, *still one of the best sellers at the visitor's center.*

The summer of 1906 I remember very well. Grandpa Wolfe had sent us train fare to Thompson Springs, Utah. We boarded a train just outside Columbus, Ohio—my mother and father, Mr. and Mrs. Ed Stanley, my brother, Ferol, and I.

Three days later we arrived in Utah. Grandpa Wolfe met us at the train. He was very glad to see us, because he had not seen his daughter since she was a little girl. He had two horses hitched to a wagon. Off we went to the Ranch. At that time it was called "Dad Wolfe's Ranch.["]

When we arrived at the Ranch, Uncle Fred met us, along with several dogs, chickens and horses. My brother and I were delighted. But poor Mom was disappointed to find a one-room cabin with a dirt floor! Mother and I had on big hats with flowers and ribbons on them. Grandpa told us "kids" to get out of our fancy-do-dads. He made us go barefoot. We waded in Salt Wash and loved it.

Grandpa moved West in 1888 when his doctor told him he had to leave Ohio for a drier climate else he would not live six months. So he took his son, Fred, and went West. He had a bad leg wound received in the Civil War in 1861, at Bull Run, Virginia.

We lived in a tent until the spring of 1907, when my dad and Uncle Fred took the horses to Grand River and brought back logs. They built the cabin that is there now. My brother and I watched them build it. Mother made them put a floor in it. Grandfather bossed the job throughout and brought his stove over from the old cabin, so we could cook in the new cabin.

Yes, children did live there when the cabin was new. My brother and I lived there for 2–1/2 years.

Grandpa's cabin was just above the Salt Wash dam. The dam washed out often and Grandpa's temper went up. He was a big Dutchman, and he used his temper on my Dad and Uncle when they let the water go down the Wash. They would just get on their horses and leave him yell.

Grandpa loved Mother, and "Dutch and Sis," as he called us. He took us rabbit hunting—crutch under one arm, his Winchester in his right hand. We carried the rabbits back for him and helped him dress them. Then he would fry just the legs in a lot of bacon fat. Two hungry kids would eat them. Mother boiled the rest of the rabbit and made pot-pie. Dad and Uncle Fred would eat a lot of it when they came from branding cattle.

When they butchered a beef Grandpa would salt and dry a lot of it. Grandpa would also feed prospectors that stopped at his Ranch.

Grandpa received his pension every three months. He would take my brother and I to meet the train to pick it up. He would order food for three months—cases of canned goods, strong coffee (and it was sure strong when he made it), and always five pounds of candy. Once he ordered mom a camera. She took a lot of pictures and printed them herself. I have some of them now.[1]

Would you believe Grandpa sent to Sears in Chicago for all of his supplies! Once he sent for a blue set of dishes which had 100 pieces in it. He gave me the butter plates and the dessert dishes. I made red sand pies in them and tried to make my brother eat them!

Wolfe (or Turnbow) cabin. The Park Service maintains this tiny building as a historic structure. Photo courtesy of Arches NP.

On the way back from getting our supplies Grandpa would open canned tomatoes so my brother and I could drink it.

Grandpa bought blankets from the Indians when bands of them stopped at the ranch. Lots of prospectors stopped with their donkeys. We loved the donkeys, so Grandpa bought us "Jenny." We rode her all the time. We rode her to the arches where mother took pictures of Delicate Arch. I have the pictures now. I also have good pictures of my brother and I at the side of the "New" cabin. We are on our donkey.

Grandpa raised large pumpkins and melons south of the cabin. There is just sagebrush there now. We would eat them until about Christmas.

Grandpa Wolfe was a good singer. He would sit on the banks of Salt Wash, on his old chair, with my brother and I at his feet and sing all of his Army songs. He was also a very smart man, and gave me my school lessons every day, some in Dutch.

My Dad was a blacksmith. He opened a shop close to the courthouse after we left the Ranch and moved to Moab. We moved into the oldest house in town. Grandpa gave us two horses, a wagon and our donkey. Our house was in back of the old IOOF [International Order of Odd Fellows] Hall. My sister, Volna Lucas, was born there May 23, 1910.

After we moved to Moab Grandpa would come to visit us. He would take Ferol and I fishing in Grand River. He was very lonely after we left him.

We all left Moab in 1910. Grandpa had lived on the banks of Salt Wash from 1888 until June 1910. We went with him for two more years, then we came back to Ohio.

Mother and I did not want to leave Moab. I liked the school. I had many friends there. I loved the 4th of July which Moab celebrated for three days. My mother made me three dresses by hand.

Moab had horse races, and races for us kids. I've never had so much fun. After school all the children in Moab would meet the stagecoach to get the mail.

I can see the Ranch as it used to be. There isn't much left of it. I have pictures of my brother and I in front of the cabin in 1908.

I am glad tourists can enjoy Grandfathers old Bar-DX. But do they see what I see? I don't think so. I see a 7-year-old girl with lots of freckles on her nose, and a 5-year-old boy, playing around the cabin when it was new. The sunsets and the early morning sunrises can't be beat—anywhere in the world.

Note

1 See the Flora Stanley photograph of Delicate Arch in James Swensen's essay later in this volume.

17

The Life of a Horse and Buggy Stage Line Operator (1972)

B. W. Allred

Berten Wendell Allred was an ecologist and historian of the range cattle industry and other Western topics. He worked with the highly influential botanists Frederic E. and Edith S. Clements. Here, he recalls his family's business.

"The mail must go through, come hell or high water," were the basic words of instruction the postmaster gave to my dad, Birt Allred, and his brother, Wilson, when in 1910 they were awarded the mail contract from Thompson Springs on the Denver and Rio Grande to Moab in southeastern Utah. Dad and Wilson formerly worked for the huge Cross H Ranch at La Sal, where some of the ranch headquarters were once homesteads of the later to be famous Tom McCarty outlaw gang....

The mail stage was the lifeline to the inland towns off the railroad, including Moab in Grand County and La Sal, Monticello, Blanding, and Bluff in San Juan County. Some of this mail eventually filtered through to Arizona, New Mexico, and southwestern Colorado via pony back or buckboard express.

Mail was only part of the business that flowed south on the Allred Transportation Company vehicles. Eighty percent of the inland passenger traffic rode with the mail.

Indians were the exception, as they went in groups on horseback. Spectacular cavalcades of Indians paraded by each summer. One year the Utes made an exchange visit with the Navajos; the next year the Navajos made a call on the Utes.

A separate contract covered our parcel post franchise, and in addition, much freight was hauled at a straight rate per pound. Parcel post and freight were carried in waterproof, canvas-top Bain and Studebaker freight wagons which moved at only a quarter of the speed of the white-top Studebaker buggies that handled mail and passengers.

The Allred Transportation Company operated from about 1910 until 1916. Uncle Wilson was president and dad was secretary-treasurer. However, dad worked early and late driving stage, so mother drew the secretarial job....

Moab was 32 miles from Thompson Springs. The Allred brothers received about $4,000 per year to carry the mail; revenue from passengers, a considerable amount, was extra. I have an old stage ticket which indicates that a passenger was allowed 40 pounds of baggage free (an interesting parallel to modern air travel). It cost $3.00 one way; a round trip was $5.00.

Roads and weather, both usually bad, bugged stage drivers the most. The roads were little more than parallel snake tracks. Below Moab, a ferry towed the traffic across the Grand (Colorado) River, and sometimes the cable broke. When this occurred the ferryman worked his drifting barge to the nearest shore where two teams were used to drag it upstream to the landing for repairs. When the crossing froze solid in winter, passengers, mail, and freight went over the ice on sleds pulled by men. Fortunately, none of our stages was aboard when the ferry cable broke.

Across nearby Court House Wash and on to the famous dugway in Moab Canyon, the road wound through shifting dunes and up a sandy draw. From there it followed a rocky-bottomed dry channel and slanting slick rocks to sandy Seven Mile Ridge; then across boggy Seven Mile Wash, on to some sticky blue Morrison shale, and finally to Court House Springs and over the sandy bed on an upper crossing of dismal Court House Wash. Next came Klondike, a nine-mile stretch of hell ending at the Valley City farm and reservoir. A half sterile Mancos shale, Klondike Ridge became a quaking loblolly in wet weather, a dust heap when dry, and a frigid zone in winter. It was a soft run from Valley City to Thompson over an easy grade with little sand.

Average annual precipitation was only 8 inches per year, but quickie cloudbursts turned normally dry washes into roaring torrents. Thompson

Wash had a bridge over it but the two fords on Court House Wash and one at Seven Mile were frequently uncrossable for 2 to 8 hours and the stage had to wait for the flood to run down. Fresh drinking water, canned goods, and crackers served as standard emergency rations, and passengers survived without hunger or thirst....

One of the stage hands was a drifter named Emmett Young. When the river froze solid and stalled the ferry, Emmett used to humor me by pretending to let me help him drag the lady passengers and mail across the ice on a sled. It was a great day for stage drivers and freighters when the Grand River Bridge was completed in January of 1912 and the ferry was abandoned....

Except for severe illness, a business meeting, or an occasional birth or funeral, dad and Uncle Wilson drove stage every day, come rain, sun, or snow. The northbound stage left the Moab Post Office at 5:00 A.M. and passengers were collected from homes or the Merchant's Hotel before then. Both mail and passengers were delivered to the Thompson D&RG depot in time to meet the 2:00 P.M. passenger train.

Our Thompson stage station consisted of a cabin for the men, a granary, and the corral and sheds for the horses. Our stage headquarters lay north across the street from J. M. Startmont's general store and the Thompson Hotel, a two-story frame building that adjoined the store on the east....

Rest stops were made at Court House Springs—14 miles from Moab and 18 miles from Thompson. Passengers from Moab took breakfast there and those from Thompson ate dinner. Incoming teams were exchanged for fresh horses needed for the last leg of the journey.

An elderly English couple presided there. The husband fed and cared for the horses and buggies. Axles were greased for the next grind over shale, rock, or sand, depending on what Mother Earth provided as a natural roadbed.

The wife served food and conversation. A dramatic person, she affected an uptown London vocabulary which certainly sounded out of tune under the red rock cliffs at Court House Springs. Her food was often delicious, sometimes plain and tasteless. If some members of Moab's 500 Club or a Salt Lake banker or politician showed up on the stage, her favorite alibi for a poor meal was, "Why didn't you let me know you were coming, and I would have cooked chicken and dumplings!"

It was hinted that the caretaker had recruited his wife off the line in a coal mining suburb of New Castle on Tyne, near the North Sea. Hardly a vestal virgin, the old lady's fires had burned out early in the exhaustion from her trade. With flaming-red dyed hair and cheeks caked with cheap face powder and daubed with brilliant rouge, she resembled a Raggedy Ann doll that had weathered a series of hard winters. She nipped on any brand of the fruit of the vine that local bootleggers provided and tried to erase the odor by chewing Sen Sen, the popular all-purpose breath purifier.

A lot of passengers were drummers, old style salesmen, and dad was loaded with their latest tales, fresh from Salt Lake's and Denver's dens of iniquity. One drummer I liked was Candy Williams, a Sweet's Candy salesman who courted our pretty teacher, who used to bring him to class. Candy was a whiz at all the latest short cuts in adding, subtracting, and dividing, and was the only person I ever knew who could make arithmetic appear as a form of magic.

Also among the regular passengers were circuit judges, lawyers, teachers, and summer stock actors in season. Local businessmen, citizens going on vacations or to hospitals, and peace officers with prisoners also used the passenger service. Not one passenger was injured during the six-year period, although several were badly scared.

Eight small passengers and the driver could be squeezed uncomfortably into three seats. Such crowding occurred only during emergencies. Most of our school teachers were ladies and when vacations arrived or schools closed for the summer they were in a rush to go home or to Salt Lake and willingly jammed themselves into overcrowded vehicles in order to reach the railway. Their voluminous baggage was sent ahead to be at Thompson when they reached there. Usually two buggies were commissioned for use when over five passengers wanted transportation. Often special passenger runs were made to accommodate groups wanting service, and schedules were arranged to meet their wishes. Fifteen hundred pounds was the maximum weight hauled, and the biggest teams pulled the heaviest loads.

There were numerous traveling show troupes that tried to elevate Moab's appreciation for the arts. I remember how I shivered through *Faust*, mourned the fate of the tragic mother in mushy performances of *The Squawman*, suffered with the heroine of *Tess of the Storm Country*, and enjoyed many other grand theater offerings held in the old Star Opera House.

Stage drivers remembered these theatrical troupers well because they hauled them and their complaints to and from Moab in the rough-riding white-topped Studebaker buggies. Theater managers who wanted Pullman car comforts and speed at horse-and-buggy prices, complained about the tedious and uncomfortable 32-mile trip. I remember the howl from a theater manager when his pet props for *Faust*, stowed in a trunk, were tossed overboard when a mean stage horse spooked at a tumbleweed and dropped a rear wheel too fast into a deep prairie-dog hole.

On one memorable occasion, the cast from the old Salt Lake Theater breezed in for a three-day stand. The manager, a meek little man with a bossy, deep-voiced wife, wanted dad to load them out of Thompson at night and drive to Moab so that the troupe would have a full day to adapt its scenery to the Star Opera House's drafty stage before opening night.

Dad had me drive an extra rig to Thompson to help move the troupe to Moab. I drove old Billy and Charley, two gentle geldings capable of making the trip both ways without a driver.

Dad agreed to haul the troupe to Moab overnight. He arranged for another driver to pick up and deliver the next morning's mail. Theater trunks were carried in my buggy, leaving the front seat for me and two passengers. Six other actors rode with dad in three seats in his Studebaker.

When the prima donna saw that I was to drive one buggy she shrilled like Carrie Nation, accused dad of violating child labor statutes, and said it was brutal to expect a baby as young as I to remain awake, let alone drive a team. I boiled inside like a teapot low on water. Finally it was agreed that the two teenage actors were to ride with me and one was to drive. I slept on a blanket under the seat and never woke up until the next morning when the trunks were being unloaded at the Star Opera House.

Dad suspected that some businessmen carried sizable quantities of money, but no stage was ever robbed. There were no banks or big payrolls in Moab, and mail pouches seldom carried enough loot to tempt road agents. The only men to carry guns openly were peace officers....

Three tough hickory bows held the canvas top and side curtains securely. Adjustable curtains could be tautly buttoned in place during cold weather or rolled up when it was warm. Isinglass windshields with slots for lines were used in wet weather to hold out cold and moisture. Woolen lap robes and charcoal foot warmers kept passengers as toasty as possible, but some of the more delicate and pampered easterners, with constitutions ruined in overheated parlors, often complained about our stage wagon heating. Many of our school teachers were easterners and several stayed and married ranchers and businessmen.

Dad and Uncle Wilson were cranky about the care of wagons and horses. They wanted no burned-out axles due to neglect in greasing. Mother used to tell dad he was more concerned about axle grease and oats than he was about his family. Stage business was built on axle grease and oats.

The Allreds invested heavily in horses that weighed 1100 to 1250 pounds and cost between $100 and $200. The stage had to roll at a trot on all roads that allowed it. Deadlines had to be met. A lot of the stage horses were former big saddle mounts. A few were former outlaw buckers that often made fast-stepping teams. A few would strike and kick and one was locoed. Dad and Uncle Wilson had an easy way with horses, and they handled the mean ones without much difficulty. Some of them scared the daylight out of passengers and me several times....

Amasa also sold us a pair of fast-stepping buggy mares—Puss and Flirt. On cold mornings balky old Puss wouldn't pull your hat off, and it was quite a circus to watch dad lay the blacksnake to her hide as she kicked her singletree all the way to the post office while old Flirt towed her and the buggy into port. Once Puss warmed up, she hit the collar and pulled her share with pride the rest of the way.

These were the only mares used. Mares in heat were temperamental, and it was embarrassing if you drove one by a proudcut gelding or stallion when lady passengers were aboard....

You expected to be taken in a horse trade occasionally but dad was rooked twice. Horse trading was a fine art of legalized swindling whereby each trader built up his horse's fine points and forgot to mention its tricks and shortcomings. A Thompson freighter had a handsome blue gelding dad wanted. The freighter was a master of the hot line and kept Prince, the blue gelding, and his mate hopping like a pair of champions. A deal was made and dad gave balky Puss and $25.00 for handsome Prince, who turned out to be a lazy, tough-hided dog, not worth his salt. The name Prince soon was dropped and Bull-O-Moose was substituted. He could open any gate with a latch on it.

One day dad showed up at home with a smile on his face. Bull-O-Moose was missing, but in his place, next to dependable old Flirt, was a snipnose brown rack of bones. Dad explained that he had luckily traded off Bull-O-Moose for Snip, a former rodeo bucker, but now a good work horse that would be a charger once he'd slicked up on oats and hay. In three months Snip had slicked up on oats and hay, his glossy brown hide shone in the sun, and he snorted and kicked like an outlaw. But once on the road, he and old Flirt made the best time of any team on the circuit.

One afternoon on the way down Moab Canyon, the dashboard on the Studebaker bumped into Snip's rump on a steep dugway, a narrow dirt fill built over a steep ledge or jump-off. The horse lunged and Flirt joined him in a stampede that lasted until the wheels were buried in deep sand and the winded team stopped to blow. Fortunately, dad was able to keep the runaways from over-turning the Studebaker.

A big drummer passenger spouted like a walrus and threatened a lawsuit, but finally said he'd never ride the stage again if dad used that brown horse. Dad managed to get into town, unloaded the mail, and headed south to deliver a timid school teacher who had been scared to complain. Nearing the schoolmarm's home, a frisky dog jumped out of the bushes and snapped at the neckyoke. The team bolted again and headed for Mill Creek. Dad finally tugged them into a strong fence post, hoping they'd stop. But the horses straddled the post and both went down. While they were struggling, dad helped the teacher out of the buggy. He untangled the repentant horses, tied them to a post, and helped the paralyzed teacher home. The wagon tongue had snapped, and the harness hung in pieces as dad led his wire-cut team home. Snip no longer bore that name; thereafter he was called Spooks. Once a spirited cowhorse, Spooks had lost his head over loco weed, became a rodeo bucker, then a work horse. Spooks was sold to a freighter, who tamed him with short rations and hard work as an off-wheeler on a six-span freight outfit.

Later dad traded our headquarters above Moab for a small farm below town near Uncle Wilson's farm. Stage horses were then kept at Wilson's and my cousin Horace cared for them. Horses and wagons used on the parcel post contract were stationed at our place.

Sometime after 1912, a few venturesome automobile buffs made some exploratory trips to Moab. It took them from three to six hours to drive from Thompson to Moab, provided everything clicked. By 1913 or 1914, a few jackleg operators with beat-up cars had decided to get rich hauling passengers to the railroad. They came and went as car breakdowns, poor maintenance, horrible roads, and inadequate revenues pushed them to the wall. It was a common sight to see one of these broken-down wrecks with passengers being towed behind a freight wagon.

Elected for four years in 1912 as a Grand County commissioner, dad was able to help upgrade the county road system and started some basic improvements on the primitive highways that were holding up progress.

Pressure from the passenger trade finally convinced the Allred Transportation Company to switch to an auto stage line on the Moab–Thompson run. Rancher J. T. Loveridge and his son-in-law, Edward Neuhart, an auto mechanic from Salt Lake City, bought shares in the company and helped start the operation. Two large Rambler cars, costing $3,000 each, and a small passenger bus were bought. The bus, even under the diligent effort of mechanic Red Jacobs, could not pull itself over the treacherous gumbos of Klondike or across the sandy floor of Court House and Seven Mile Washes. The Ramblers did nobly as pioneer autos. They were powerful and tough but still they broke down regularly and kept Ed Neuhart busy patching them. Several punctured tires per trip were not unusual.

Court House Wash was a temperamental hussy. When floods dumped tons of quicksand onto road crossings the cars bogged down. When dry, the new debris became deep sand that fouled the footing for power driven vehicles. Teams were kept at Court House Springs to help stalled Ramblers across Court House and Seven Mile Washes. When motors balked or axles broke, the teams pulled the autos and passengers to Moab or to Thompson. A lot of cars were broken to lead in those days.

During spring runoff, the Colorado River's backwater flooded the mouth of Court House Wash until the road bed was covered to a depth of several feet. Horse-drawn vehicles were diverted around the backwater over a gooseneck too narrow and unsafe for cars. Therefore, during the month of high water, the Ramblers were left on the north side of Court House Wash and passengers and mail were hauled to Moab in horse-drawn Studebakers.

One night someone tampered with the car brakes after the driver left and the Rambler rolled out of sight into Court House Wash. A diver hooked a chain onto the car, and it was pulled out after a week's bath. Ed Neuhart had to tear down the motor, repair and oil all sensitive parts, and reassemble them. The other Rambler did double duty, and much of the time horses and Studebakers were also put on the road to the mail....

Over 50 head of horses were used during the six-year period that the Allred Transportation Company operated. Old, stoveup, and mean ones were replaced. So far as I know old Dan was the only horse to die on the job. He was naturally colicky, and had I been old enough to know what was wrong we might have saved him.

Late in 1916 or early 1917, Ed Prewer and Andrew Tangren of La Sal bid in the Monticello mail contract and the Allred Transportation Company was dissolved. Wagons, buildings and miscellaneous equipment at the substations were sold to the new contractors. Dad and Uncle Wilson kept some of the horses. Dad took Don and Rowdy, the sorrel team. He also bid for the two grays and Midnight for saddle horses as he now owned about 300 head of range cattle being cared for by G. W. Johnson, my uncle. Shortly after, we bought the Huff Ranch and moved there. Wilson moved his family to Monticello where he owned some ranches.

Dad's pencilled notation on the back of the only remaining stage ticket shows that equipment and stations sold for $14,998 and remaining horses and miscellaneous effects brought $3,779 for a total of $18,777. This amount was for all property used on the Thompson to Monticello contracts including Ramblers and the passenger bus.

Rate of income per dollar invested in sheep then was much greater than from cattle. By 1918 dad sold half the cattle and went into the sheep business with kinfolk.

A group of auto-minded businessmen organized the Moab Transportation Company and, through patience and hard work, pyramided the automobile stage line into a prosperous enterprise. Model-T's kept the company mobile until the state and county constructed roads negotiable by heavier cars with less clearance. By the time U.S. soldiers returned home at the end of World War I, there was a full-blown automobile stage line in operation, including a new car sales service. The passing of the Allred Transportation Company's horse and buggy stage line was a sign of the times.

PART III

A WONDER FOR THE WORLD

Alexander Ringhoffer, “discoverer” of Arches.
#321 Photo courtesy of Arches NP.

18

The Man Who Discovered the Devil's Garden (1928)

Alexander Ringhoffer

Prospector Alexander Ringhoffer, a Hungarian-born immigrant, saw the area he called "the devil's garden" when he and his sons wandered into what is now called Klondike Bluffs on a deer hunt. Ringhoffer was the first person known to suggest that the Arches had potential as a scenic attraction. Here Ringhoffer (with distinctive spelling) writes the Department of the Interior, insists on his status as discoverer, and lays out ambitious plans for development.

January 28, 1928

Gentlemen,

I beg to ask information [through?] your office.

I am the man who Discovered the Devil's Garden, in Grand County, Utah in 1922—and 23-. Photos Send to Your office,—after Years of eforts I now Succeeded to git Some of the Major—Movie Studios Directors Interested to come to Eastern Utah and cast some of there Movie Plays in this Wonderful Region give it a worlds wide advertising.

And as I have Mineral Claims in the Devils Garden and would like to Stake Some more I ask if I am alowed to do so as Citizen of the United States?

And as I am also asked to provide for good wholesome water for domestic and Stock purposes for the Temporary Movie Town am I allowed to dig wells, a series of them, were natural Seap water apears on Public Domain? in open Range Country in the Desert.

Also I shall build Roads -, so as to be posible to Reach the Devils Garden, can I have the Privilage to build on Public Domain (Some Unsurvayed Lands) Roads to Reach the Devils Garden?

Please advise me if convenient So that I not do anything contrary to the Laws of Your Department will greatly apritiate any advise extended towards me.

I am the originator the Discoverer of Said Devils garden, one of the Greatest natural wonders of America, its in the U.S.A. and State of Utah, County of Grand.

Any advise extended towards me will be very much apritiated.

I am Respectfully Yours,

Alex. Ringhoffer,
Thompson, Utah

19

Devil's Garden

The Case of the Perambulating Place-Name or, How Arches Became Part of the National Park System (1981)

John F. Hoffman

John Hoffman wrote perhaps the best and most complete guide to Arches National Park. It was published in 1981. Here he tells the tangled tale of how arches became Arches and demonstrates how hard it can be to describe a particular part of its extraordinary landscape.

Occasionally a name given first to one area will eventually end up designating an entirely different locale. Devil's Garden is an example of such a place-name mix-up. Originally this name was applied to the area now known as Klondike Bluffs, a ruggedly scenic maze of reddish sandstone on the western ridge of Salt Valley. Significantly, it was this locale under its original name—Klondike Bluffs as "Devil's Garden"—that generated the National Park Service's interest in the Arches area, leading to its eventual inclusion in the park system.

Klondike Bluffs was first named "Devil's Garden" by Alexander Ringhoffer. On December 24, 1922, with two of his sons and a son-in-law, Ringhoffer made his first visit to the spectacular area. He was greatly impressed by its many strange and wonderful landforms. In July 1923, Ringhoffer, a Hungarian-born prospector and miner, wrote to officials of The Denver and Rio Grande Western Railroad urging them to send representatives to view the area's erosional features.

Frank A. Wadleigh, the railroad's passenger traffic manager, and George L. Beam, also of the passenger department, met Ringhoffer in September at the railroad station in Thompson, about forty miles north of Moab. Ringhoffer escorted them to the place he called "Devil's Garden," approximately thirteen miles south of Thompson. Beam photographed what is now designated Tower Arch, the principal attraction of the area, thus establishing indisputably the location of Ringhoffer's "Devil's Garden."

After his trip, Wadleigh—obviously awed by what he had seen—wrote to Stephen T. Mather, then director of the National Park Service, suggesting that the area be made a national monument. Interested, Mather requested William Spry, Commissioner of the General Land Office, to have a survey made of the area. The field work was conducted by T. W. McKinley, from July 12 to 14, 1924. However, he could not find anyone at Thompson or Moab who had heard of "Devil's Garden." McKinley then went to Salt Valley but was unable to locate an area fitting Wadleigh's description of "Devil's Garden." So he returned to Moab, where he met Heber Christensen and described to him the place he was looking for. Christensen guided McKinley to a somewhat similar locale, The Windows, a section of today's Park approximately ten air miles from Ringhoffer's "Devil's Garden." McKinley mistakenly concluded that The Windows and "Devil's Garden" were the same.

Moab's newspaper carried a story and photographs about McKinley's examination of The Windows. The July 17 article was seen by Wadleigh, who noted that the location given for The Windows did not coincide with the location of the area he had visited. On August 21 Wadleigh wrote to Mather, calling the apparent discrepancy to his attention. Arthur E. Demaray, administrative assistant to Mather, replied on August 26, saying that McKinley's report had not yet been received by the Park Service, and promising to write again once the report had been delivered and reviewed.

Demaray sent McKinley's report to Wadleigh on November 10, 1924. After studying the report, Wadleigh was doubtful that the "Devil's Garden" he had been shown by Ringhoffer was the same area as The Windows that McKinley had been shown by Christensen. Wadleigh wrote to Demaray on November 24, stating his suspicions.

On February 14, 1925, Demaray wrote Wadleigh that a new field survey would be made by the General Land Office. The second examination was conducted by F. J. Safley, between June 11 and 14. Safley resurveyed The Windows section and examined an extensive area of fins and arches on the east

Tower arch, by Frank A. Beckwith. Photo courtesy of Jane Beckwith.

ridge of Salt Valley which he thought to be Ringhoffer's "Devil's Garden." It was not, but the area has ever since carried that name.

While Safley was engaged in his field investigation, he met Dr. and Mrs. Frank R. Oastler of New York City, who at the request of Mather had just completed a private examination of the original "Devil's Garden" under the guidance of Ringhoffer. Safley did not realize that the area he thought was "Devil's Garden" was not the same locale visited by the Oastlers. Safley never did survey Ringhoffer's "Devil's Garden."

Wadleigh wrote Mather on January 2, 1926, inquiring about the results of the second survey. Mather, who had decided to seek monument status for Arches, responded on January 8 that Hubert Work, Secretary of the Interior under President Calvin Coolidge, was opposed to the establishment of any more national monuments. In fact, Work advocated returning some monuments to the individual states for state parks.

Park Service officials decided to wait until a secretary more favorably inclined to their goals, including their plans for Arches, was in office. Mather, however, continued to push for Arches, but now concentrating his promoting outside of the Interior Department. He convinced John H. Mc-

Neely to prepare an illustrated feature article, using photographs supplied by Dr. Oastler, for the *New York Times Magazine* of May 9, 1926. Mather was quoted in the article as saying: "The national park system contains many marvelous prodigies, yet none of them exceeds in interest the extraordinary specimens of natural sculpture and architecture found in [Arches]." The article also forecast eventual park-system status for the area.

Pressure generated by this article had its effect in Washington, D.C. Secretary Work relented somewhat, and agreed to recommend temporary withdrawal of not more than eighty acres around each of the arches in The Windows section and in Safley's Devil's Garden. Park Service officials recognized that this plan was impracticable, and did not expedite the project while Work or his successor, Roy O. West, were in office.

The election of Herbert C. Hoover in 1928 heralded brighter prospects for Arches. The month after Hoover's inauguration, his Secretary of the Interior, Ray Lyman Wilbur, recommended to the president that he sign an executive order to create Arches National Monument. President Hoover affixed his signature to the order on April 12, 1929. The new monument consisted of 4,520 acres in two detached sections: The Windows, containing 1,920 acres, and Devil's Garden, with 2,600 acres. The monument's name was suggested by Frank Pinkley, superintendent of the Southwestern National Monuments, in a letter to Mather on July 24, 1925. Administration of Arches was placed under Pinkley as its first superintendent.

Ironically, when Arches was proclaimed a monument, it did not include Ringhoffer's "Devil's Garden," the very area that had been the impetus for establishing the monument. Not until President Franklin D. Roosevelt greatly enlarged the monument's area to 33,680 acres on November 25, 1938, did the original "Devil's Garden"—by then called Klondike Bluffs—finally became a part of Arches National Monument.

20

Good Roads (1933, 1934)

Frank A. Beckwith

Frank Beckwith was a man of wide-ranging interests and skills. An amateur scientist, he was editing a newspaper in Delta, Utah, when Southwestern Monuments Superintendent Frank Pinkley chose him to lead the Arches National Monument Scientific Expedition in 1933–34. For two summers Beckwith and about fifteen others explored, surveyed, and measured sandstone formations in the region. The Expedition gave lasting names to several features, including Delicate Arch and Landscape Arch. In this excerpt from his report, Beckwith makes clear that he saw the promotion of tourism as part of his remit.

Why does a motorist visit a place?—Because he has been "sold" for that place by friends who have visited it, by direct advertising, or by general reputation. And at the present time the motorist will demand good roads and first-class accommodations. He is used to it, gets it elsewhere, maybe slightly spoiled—but without good roads the Arches National Monument may just as well "fold up."

Good roads and good accommodations: By good roads, coupled with good accommodations at the end, the tourist is quickest sold to any prospective region. It is a task before the Lions Club of Moab, the County Commissioners of Grand County, and to even the Federal Government to get this Region onto the plane of a real enticement to the motoring public, used to luxury as they are, to visit the spot. The present trail to it cannot be called a "road" under any flattery; it ends four miles from the Arches, and for the first mile and a half is so repellant that it will damn the rest of the trip. So a ROAD to it must come first; then with Government aid, an inn, accommodations, water, showers, cabins, horses for those who wish them, guides—the story is too well known to dwell on it further.

The writer visited Zion National Monument when he went to it over a vile road; ate in a wood-floored tent not superior to the mess tent our party had at Willow Spring in 1934. Quite a step from a mere half dozen score of us who visited it that year, to when I went in 1933 to Zion National PARK, one of 42,000 others; and what induced that forty-two thousand people to visit Zion—Scenic Attractions, Hotel accommodations, and GOOD ROADS.

So, seeing the necessity for a good road into the Arches, let us continue on that same (forecasted) good road we ascended when we got the first whetting glimpse at Observation Point.

We followed that road through COURTHOUSE TOWERS; we continued on it to the ARCHES sector. Now where does it go?

Up through the very center of the DEVIL'S GARDEN;—with fascinating and marvelous sights on either side.

Down the outcropping of the Arches, the road zig-zags down the hill by a series of easy switch backs, and attains the bottom of Salt Valley at the southeast end of the Devil's Garden; then right up through the very center of it for EIGHT miles, with a riot of beautiful, bizarre, and enjoyable sights in a prodigality.

21

Managing the Monument

Excerpts from Custodians' and Superintendents' Reports, Arches National Monument (1940s–1950s)

Arches National Monument custodians (later superintendents) were required to file monthly reports about activities at their units. The following selections demonstrate the great variety of mundane labor that they performed, often with tiny staffs, before mass tourism remade Arches. Superintendents, their rangers, and especially their maintenance men, did a little bit of everything: plumbing, carpentry, wiring, wrangling, diplomacy, guiding, search and rescue, and (endlessly) road repair.

Even in these early days, one persistent theme emerges. The Park Service always worked to increase visitor numbers (within its budgetary limits) and kept careful track of those visits.

January 1941
Mr. Hugh M. Miller, Superintendent
Southwestern National Monuments
Coolidge, Arizona
Dear Hugh:

This has been a very short but very busy month for us. We returned from California on January 5th and found a small mountain of mail, both personal and official, awaiting us. It took us a day or two to dig our way out and then we buckled down to the real work ahead of us. The CCC camp has had the appearance of a ghost-town, for the past month, but the arrival of new men on the 10th to bring the company up to regular strength has changed all that. They will be turned over to us in another day and I hope the ball will then start rolling. We have just started the tests on the headquarters well and I will be able to give you a detailed report on it within the week. This test was made possible through the cooperation of Fred Jewekes, Project Superintendent of the Dalton Wells, Grazing Service, CCC Camp and James Andrews, District Grazier, Moab, Utah. These two men have always been willing to help us in any way they could and they surely filled the gap this time just when it looked as if the tests would have to be postponed through lack of equipment.

ARCHES
By Henry G. Schmidt, custodian
Moab, Utah
Travel this month, 49 Travel year to date, 660.

Weather:

The first part of the month was spent in California, on annual leave, and I unable to vouch for the Utah weather during that period. However, I will pass on the word of our Moab friends and report two weeks of snow, rain and blustery weather. Since our return to Moab, the weather has been clear and warm, with just a day of snow and rain. We didn't bring this sunshine back with us from California; it is just a sample of the weather ordinarily enjoyed in southeastern Utah during the winter. We can't boast about our roads, but we do boast about the climate.

Roads:

There are, at present, nine miles of parallel ruts leading into the Windows Section of the monument. The abnormal amount of precipitation during December, plus the recent warm spell, left portions of the road in very bad condition. It is still possible to navigate the entire distance during the daylight hours without a great deal of difficulty, which condition, according to my guess, will place us next to Chaco and El Morro in the road classification. Lack of man-power at Camp NP-7-U has slowed down the road maintenance during the past month, however, the recent arrival of enrollees assures us immediate continuation of work on the road and it can easily be put good condition within a month.

Bates Wilson, Lloyd Pierson, and Pierson's daughter, examining dinosaur tracks at Williams Bottom. Photo courtesy of Arches NP.

The road to Devil's Garden and Delicate Arch sections, via Salt Valley, is impassable at present. A few more warm, clear days will help dry out the mud and patrol of these sections by car will then be resumed.

Visitors:

A few out-of-state visitors skidded into the Windows Section this month and kept our visitor count from dropping down to nil. A total of 49 visitors signed the register at the end of the road and of this number, 23 were from Colorado, 9 from California, 6 from New Mexico, 3 from Texas, 3 from Illinois, 3 from Utah and 1 each from Washington and Alaska.

Seven parties, with 26 visitors were conducted through the Windows Section....

General:

The recent trip and vacation in California gave me a chance to try out my collection of [K]odachrome slides of Arches and vicinity on quite a number of people. During our stay in California I gave 5 illustrated talks to 193 people. The largest gathering appeared at the Visalia Lions Club, where the slides were shown to 62 members and visitors....

We end this report with the expression of hope that we will see all of the "Outfit" at Coolidge, sometime during February.

Respectfully submitted,
Henry G. Schmidt.
Custodian

June 1941
Mr. Hugh M. Miller, Superintendent
Southwestern National Monuments
Coolidge, Arizona

Dear Hugh:

It is hot enough today to fry eggs on the "slickrock," but there are things to be done so I may as well ignore the heat and get my monthly report on paper. Since the 21st I have been trying to catch a few minutes for the reports in between almost continuous contacts with out-of-state visitors. Travel for the month was more than double that of June, 1940. Just to give you an idea of where our visitors are coming from the travel for Sunday, June 22, consisted of 16 parties with 82 people, registered from 11 different states. Only 2 of the parties were from Utah.

The trip through the monument with Dr. Maxwell was very instructive and extremely well worthwhile from several view points. I have always thought that this area was one of the outstanding outdoor geological laboratories in the nation, and now I am convinced of the fact. Dr. J. LeRoy Kay, Curator of Vertebrate Paleontology at Carnegie Institute, accompanied us on the entire trip, and his technical assistance was of great help to us. I will make a complete report of this trip as soon as I return from the fire school at Bryce Canyon.

ARCHES
By Henry G. Schmidt, custodian
Moab, Utah
Travel this month, 472 Travel to date, 2387 . . .

Roads:

The Windows Section road was badly washed by the rains during the first part of the month and was closed to travel for three days. Most of the damage was centered in the vicinity of Courthouse Wash crossing, but this damage was repaired by CCC maintenance crew and the road is now in good condition.

The heavy rains further damaged the road down Salt Valley, many sections of the existing road being entirely washed out. This road is passable but only to experienced desert travelers.

Visitors:

Travel to the monument more than doubled over the corresponding month in 1940. California, Colorado and Utah sent us the largest number of visitors with the balance of travel originating in 27 other states.

Twenty-seven parties, with 132 people, were conducted through the Windows Section and 20 parties, with 170 people, were contacted at the Willow Springs Ranger Station or on the entrance road. Two parties with 11 people hiked into the Courthouse Towers section....

Newsworthy Visitors:

Arches has been visited by more than its share of newsworthy visitors this month. Dr. J LeRoy Kay, Curator of Vertebrate Paleontology at Carnegie Institute, and family, of Pittsburgh, Pennsylvania, visited in this section for two weeks. During this time, Dr. Kay toured the greater portion of the monument area and points of interest outside the monument.

Dr. Lawrence H. (Larry) Gould and wife, of Northfield, Minnesota, spent two days re-visiting the Windows section.

Dr. C. L. Hess and daughter, Charlotte, of Bay City, Michigan, are now re-visiting the Arches. While on their trip through the Arches last summer Dr. Hess made 200 [K]odachrome slides of the area. He has used them in lectures throughout the state of Michigan during the winter and stated they were so well received that he returned this summer to complete the photographing of the Arches area.

Project Progress for the Month:

The maintenance of the Windows Section road continued to June 18. On that date the company strength of the Arches CCC Camp was cut to a minimum; this project, consequently, was discontinued until the replacements arrive to bring the company up to normal enrollment again.

The collecting of flower specimens has been rather a disappointment than a project showing progress. Just at a time when the desert flowers were at their best, the rains came accompanied by hailstones and wind, making it necessary to postpone the collection of additional specimens until next Spring.

Patrols were made in all sections of the monument.

Dr. Ross Maxwell, Regional Geologist, and I made a very complete survey of the entire area. A pack trip of 6 ½ days duration took us through Devil's Garden, Delicate Arch, Fiery Furnace and Courthouse Towers sections. Specimens of the various formations were collected and notes and data compiled for preparing a geological map and report on the area. Dr. J. LeRoy Kay accompanied us on part of this trip and his assistance is greatly appreciated. A detailed report of the trip will be made within the next 10 days....

Notes of Interest:

One of the interesting discoveries made on the pack trip with Dr. Maxwell is that of a new arch, located in a very inaccessible part of the Devil's Garden. The newly discovered arch is similar in shape to the North Window in the Windows Section and is approximately 130 feet in length and 45 feet high. It is framed in a great sandstone fin and is sided by an arch in the making, approximately 30 feet from each buttress.

Part of our trip carried us into the side canyons of the Salt Wash, in Yellow Cat district, just east of the monument. During this portion of the trip we discovered several caves that showed distinct signs of early habitation. The largest of the caves and the most interesting, is approximate ½ mile east of the Devil's Garden. The cave is approximatery 350 feet in length and 150 feet deep. We were able to trace several walls of inner buildings that have been covered, apparently, for many years with the accumulation of sand and debris. One fine mano was found in the cave.

Respectfully submitted,
Henry G. Schmidt
Custodian

October 1941
Travel this month, 234 Travel to date, 234....

Roads:

The road to the Windows, or rather what was left of it after the September storms, is something to make the Angels weep. Repeated heavy rain storms washed out all the old wash crossings and several new washes have developed. All sections of the road having steep grades were washed badly, leaving ruts from 1 to 4 feet deep. My 2-man CCC maintenance crew and I have been able to keep the road open for travel with the exception of 5 days, October 13 to 17 inclusive. Constant patrol of the road is necessary to make sure those brave travelers who attempted the drive to the Windows were able to reach the highway again. Sixteen cars were towed or dug out of washes and ruts in 3 days—this may be some kind of a record, but not one to be proud of I am sure. Visitors' remarks about this road are monotonously the same; I quote, "A disgrace to the Park Service" or "A shame that such a fine area is kept so inaccessible", and many other remarks that are better not mentioned. We are doing our best to keep this road passable, but it is a heartless job. I look forward to the day when visitors can make this trip over a good highway, in comfort, and will then confine their remarks to the grandeur of the Arches instead of the impassibility of the road.

Once there was a road down Salt Valley.

This road topic reminds me of a bit from Omar Khayam but, perhaps, it has no place in this report.

Visitors:

The travel year of 1942 started off with an increase of 66 visitors over 1941 for corresponding periods. Two hundred thirty-four people, the greater majority of them from out of state, bumped, sloshed, cussed and skidded their way from Hiway 160 to view Nature's most spectacular spectacle—The Arches. Almost the same number took one look at the road and decided they preferred to drive their car another year or two without willfully abusing it, and went away disappointed. Forty-one parties, numbering 169 people, were guided through the Windows Section; 2 horseback parties made the trip through Courthouse Towers and to Delicate Arch; and parties numbering 44 people were contacted at Willow Springs and urged to risk a little more of it and drive on to the Windows.

Regional Biologist McDougall was our only Park Service visitor during the month. Everyone else must have heard about our mud and water in advance....

Project Program for the Ensuing Month:

Since I expect to be on annual leave from November 7th to December 7th, inclusive, no project program has been planned for the month. The above dates are tentative and the commencement of my annual leave will, of course, depend upon Russ Mahan's arrival. His project program, I suspect, will be trying to keep the Windows section road from floating to the Colorado River.

Respectfully submitted,
Henry G. Schmidt,
Custodian

July 27, [19]45

MEMORANDUM for The Director:

The following is an Annual Narrative Report for Arches National Monument for the Fiscal Year of 1945:

GENERAL:

This custodian reported for duty at Arches National Monument on August 30, 1944 to relieve Lewis T. McKinney, resigned.

PRIVATE LANDS:

Upon investigation of land descriptions for Utah State lands included in Arches National Monument it was found that the Utah State Land Board claimed more land than the General Land Office records disclosed. This matter has not been cleared up yet.

The 160 acre Wolfe Ranch (Turnbow Homestead), included within the monument, was leased by Emmett Elizando, Colorado sheepman, for access to water in the Salt Wash. If the present owner, Mrs. Susie Turnbow, sells to this man, under an option she has granted him, this problem will be a continuous headache.

GRAZING:

Permits were issued to four sheep operators during the year. Two of the permits covered crossing of the monument to gain access to isolated sections of Grazing Service Land in the Salt Valley and the Windows Section. One permit was issued for the use of Freshwater Spring, near Wolfe Ranch, during dry periods and the other covered a driveway down Cache Valley, for access to water in the Salt Wash at Wolfe Ranch, under lease....

Russell L. Mahan
Custodian

April 27th, [19]47

MEMORANDUM for the Regional Director, Region Three:...

SPECIAL ACTIVITIES:

An investigation was made on April 12th of unauthorized excavation of dinosaur remains in the vicinity of Dalton Wells, 15 miles from Moab. It was found that Mr. Cole Godsey, owner of a small private museum at Idaho Springs, Colorado, had hired local boys and was collecting some very good specimens on public domain. After learning that he did not have the necessary permit I advised him that he could not rightfully remove the collection until he had received permission from the Bureau of Land Management, who control the land. The specimens were unloaded and he returned to Moab to contact representatives of the Bureau. This deposit should have protection to prevent recurrence of this type of promiscuous collecting as it will eventually make an interesting exhibit.

RESEARCH AND OBSERVATION:

A party of Brigham Young University professors and students, 8 in all, are making a three-day survey of plant and animal life in the monument. They left headquarters on May 25th, with a string of 19 horses, for the base camp site at Freshwater Spring. They intended to return late on the evening of April 27th. Check lists will be made up and submitted to the Service at an early date.

Russell L. Mahan
Custodian

July 29, [19]47

MEMORANDUM for the Regional Director, Region Three:

The following is a narrative report for Arches National Monument for the month of July, 1947: ...

PUBLICITY:

The June issue of Utah Magazine contained an excellent write-up and pictures on Arches. This is the result of the expedition made into the area by Dr. D. Elden Beck and other professors from the Brigham Young University of Provo, Utah during April.

The August issue of National Geographic contained Jack Breed's pictures and article on Arches. Requests have already been received from people who have seen the article and pictures for information on the area. This is excellent publicity and should boost our travel considerably.

Representatives of Graphic Pictures of Los Angeles, California visited the area on July 11th and shot colored movies and 4x5 black and white of features in the Windows Section....

Russell L. Mahan
Custodian

October 28, [19]47

MEMORANDUM for the Regional Director, Region Three:

The following is a narrative report for Arches National Monument for the month of October, 1947.

GENERAL:

Despite heavy storms during the month the exceptional visitation to this area has continued. Most of our visitors are the type who want to spend several days in the country absorbing the scenery of the area and not the stop-look-run type, but we have had to discourage their visiting the outlying sections due to impassable roads. Many of these parties, not to be discouraged, have made the hike from Balanced Rock to Delicate Arch, a round-trip of 12 miles, and stated that it was certainly worth the effort. The Courthouse Towers area continues to be one of the most popular sections, despite the two mile walk over rough country with no trail.

TRAVEL:

Again this month our travel was well above normal with 181 cars and 463 people visiting the area, as compared with 70 cars and 185 people for October, 1946. We had representation from 28 states and Canada. Approximately 75% of the travel was out-of-state.

The Moab Lions Club held a picnic at the Windows on September 28th, honoring visiting Lions from Grand Junction, Colorado and Monticello, Utah with 75 people in attendance....

The heavy storms experienced during the month raised havoc with our roads. On October 13th three cars containing 6 people, were marooned near Courthouse Wash due to high water, and had to spend the night there. They were all good sports and enjoyed the experience very much. We have been able to keep the road to the Windows passable after these storms but for most of the month it has been very rough. The state hauled shale to Courthouse Wash and other bad spots on October 24th and 25th and the patrol graded the road from the highway to Balanced Rock on the 27th. The headquarters loop road was washed out in three places when a retaining wall gave way in the wash above quarters and flooded the headquarters area.

The road to the Devil's Garden and Delicate Arch, through Salt Valley, has been impassable since October 10th and I don't know when the county will be able to put it in passable shape.

PUBLICITY:

The Viking Pictures Corporation of Chicago, Illinois have signed a contract with the Utah State Department of Publicity and Industrial Development for the making of two reels of color film of Southeastern Utah. Representatives of the company, Mr. Sullivan C. Richardson and Mr. Arnold Whitaker arrived on October 15th and the matter of the filming of Natural Bridges and Arches National Monument was discussed. They left for Natural Bridges on the 6th, to complete filming there before snow closed the road over the Elk Mountain. They returned on the 15th and shot the Windows and Courthouse Towers sections, after which they went to Monument Valley and finished their work there. They are at present filming the features of the Devil's Garden and Delicate Arch sections....

PRIVATE LANDS:

Funds have been made available for the purchase of the 160 acres of private land included in the monument, the Turnbow Homestead, and negotiations are under way for the acquisition of same.

MAINTENANCE:

Our water pumping system ceased functioning on October 9th and upon investigation, it was found that the main shaft in the pump rack had broken. A new shaft was made in Moab and it was again in operation on October 9th.

Signs are being constructed for the new roads to Devil's Garden, Fiery Furnace and Delicate Arch and also for the trails in these sections. We hope to have all roads and trails adequately marked by the next travel year.

NATIONAL PARK SERVICE VISITORS:

Mr. Jesse Nusbaum visited the area for a short time on October 9th and discussed the investigation now being carried on by the Bureau of Land Management of unauthorized archaeological excavations in San Juan County. He continued on to Blanding to contact Mr. Koch, who is making the investigation.

Russell L. Mahan
Custodian

January 27, 1950

Memorandum
To: Regional Director, Region Three
From: Superintendent, Arches National Monument
Subject: Monthly Narrative Report for the month of January, 1950

WEATHER:

We certainly were not bored by the weather this month, for winter made its appearance five times, March blew in and out for three days and spring, with warm sunny days, visited for almost a week. At present winter seems here to stay....

PERSONNEL:

On January 22 Maintenance man Winbourn was stricken with a heart attack while at his residence in Moab. He is now in the Grand County Hospital and the Doctor has informed us that he will not be able to return to work for three or four months. We will miss him and his fine work, but I believe we can get along until he returns.

GRAZING:

Sheep crossing permits were renewed for Mr. Emmett Elizondo and Mr. Frank Paxton. A cattle crossing permit was issued to Mr. Ross S. Musselman. A thorough investigation was made concerning the watering and crossing problems of Mr. James S. Westwood's cattle. His grazing permit expired last year, and it is a little difficult to teach old cows new tricks without a fence. Our only solution to this problem, at present, has been to issue a crossing permit to water and enlist the cooperation of Mr. Westwood....

Bates E. Wilson
Superintendent

To: General Superintendent
From: Superintendent, Arches
Subject: Monthly Narrative Report for May, 1950...

NATURE TRAIL:

Valuable assistance was received in identifying plants along our proposed nature trail from two botanists out of Dr. Hayward's B.Y.U. group. Numbered blocks have been painted and carved and when time permits a rough draft for the mimeographed leaflet will be submitted to the Regional Office.

PERSONNEL:

Maintenanceman Winbourn's health has improved a great deal since his return to duty, but we are still trying to keep him on light duty. Ranger Worthington took annual leave on May 24th and will return to duty June 5. At the annual election of officers of the Moab Lions Club Ranger Worthington was made a one year Director and Superintendent Wilson brought up the rear as Tail Twister....

RESEARCH & OBSERVATION:

A group of 12 men under the direction of Dr. Lynn Hayward, Brigham Young University, spent the week of May 7th thru May 12th completing the Natural History Survey which has been in progress since 1947.

CONCESSIONS:

Mr. Ross S. Musselman, Four M Ranch was the successful bidder on the Pack & Saddle Horse Concession. He intends to start operations as soon after June 1st as possible.

Copies of Form B permit for the operation of the Food & Drink concession by Mr. Keith Bateman, Moab, have been received in this office and returned to the Regional Office for further handling....

SPECIAL ACTIVITIES:

Mr. John Ford will start the filming of a picture called "Rio Bravo" for Republic Productions on June 10, starring John Wayne and Maureen O'Hara. The company of 160 will stay in Moab and most of the shots will be made on the Colorado River 12 miles above the bridge.

SPECIAL TRIPS:

A trip was made to Navajo National Monument in order to deliver a horse trailer and [?] and also pick up a kitchen range and hot water heater for Arches. It was my first trip to Betatakin and I thoroughly enjoyed it in spite of the Monument Valley roads.

NATURAL BRIDGES:

John Wiley Redd went on duty May 22nd and officially opened the monument, but as I have received no mail from him I am unable to give a very detailed report. The lateness of this report is due to unforeseen happenings and a great rush of travel.

Bates E. Wilson
Superintendent

February 23, 1954

Memorandum
To: General Superintendent
From: Superintendent, Arches
Subject: Narrative report for February, 1954

WEATHER:

Only one light storm interrupted the unusually clear, warm weather which has prevailed during the month.

TRAVEL:

Taking advantage of the pleasant weather, most of the newcomers in Moab, of which there is an astounding number, have set out to see the scenic sights and our travel count shows an increase of 79% over the same period last year. A total of 951 people entered the area in 297 cars.

INTERPRETATION:

The register at the Wayside Exhibit was signed by 373 people and we estimate the same number used the Cove Nature Trail. Ranger Morris has completed the project of casting the Nature Trail stakes and they will be placed when we receive the new edition of the leaflet. To cut down on the loss experienced last year on the trail leaflets Bob has constructed a collection box at the end of the trail, which will act as a tactful reminder to either pay for the leaflet or leave it. Bob is also well along with the construction of the Layman's Herbarium and publications display case.

The prefabrication of the Wayside Exhibit for Natural Bridges was completed by Merle Winbourn and it will be erected at the headquarters site in May.

Information requests are making quite a dent in our supply of postage stamps, averaging about 1/3 of the total used for the month. Thirty-two requests were answered this month.

COMMERCIAL POWER:

The formal contract from the Utah Power and Light Co. for power at Arches has apparently been received by your office and we hope to see a line crew here in the very near future. We are keeping our fingers crossed for the operation of the old light plant until this project is completed.

BOUNDARY POSTING:

Nine days were spent in posting the monument boundaries to ward off the mad scramble for Uranium claims which hit its peak this month. Twenty-nine miles of the boundary were posted on all roads, trails, section and quarter corners. The transit was used on almost all corners as most of the old posts and signs were missing.

ROADS AND TRAILS:

A sign has been placed at the end of the Delicate Arch Trail reading, "END OF TRAIL, PROCEED AT YOUR OWN RISK." With most of the odd jobs cleaned up Merle Winbourn will go back on the job of shaling our roads. All of his road equipment except the dump truck has been put in good shape.

Bates E. Wilson
Superintendent

August 25, 1954

Memorandum
To: General Superintendent
From: Acting Sup't., Arches
Subject Narrative report for August 1954

WEATHER:

High temperatures have dropped to around 97 degrees. There was one hard rain in Salt Valley on Aug. 13 causing some damage to the Devil's Garden and Delicate Arch roads. The Windows Section got a nice shower and at headquarters we have had no rain at all....

COMMERCIAL POWER:

The Utah Power and Light Co. went to work on a structure at the AEC Sampling Plant that resembled a sub-station. We all got excited—the Moab Electric Co. came out and installed meter bases, breaker boxes and made all connections for 110–220 volt power to the residences and utility area. The power crew completed the structure and ran a line to the AEC plant, then pulled out. However they did not tie in the sub-station with the main line and they did not underline back to us as they said they would do. Rumor has it that the substation could not pass inspection. At least there has been no activity for the past two weeks and it seems that not even the AEC can speed them up....

ADMIN. CONT:

Rumors are flying in Moab that Arches is to be opened up for Uranium mining. The personnel at this monument does not know a thing about it and in the past three weeks we have seen several faces fall and a few million dollars fade from the eyes of would be miners who are sure they would be another Charley Steen if the monument were only opened up.

ROADS & TRAILS:

Entrance route #93 has been very rough all month. The monument roads are in good condition....

NOTE WORTHY VISITORS:

Mr. Alfred A. Knopf, Chairman, Advisory Board on National Parks, Historic Sites, Buildings and Monuments; and companion Mr. William A. Koaleland.

Robert L. Morris
Acting Sup't

22

Utah's Arches of Stone (1947)

Jack Breed

Southern Utah's spectacular geology became a favorite magazine subject in the mid-twentieth century. Jack Breed was a prolific photographer-journalist whose work often appeared in National Geographic. *His article points up how undeveloped and relatively unvisited the Arches and Moab area were.*

"Beyond those mountains," said Harry Goulding one evening as we watched the sunset from the porch of his Monument Valley trading post, "is a natural arch as long as a football field!"

Harry was looking north toward the Blue (Abajo) Mountains in southeastern Utah. Beyond this range we could clearly see, 100 miles from us, the La Sal or "Salt" Mountains, which served as a towering landmark for Arches National Monument of Utah, to which Harry was referring.

An arch that almost equals a football field in length was worth investigating!...

Moab, with a population of about a thousand, is the county seat for Grand County and the center of an extensive sheep- and cattle-grazing area for a little-known sector of eastern Utah. The valley in which the town is located was first settled in 1855. Continuous trouble with the neighboring Piute and Navajo Indians, however, prevented any permanent settlement for nearly 25 years, when in 1879 the town itself was established.

Moab has never grown large. Many of its people are descended from the original settlers of the region.

Most travelers pass right through Moab and remember the place as a verdant farming community sleeping amid a settling of brilliant red cliffs. However, the speeding traveler is really missing some of the most spectacular scenery in the United States.

Behind the ruddy abutments of Moab Valley lies a veritable galaxy of natural wonders—delicate arches, giant natural bridges, and the deep canyons of the Green and Colorado Rivers, climaxed by the startling vistas from Dead Horse and Grand View Points.

Nestled against the slopes of the La Sal Mountains are lovely lake and aspen glades to tempt fisherman and hunter, lonely Castle Valley, and awe-inspiring Fisher Towers, which dwarf modern skyscrapers.

The most readily accessible attraction is the maze of sand-blasted formations included in Arches National Monument, which lies just a few miles north and west of the town.

Wagons Lowered by Rope to Valley

With Custodian Russell L. Mahan of the National Park Service as guide, I set out toward the Windows section early one morning to study and photograph its geologic wonders. We sped northwest on the paved highway up the steep incline of Moab Canyon, following the route of the old Mormon dugway.

"Over here," said Russell, "you can see where some early settlers lowered their wagons over the rock. They had to dismantle them and let them down piece by piece through these clefts."

Paralleling the road in many places are unusually regular steps cut into the rocks, and on close examination we could still find the marks worn by the old wagon wheels.

Near the top of the dugway, where the highway bursts out of the red-rock canyon into the open prairie, we passed the original jumping-off place, a perpendicular ledge which offered Mormon settlers their first real obstacle in reaching the fertile valley beyond.

A few miles along on the prairie we turned off to the right on an unobtrusive dirt road that leads to the Windows section of the Arches, nine driving miles away.

In the fall of 1936, Harry Goulding of Monument Valley, in his specially equipped car, managed to traverse the rugged sand and rock of the Arches region and thus became the first person to drive a car right into the Arches. Soon afterward a bulldozer followed Harry's tracks and made a passable trail.

Little improvement was done on this rough road to the Windows section until recently. Mahan, aided by members of the Highway Department, has done much to make the way an easier drive for the most discriminating motorist.

We followed Goulding's original route, twisting and winding over small dunes and tablelands, across "slickrock," and through several washes which are invariably flooded after heavy rains or during spring thaws.

Windows Section Most Easily Accessible

At the end of eight miles we were in the midst of the red-rock formations that could be seen from the highway, and began to pass many weirdly eroded towers, spires, balanced rocks, and finally some arches. We parked the car, and after a hike of a few minutes and several hundred yards toward Double Arch we passed between two huge buttresses jutting out on either side of the trail. Strewn on the ground below were the chunked remains of a former complete span.

"That used to be a fine big arch," said Russell, "but it eroded too far and fell through. You'll see arches in all states of erosion here."

In the Windows section the basic geology of the Arches can be studied. The rock strata stand out in bold relief; it is easy to see where one layer ends and another begins.

The arches are holes blasted mainly by the wind through long sandstone reefs. Throughout the Monument I noted that these thin reefs or fins are sometimes 300 feet or more in height, and often hundreds of yards in length.

The freezing of rain water in cracks and joints in the rock mass, along with subsequent thawing, enlarges the cracks until big chunks become loosened and start to fall out.

After this process has been repeated for several thousands of years, huge caves develop in the reef and eventually, in many instances, a complete break results. Fine sand, driven by high winds, helps speed the process and smooths out the jagged breaks into finely sculptured contours.

In the Arches these windows have been formed in a 300-foot layer of rock called the Entrada sandstone called the Carmel formation. Below is the better-known Navajo sandstone, common throughout southern Utah and northern Arizona.

Since geologists class these rocks in the Upper Jurassic period, it would mean that the general rock matrix of the Arches is some 40 million years old!

It took us a full morning to hike around the Windows section of the Arches to visit each of the major features. In the afternoon we returned to Mahan's headquarters to prepare for the climb to the Courthouse Towers sector.

I could see little sign of a trail to Courthouse Towers. We started climbing up the talus slope and slickrock immediately behind the Monument headquarters, picking the easiest way over or around the huge sandstone boulders. Mahan showed me where some work had been started during C.C.C. days to build a road by means of hairpin switchbacks up the face of the escarpment.

This feat has not yet been completed. Eventually it will make the Courthouse towers section available to travelers in their cars.

Fifteen minutes of steady climbing brought us to the base of the sheer sandstone cliff that forms the north wall of Moab Canyon.

Beneath us was the black thread of highway US 160, which follows the route of an old Mormon trail.

To the left, three miles away, we could see the break in the south wall of Moab Canyon where the Colorado River starts winding through hundreds of miles of high red walls that will eventually bring it into Lake Mead, Nevada.

The pattern of deep-green fields and trees around Moab contrasted sharply with the brilliant red walls of Moab Canyon and the "behind-the-rocks" escarpment which hems in the town from the south. Farther to the eastward, receding rain clouds atop the 13,000-foot La Sal Mountains formed a backdrop to this breath-taking sight.

We continued along the base of the cliff, working our way back over the rim on to the sandy juniper flat that leads to the junction with Park Avenue Canyon.

At the head of this hidden gorge there is a sudden but easily traversed drop-off into a winding dry wash that runs the Courthouse Towers section.

Park Avenue of the Arches

Arches' Park Avenue is well named indeed. For a mile down to Courthouse Wash, huge, silent, sandstone skyscrapers looked down on us as we made our way toward Great Organ Rock at the far end.

The monoliths in this section were named by the citizens of Moab who have explored the area, and the visitor can readily recognize such formations as Sausage Rock, the Three Gossips, Sheep Rock, the Tower of Babel, and many others.

Early the next morning we set out to explore the more distant sectors of the Monument and selected as our first objective remote Delicate Arch.

We sped northwest on Highway 160, up the old Mormon dugway again and past the turn to the Windows section. Twelve miles beyond, we cut off to the right on an unimproved dirt trail used by sheepherders and cattlemen to reach grazing lands in Salt Valley, which we soon entered.

Twenty-two miles from the highway turn-off, the trail drops to the floor of Salt Valley Wash, and the rest of the drive was tedious and rugged going.

We plowed through sand, bumped down over rock ledges, straddled boulders, and finally were forced to stop on the brink of a three-foot embankment.

We continued on foot for the remaining half-mile of the trail down the wash to a dilapidated log cabin, known as the Turnbow Cabin, which ordinarily marked the terminus of the automobile road.

The little hut had been tumbling to ruin so long that it virtually melted into the landscape. Years ago sheepherders used it as a camping headquarters, but it has long since passed its usefulness. From here a trail leads across sandy grasslands to the foot of a smooth slickrock ridge where the ascent to Delicate Arch begins.

Delicate Arch is Well Named

Another mile of easy climbing brought us to a gnarled and weirdly eroded mesa top of gorgeous coloring and commanding views of the surrounding countryside. However, the indescribable beauty and unbelievable formation of Delicate Arch itself made everything else insignificant.

Isolated and alone, the arch seems to sprout from the rim of a natural rock bowl. The matrix reef in which it was originally carved has been eroded away, leaving only this finely shaped sculptured semicircle of more resistant sandstone.

"Delicate" is indeed an appropriate name for the arch, for one leg of its 65-foot span is not more than 6 feet thick at its narrowest! Its beauty is further enhanced by the pastel colors which change continuously throughout the day as the sun moves around to the west. On clear days the arch perfectly frames the whole range of the La Sal Mountains, 20 miles southeast, and at any time an inspiring view of Cash Valley may be seen immediately below.

The Devil's Garden section of the Monument is not far from Delicate Arch. We drove in there the day after our visit to Delicate and cut off to the extreme northwest corner of the Monument before reaching the difficult wash we had to traverse the day before.

Leaving the car at the base of a steep, rocky escarpment, we started climbing toward the plateau area that forms the base of Devil's Garden. Our guiding landmark was a massive 125-foot, black-rock pinnacle, the Dark Angel, visible from most sections in this part of the Monument.

On some of the cliff walls along our route we encountered our first visible signs of Indian peoples believed to have frequented this area. Hundreds of petroglyphs, depicting human figures and animals, are scratched into the blackened walls. Because of the present lack of potsherds or other concrete signs of early Pueblo culture, some archaeologists think these drawings may have been made in comparatively recent times by the Ute Indians, whose range includes the Arches area.

Of the Monument's 83 known arches, 64 are found in the Devil's Garden. We first paused to examine unusual Double-O Arch, a phenomenal feature where one arch has been carved immediately above another.

Beyond Double-O the trail enters an unbelievably rugged maze of fins and reefs that seems to form an impenetrable forest of wildly eroded slickrock. The most concentrated group of these fins, known as the Fiery Furnace, is located at the lower end of the appropriately titled Devil's Garden.

Longest Known Natural Arch

Mahan led the way over dozens of these fins, each one of which looked just like its predecessor, and at times even he had trouble making certain we were not lost. Our goal was the giant sandstone fin in which ribbonlike

Landscape Arch has been carved—the longest known arch of its kind in the world. After an hour of laborious hiking we came upon it suddenly, hidden in its own little canyon draw that frames the lovely desert landscape from which it gets its name.

"This is one place that few people get to," Mahan told me. Remembering the ruggedness of the terrain, I could understand why. A friend who visited the Monument sometime later told me he had spent a day wandering hopelessly among the hundreds of fins trying to find Landscape arch. He never did catch sight of it until nearly sundown when it was too late in the day to approach it.

Admiring Landscape Arch, which averages more than 100 feet above the canyon floor, I could not help wondering if it would fall through in the next windstorm. Its 291-foot span, just nine feet short of the length of a football field, has been eroded down to six feet at one point!

23

Mitch Williams's Story (2004)

Mitch Williams lived a long, eventful life that included some of the seminal events of Moab's (and the nation's) history. At 87, he recorded this rambling tale of his father, uranium mining, and the birth of the "adventure tourism" industry.

My name is Mitchell Marvin Williams. I am a native of Moab, Utah. My father was Moab's first doctor in the 1890s. My father met my mother here in Moab, they were married May 19, 1900, and had 5 children, 3 boys and 2 girls. My father brought all of his children into the world. I am the youngest and my father was 62 years old when I was born in 1916....

Justus Noyes Corbin, who was called J. N., in Moab found out about Dr. Williams and wrote some letters to him to come to Moab, Utah. (I still have a couple of those letters). J. N. was quite the entrepreneur; he owned the *Grand Valley Times*, which was the first newspaper in the area. The *Times Independent* is the current newspaper and is a direct descendant of the *Grand Valley Times*....

I had a truck and hauled vanadium for many of the mine owners. Vanadium was used for hardening steel and the ore was sold to different mills. There was one mill in Uravan, Colorado, which was the largest mill. They paid for vanadium, but not for uranium, even though they saved it. When the Manhattan project came along, they used the stashed uranium.

I would ask people to watch the gas station for me while I hauled the ore. It was a tough job now that I look back on it, but at the time, I would help shovel the ore onto the truck, and then shovel it off the truck by myself at the mill without stopping. Each truck load weighed around 6 to 7 tons! I would drive the truck for 24 hours between loading, unloading and getting back.

Lloyd wanted me to be his partner in the mine. It sounded better than the gas station, so I sold my interest in the gas station and went to work with Lloyd. I mainly drove the truck to Uravan and back. It was a 24 hour trip with no sleep or rest. There weren't many places to get gas, so I carried a barrel of gas in the bed of the truck. I drove until the tank was empty, and then siphoned gas from the drum to fill it up again. I used the back roads and they were pretty bad....

[Williams served in the Pacific Theater in WWII, then returned to Moab.]

I flew part of the time and took tours out part of the time for Pack Creek Ranch and I also took care of our trailer court. I liked jeeping around Moab so well that when I realized I wasn't going to get rich with uranium, I decided to go into the tourism business....

I had a jeep station wagon I used on tours. People liked to go and I loved to take them out to see this beautiful country! Before the war, there were no roads or jeeps. The war gave us jeeps and uranium prospecting gave us the roads. The two things made a jeep tour company possible, along with Dad's interest in and promotion of the tourist business. Dad was a real booster of this country. The plains of Colorado and cow country of Missouri gave him an appreciation of Moab's scenery....

Dad had many Indian friends and tried to learn the language, but wasn't very good at it. Ute Indians migrated in the spring and fall to a reservation near Roosevelt and back to the southern reservation. There were men on horseback and long caravans of wagons—it was quite a sight to see!...

The "tourism" business is now the "expedition" business. My son, John, owns NAVTEC Expeditions. The name of my old company was Tag Along Tours, now called Tag Along Expeditions....

I took a prominent group to a special place called Chesler Park. Chesler Park was named after a man named Chesler by the cowboys. It was circular with an island. (An open area was called a park in those days.) We cooked a special meal for them. Dr. Mayberry loved to cook and go on trips, so he was my cook on that trip. It was the National Park Advisory Board—very prominent citizens from all over the country. The publisher of the National

Dr. John Williams, indefatigable booster of Arches, on his 100th Birthday. Photo courtesy of Arches NP/Bev Spencer, 1954.

Geographic, Mr. Grosvenor, was there. I got to know many of those people. Senator Ted Moss from Utah was there, as well.

All of these people were very much in favor of making the area a National Park (now Canyonlands) and this trip helped push it over. I took some travel agents down to camp there. Someone flew down and dropped a note from his plane that we were now camping in a National Park. That was his way of letting us know that the bill had passed!

My father was called "Father of the Arches" because of his promotion of the area. The Lions Club helped him get Arches declared a national monument. They asked Dad to join, but he declined. A couple of months later, he told them he would join if they would help get Arches declared a national monument. That happened long before Canyonlands.[1]

At every meeting, no matter what they talked about, Dr. Williams would bring up the subject of Arches. Dad was a huge promoter and often guided people through Arches and he wouldn't let them pay him.

The editor of the paper, Mr. Taylor, called Dad "Moab's Grand Old Man". Mr. Taylor took over the job of writing all the letters to promote Arches. He was very inspired and supportive of Arches himself and he was also a member of the Lions Club. They were representing the Lions Club's views to show that a lot of people were behind it, but my dad was "the man"....

I wasn't good at marketing, but I got some good ideas from Harry Goulding. Harry was an old-timer in Monument Valley and friend of my father and me. His age was between ours and he was a good friend to both of us. Harry said, "A good way to get business is to get writers to come in and write about what you're doing and take pictures." I followed Harry's advice and it worked....

Our company was the first on the stretch of river above Moab to provide a day tour with lunch included. We called it "The Daily". Some companies still do this today. We made coffee over a campfire, provided sandwich fixins and laid a board covered with a tablecloth over some rocks for a table. After we went over the rapids and got to smooth water, we cranked up the motor and went to the Moab boat dock just above the bridge. Everyone does this now.

When we ran our jeep tours, we used thirteen 4-wheel drive Toyotas, one International and one 4-wheel drive Ford van. We had a total of 35 vehicles including busses trucks, etc.; sixty-five outboard motors and twenty-one flatbed trailers for rafts and a jillion other things. Many of the employees became experts in repair and maintenance. We had a repair shop and mechanic and sometimes and assistant for the mechanic. It was a good-sized operation for the "little guy in a little burg".

Note

1 John Hoffman explores the "father of Arches" title at some length. He notes that Dr. John Williams and newspaper editor Loren "Bish" Taylor are sometimes accorded that title, but Hoffman concludes that neither man was deeply involved

in the 1929 proclamation of the Monument. Hoffman credits Alexander Ringhoffer instead; see Ringhoffer's letter and Hoffman's essay earlier in this volume. Williams and Taylor and the Moab Lions Club did promote Arches and helped convince Franklin D. Roosevelt to greatly enlarge the Monument in 1938. See Hoffman, *Arches National Park*, 62-70. Mitch Williams's son John proudly displayed a thank-you letter from FDR to his grandfather on the wall of his NAVTEC Expeditions office when the author visited on April 19, 2016.

Plate 1. Cove of Arches and Cove Arch at Night. Arches National Park, Utah, USA, 2013, QT Luong. Photo courtesy of QT Luong/terragalleria.com.

Plate 2. Len Jenshel, road leading to Bluff. Photo courtesy of Len Jenshel.

Plate 3. Josef Muench's Delicate Arch, *Life* magazine, April 13, 1953. Photo courtesy of James Swensen.

Plate 4. Mountains + Valleys (Arches, Diptych), Millee Tibbs, 2013. Photo courtesy of Millee Tibbs.

Plate 5. Impossible Geometries (Arches, UT), Millee Tibbs, photograph and thread, 2014. Photo courtesy of Millee Tibbs.

Plate 6. Indian Paintbrush and North Window, Tom Till. Photo courtesy of Tom Till.

Plate 7. Mules ear flowers and the Organ, Tom Till. Photo courtesy of Tom Till.

Plate 8. Lightning strike at Balanced Rock, Tom Till. Photo courtesy of Tom Till.

Plate 9. Tiny moguls at Turret Arch, Tom Till. Photo courtesy of Tom Till.

Plate 10. Three Gossips, Sheep Rock, and Courthouse Towers reflected in flashflood pool, Tom Till. Photo courtesy of Tom Till.

Plate 11. Navajo Arch reflected in muddy water, Tom Till. Photo courtesy of Tom Till.

Plate 12. Rare winter snow at Delicate Arch, Tom Till. Photo courtesy of Tom Till.

Plate 13. Morning fog with the Three Gossips, Tom Till. Photo courtesy of Tom Till.

Plate 14. Milky Way over Balanced Rock, Tom Till. Photo courtesy of Tom Till.

Plate 15. Delicate Arch Thrust, John Pfahl. Photo courtesy of Estate of John Pfahl.

Plate 16. Arches NP #54, 2017, from the *RV Landscapes* Series. Photo courtesy of James Swensen.

Plate 17. Looking up at Delicate Arch, Stephen Trimble. Photo courtesy of Stephen Trimble.

24

Tug Wilson Remembers (2012)

Bates Wilson may be best remembered today for successfully championing the creation of Canyonlands National Park. But he was also superintendent of Arches for years, a period that saw an enormous increase in visitors while Moab experienced a uranium boom. Bates's and Edie Wilson's son Alan (Tug) provides a wonderful, digressive version of living and working in Arches. He offers insight into his father's popularity and long tenure, his rough-and-ready management style, and Tug's own decidedly irregular utility work. The interviewer is Chris Goetz of the National Park Service.

Alan Wilson: So we go to El Morro, from El Morro to Moab in April 1949. At Arches, the office was the CCC barracks, not right at the house. The Rock House was fairly small, not as nicely built as the one at El Morro. Anyway, for me, I don't...want to go into the end of sixth grade at Moab, so I just troop around with my father, learning whatever there was to learn. Wherever he would go, I would go along and we would explore, trying to find out what is what, where do the trails go, what are the things that people don't know about and that sort of thing. And that was the beginning of April [1949] through early summer.... I don't know exactly how it all happened, but he was well accepted. And immediately he became involved in the community in Moab, and there are several incidences. Let's go to, I think it's the fall of 1949, John Ford was making a movie called Wagon Master, I think that's the name of it, a black-and-white film, in Moab, using the White Ranch to cross the Colorado River and fording the river, so to speak. There was a pretty large crew living in people's houses in Moab, to a large extent, and a couple of motels that existed. And Father somehow got into being the March of Dimes chairman. You know, he joined the Lions Club, and he was involved with lots of people in town and immediately became, because he's the new guy on the block, to take on the responsibility for the March of Dimes. So how do you earn money for the March of Dimes? Polio was a pretty big issue that March of Dimes was addressing at that time. And he somehow convinced John Ford and his troop to put on a benefit show in the high school. The high school had a really nice auditorium. The Mormons liked having entertainment, music, etc., and that high school had a stage with footlights and overhead lighting and had a really nice set of lighting system, although they didn't really know how to use them. I ended up fixing some of it. So he got the movie company to put on a series of small bits, and those little bit acts were very, very popular, and they brought in a lot of revenue. Some of them I remember. One of the little bit acts was two of John Ford's actors that went something like this. There's a couple of hillbillies dressed, a man, a brother or a son and a mother. And the son and the mother are on stage in their country clothes. And she asked him something, where's Dad. And he says, he hung himself. Long pause, etc. And then she says something, did you cut him down? The son says, ain't dead yet. And they had this great timing with these little mini short bit acts. So he fit into the community very quickly. I suspect that helped him with a whole variety of things, dealing with Arches problems, dealing with what later became Canyonlands, to some extent, but certainly in the local community and getting the people in Moab to realize there's some value to the park, which, prior to that, they didn't have any idea. If you drove into the Robertson's gas station, which is roughly where MIC is now, on the corner there, except maybe one street farther down, and said what's that Arches stuff, the guy pumping the gas, which was 10 cents a gallon at the most, would say, just a bunch of rocks with holes in them. Delicate Arch was called Old Maid's Bloomers or something like. Dad held little sessions, and he would get people to understand how to answer questions and get people to think, if you stayed a day longer, maybe they'll eat another meal, motel, buy more gas, etc. So he started that very early in 1949. And my role was to go with him and find things instead of go to school.... Merle Winbourn, when he was at Arches, would arrive no later than 5:00 in the morning to do his work. In the old days, we didn't have the time clock kind of thing, and my father was not an administrator that required that. He was more interested in the result versus the activity. So Merle would arrive as early as he possibly could in his little Jeep. He parked the Jeep at a little shed where the forge was which is just a little bit towards the current road from where the gas tank where you saw my father pumping gas and smoking a cigarette. He had a little forge because he was a blacksmith of skill then, and he parked his Jeep out of the sun in there. He would drive out on the old road with a #2 shovel and a dump truck, and he would load the dump truck with either sand or shale. If he was trying to stabilize the sandy road, he would put shale or clay in it and fill it with a #2 shovel. And then if he was going to stabilize the slickness of the clay, like on Blue Hills going down into Salt Valley, he would fill it with sand. He did it day after day. But it was very early in the morning because it got hot. He would work his eight, nine hours and that's it.... He never went anywhere without a case of dynamite. His family had been miners, and he had done mining in Pack Creek, and his mine produced vanadium, a byproduct of which is radium which he sold to Madame Currie. And in his mine, long defunct, in the 1950s he set it up as a little hunting camp for us all.

The old trail to Landscape, you probably never took it because you're way too young, used to go down to the sand, terrible trail. So Dad decides to change the trail route. He didn't exactly always do things according to planning in Washington. He wasn't known to do that. Why, I don't know. Anyway, he worked out with Merle a new trail which is the trail you take today to Landscape. But there was a great big rock about four or five times the size of the vehicle that you and Jim just drove here in, blocking the fin on the way. Merle had taken his Jeep and made a little box in the back to haul either sand or gravel when doing the trail. So he used his Jeep, I don't know if he was paid, I don't know how that worked. But now you come to the rock and there's no way around it. So my father is showing this guy Landscape who is coming there that this'll be the new trail and so on. Merle's working and the guy says, you'll never get that rock out of there, never, ever. Well, they go to Landscape and hike on to Devil's Tower and then come back and guess what, there's no rock. His half case of dynamite took care of the rock, completely got rid of it. So he was an entrepreneur in that sense. He was a miner, he knew what to do....

Chris Goetze: How did these trips get arranged?

Alan Wilson: Well, that's hard to say. In every motel room, I had a 5 x 7 card that my mom helped me put together, and Bish Taylor printed it. Tug Wilson Guide Service 50 cents an hour. And the phone number was 2313. Does that ring a bell to you? That's the Arch's headquarter's number....

So they would call that number. Sometime they would just come into the Arch's CCC barracks and ask, can someone take me somewhere or something like that. I made a little list of some things that, some places that people asked me to take them. And I probably did 20 or 30 tours, in a sense, or day-guiding, but the only one that was memorable is the one to Bridges which I'll explain. But I did the Fiery Furnace many times for people because there was no path, no trails or anything. Harry Reed, who was a photographer in Moab who worked as a summer seasonal, he took Dad and I first into Fiery Furnace, so I then knew the path. Once I had been on a path, I had never forgot it. So I went to Bridges, took people to Bridges. People liked to go up to La Sal Mountains, cooler. They didn't want to drive the roads themselves. I often would drive them, though I wasn't very old. Dead Horse Point, Grand View Point.

Chris Goetze: You would have been 15 on some of things.

Alan Wilson: Yeah, 14, 15, 16.... I would carry people's water or cameras to like Landscape Arch, Delicate Arch. Delicate Arch was hard to get to in a certain sense. The Windows section, not where the road is now, would be a mile and a half. And people in the 1950s didn't have lightweight gear like you do today. They were not as rugged. They were very interested, but they didn't have...The desert was a rare experience for them. There weren't guide books, weren't any of those things. So they wanted someone to go with them, and I would take them....

Sometimes people have no aesthetics in terms of approaching an arch. You take Delicate. Delicate used to be awful. Probably related to Mission 66, Dad was talking to Merle about using the theme to shoot a trail out. Merle says, yeah, I can do that. So they hire a couple of Navajos and they get a little V8 engine bulldozer, half the engine is an engine, the other half is an air compressor and it's on tracks. It was very tippy because I rolled it once. Merle inched that thing up with his Jeep as well to a flat area before the trail goes up today. And they shot that out very, very carefully and used the little dozer and picks to throw the debris off the side and made that trail that's on the scene that naturally slopes inward, and you come around that right up and there's the arch in front of you. And the two of them decided this is how we're gonna do it. And Merle said he could do it without damaging anything, so they did it. I don't know if there was any approvals done or not, I have no idea.... And then, of course, there's the other viewpoint for Delicate, and this is related a little bit to my father's desire to have people have a, both be preserved, the park areas, but also good visitor experience. Many visitors could not get to Delicate. Many were very disappointed. And we had driven a number of times up Cache Valley, we did some uranium prospecting up there and also just to go look and see. So one day, having been there in my Jeep a number of times, he asked Merle, do you think we could build a road or a trail, pathway up to where we can see Delicate Arch, where someone in a car can see it or someone handicapped can see it? Merle probably answered something, yep. A few weeks or a month later, Dad writes in the monthly report to Washington, the viewpoint road to Delicate Arch has been completed. Well, all hell broke loose because it wasn't in the master plan, it hadn't been surveyed by the engineers, corps of engineers across Salt Wash, you know, all of this stuff. So they were livid, a lot of bad correspondence. I think they probably sent somebody out. But, of course, eventually, gee this is pretty nice, I mean, today it's quite popular. So Merle and Dad used to do things that way....

...But I don't think I got paid anything at Arches for actual work. They did at times give me gasoline when I would use my Jeep for rescue, they would fill the tank up. Then when I was working for A&E Electric, we wired, what was new then, the visitors' center and got paid for that. But that's through contract with the building contractor. But I don't think I got paid when we built septic tanks. I helped Merle build the Delicate Arch suspension bridge. I actually taught him how you don't want to make the cables too tight because they'll break, the stresses get very high. I wired the CCC workshop for AC current and converted all the table saws, planes and things to AC motors from DC motors and the lathe. But that's because I wanted to use the power tools also, and I wanted to work in there at nights, so I put lighting into it. The antenna work, I don't know, I must have been 15, maybe 14 or 15, but I was interested in radios. I had what was called a radio engineer's handbook. It's kind of a technical book. But I designed the antenna to work for that frequency and used at Bridges. The best ground that I could find was the root of a pinion tree. And once I put that ground in, that radio worked unbelievably. It swamped out all the radios in a big fire in Saguaro because the guy detuned the transceiver and he was yakking that he couldn't hear anyone tell him to get off. That was a very powerful radio sitting on that ridge, and the antenna was perfect....

Chris Goetze: Well, now that you've brought him up, did you ever meet Ed Abbey?

Alan Wilson: Did I meet Ed Abbey?

Chris Goetze: Yes.

Alan Wilson: More than I wanted to.

Chris Goetze: Can you tell me anything about him?

Alan Wilson: Well, I think he was probably a very good writer. He had a nice young family in the trailer at the Balanced Rock which he suddenly got rid of. I think he took advantage of the park service and my father in time because I think he spent more time on his things than what he was hired to do....

Alan Wilson: You know, you talk about uranium days, you asked a couple of questions about it. It was really pretty friendly. And in the Arches in particular, I'd get two things going on and parallel with the uranium boom. You had people coming from California with pickups and dump trucks, looking for dinosaur bone and flint and jasper and so on. So they would drive through Arches, and they would load this stuff in their trucks and haul it out for selling it to California rock hounds. At the same time, concurrent with that, you had people staking uranium claims. And one of the funniest ones, I think, is Dad caught a guy one day where he had staked quite a bit of the Arches road, this is before the new road, this would be Willow Flats within the monument on the old dirt road. He had a red VW and he tied a red ribbon of some sort, like on the valve stem, and he was counting the number of rotations and then every 600 feet, he'd put a claim stake in. This is in Arches. We had this happening everywhere. There wasn't a place you could go without finding a uranium claim, a stake, a marker, a center stake. Rarely did they put the back stakes in, if they could do it along the roads. We had that going on in Arches all the time.

Chris Goetze: But those would be totally invalid claims.

Alan Wilson: Of course. But these people didn't know or care about that. They were just staking claim....

Alan Wilson: But if you look in the Arches archives, there was a map, Gregory's Map of Geology, but a large scale, not to do navigating and so on. By the way, Charlie Steen used to come in, in 1952, in his little red Jeep, into the CCC, Arches headquarters, and pore over that Gregory geology map with Father, and that's how we figured out what some people say is, the water course for the Dolores River went south over the La Sals versus it goes north now. And that's how he tracked where he might find uranium because it's deposited by water. So he used to pore over the maps at Arches headquarters.

Chris Goetze: Is that how Bates and Charlie got to be friends?

Alan Wilson: Yes.

Chris Goetze: And they stayed friends the whole time that Charlie was in Moab, even after he became a multi-multimillionaire?

Alan Wilson: Oh, yes, the whole time....

Chris Goetze: Do you remember anything about the parties that they used to have up there?

Alan Wilson: Yeah, they were big parties. Now the Sunset Café. Large parties, lots of people.... There were lots of famous people who came through before the park and I'm sure many others afterwards, John Ford, film directors, Barbara Rush, Jess Jennings, the archeologist from University of Utah.... Bates got along with most everybody in Moab, whether it was the Mormon bishop or whether it was the miners or the cattlemen, etc. He was not loved in San Juan County. Calvin Black hated him. San Juan County, well because a lot of San Juan County was carved out and taken over for making Canyonlands, but the headquarters and all those things were established in Moab. So the San Juan people were extremely unhappy with all of that, not that they promoted business but they saw it as a government grab, and they [?] a Sagebrush Revolution kind of attitude. They considered the government lands theirs, not the government's....

Chris Goetze: Was Lloyd [Pierson] hired as an archeologist or was he hired as like the first resource guy?

Alan Wilson: I think he was hired as the long-haired ranger. I don't know. I don't think he was hired as an archeologist, per se.

Chris Goetze: I don't think he had any hair.

Alan Wilson: No, he never had any hair. He was known to all of us as the long-haired ranger, but I don't know at that time whether the classification had an archeologist designation to it, I doubt it. Firstly, I'm not sure archeology was on the focus point except for places like Chaco. I'm sure there were petroglyphs, pictographs, the Indian ruins around. But the biggest problem with Arches was the beginning of Mission 66, it started in 1956 timeframe, expansion and growth of visitors.

Chris Goetze: So I'm guessing Arches got extra money as a result of Mission 66 and the influx of tourists after the new road was built.

Alan Wilson: Yes.

Chris Goetze: So they were then able to hire some extra...

Alan Wilson: Yes, many, many more people. Not large numbers but some. In addition, that meant you got electricity. Didn't have electricity. Didn't know electricity. I grew up in high school with no electricity. I don't think my parents had continual electricity until maybe 1955 or 1956 when the substation, when the new power line was built to drive the uranium mill. Arches didn't have continuous power. We had a generator run by a Jeep engine, and once in awhile we'd turn that on in the evening or the daytime. My mother could do laundry and the ranger wife could do her laundry. The range was gas, the refrigerators were gas, the furnace was gravity fed, air-fed coal furnace. There was not continuous electricity. No air conditioning.

Chris Goetze: No air conditioning.

Alan Wilson: No. Living in the Rock House in the summer was really an ordeal because the rocks heated up in the daytime and they would radiate all night long. And there were no fans, no air conditioning. A lot of mosquitoes.

Chris Goetze: Mosquitoes?

Alan Wilson: Yeah, a lot of mosquitoes. And that's one of the little minor jobs I forgot. I think the scouts took on the job of mosquito abatement which meant Sam Taylor driving a Jeep, and I don't remember whose it was. We had a 55-gallon barrel in the back of it with two of us scouts pumping that and spraying for mosquitoes around the swamps as we called it, Skakle Farm, now Moab Spring, whatever, 400 West or whatever the street is that runs by Westwood's old house. That was mosquito abatement. One time we flipped the Jeep over near the bridge, he turned too quick to turn around and the Jeep rolled over with the 55-gallon barrel of DDT in the back. So we all got soaked, but we tipped it up, drove back and continued to spray for mosquitoes. But there were a lot of mosquitoes. These were primitive days. Moab had a little diesel generator and the power dam for electricity before the uranium mill and the mines in Lisbon Valley needed electrical power. Also at that time, by the way, was the El Paso Texas gas line that went through the big steel pipe that blew up as it headed towards Arches, so that was all in the 1955–1956 timeframe.

Chris Goetze: So the infrastructure that came into Moab really came in because of the uranium boom, which put Moab on the map and they needed...

Alan Wilson: Yes, it did. I think that's true, yeah....

25

Caroline Wilson Remembers (2012)

Caroline (Cindy) Wilson, daughter of Bates and Edie Wilson and sister of Tug, grew up with Arches as her backyard. She became a naturalist and interpretive ranger with the National Park Service. Joette Langaniese, a longtime health care professional, executive director of the Friends of Arches and Canyonlands National Parks, and mayor of Moab, conducted this interview.

Joette Langaniese: So what was it like living here in Arches in the Rock House?

Caroline Wilson: What was it like. It was windy. It was dusty. It seemed like it was a long ways from town. I can remember saying, even at a young age, well I live five miles from town which seemed like...now it doesn't seem like anything, but at that time, it was a long ways. It was a wonderful childhood. My sister spent a lot of time inside reading and eating chocolates. I was outside running around, and I'm still running around and she's still inside. We're sort of different in that way.... But the interesting thing, too, about all those places in the rocks, the Navajo sandstone right here where we played, we found certain spots that had some special little aspect to them as kids. Now maybe it was a really nice smooth piece of slickrock, or there was certainly the cave we nicknamed Indian Cave down the road aways, but we named them places. There was the Princesses Ballroom which was right up here in the rocks, Indian Cave and a bunch of others. They were mostly sort of houses and palaces and ballrooms and things. And when I came back years later after being in college a few years and, I can't remember if my dad was still here or not, I guess he was, anyway there were new little park kids living here. And I said, not here in this house but in the community, and I said, let's go for a little hike in the rocks and they took me to some of the same places. And we got to the Princesses Ballroom and I said, oh this is the Princesses Ballroom. Nope, they said, this is the Palace. Okay, a new name but the same spot, so that's interesting. Something about the configuration of the rock or whatever. So that was fun. Playing in the rocks and just being here. It was a real adventure for us to pack us peanut butter and jelly sandwiches or maybe it was just sugar and butter sandwiches, ugg, could have been. Anyway, sandwiches. My sister and I would hike up, this was long before the entrance road was in, we would hike up to what we called Opening Doors. There's a rock formation over here that looked like a door and then around the corner where the new entrance road goes now where you can see the La Sals. That was a really big adventure because we were outside of the houses and of the community. And that would be like a half a day hike, we would go up there. And some of the places where we used to go, now I look back and I just think, my God, if our mother had known and if Daddy had known where we were hiking. There's a big rock fall right over here, I think the road just goes right under it, and you can go up that rock fall up to a ledge, so you know about that? And then you can walk right out, is it called the Three Penguins or whatever it is, on that rim of rock. But there was a big rock that leaned up that you had to walk out around, and the area that you walked around was sort of slanted, and then it was about a 300-foot drop. But Daddy always told us to never go under a rock because it might crash on us (laughter). And we scampered around on the outside where we could have easily gone over the edge. That's scary. When I went back up there as an adult, I just said, oh my God, I was doing that. So living in the park was fun. You know, way back in the early days before the visitors' center was built which was, what year, was it 1956? It was a Mission 66 building, so it was at least complete by 1966. But, there used to be a little, it was like a Quonset hut, a little kind of rounded structure, as I recall, long, that sat down there. And that was my Dad's office and that was the park headquarters. And when people would come in, they would stop there. And there was a pit toilet hidden kind of discretely up behind some rocks. And as they got out of the car, there was a sign on a three-inch swivel pipe that said, directed, Toilet or whatever. And our fun thing to do was to wait for a car, we could see it coming in over the bridge, and when it would come in we would turn the sign about 180° so it pointed out in the flat area, then we would hide behind the rocks and we would wait. And she would get out with her handbag, and she'd look at that sign and she'd look out into the flat. And then she'd kind of go into the building. And then my dad would come storming out, and he would turn the sign again. That was fun.

26

Quiet Times at Arches National Monument (2013)

Jim Stiles

Jim Stiles followed his favorite author, Edward Abbey, into Arches in the 1980s. First as a seasonal, then a full-time National Park Service ranger, Stiles came to know the park as well as anyone. In 1989 he began publishing the Canyon Country Zephyr, *which often highlights Arches, Abbey, or both; several such stories are included later in this volume. In this piece from the* Zephyr, *NPS veterans Lloyd Pierson and Lyle Jamison reminisce. The first paragraphs in italics are by Stiles, and his voice is heard throughout.*

Arches National Monument was created on April 12, 1929, when President Hoover affixed his signature to an official proclamation. Since then the size, status, and popularity of Arches has increased drastically, from a meager 5,000 acres then, to over 70,000 acres today. Only a handful of intrepid and adventurous souls braved quicksand, blowsand, and jagged rocks on the old unimproved entrance road to see the arches and slickrock sentinels in those early days. In 1996 more than 800,000 visitors came to Arches.

Today, of course, the park is accessible by 28 miles of paved roads and made increasingly convenient by a "modern" fully equipped campground, running water, flush toilets, and an air conditioned visitor center, museum, and book store. Arches National Park has in many ways become a business, with its own mega-budget, computer room, and burgeoning management problems. The tourists swarm to the park seeking peace and quiet and often find long lines at the entrance station, waiting lists for park walks, bumper to bumper traffic, and a campground that fills by noon. And the rangers are slowly going nuts.

It wasn't always like this, of course. Arches National Park has led two lives—from its creation in 1929 as a national monument, the first 30 years were lazy, quiet times, with low visitation and primitive facilities (an "inadequate infrastructure" would be the term used today to describe the old dirt roads and shacks that passed as offices). The watershed year of 1956, marked the beginning of the end of those times. It's been getting busier, and more frenetic ever since.

Lloyd Pierson was the Chief Ranger at Arches from 1956 to 1961; Lyle Jamison worked as the administrative officer from 1959 to 1960. Lyle later returned to Canyonlands National Park in the early 70's. Lloyd and Lyle retired from government service many years ago; in January 1989, I coerced both of these guys to take a ride with me through Arches to remember and recall the "good old days," and observe the changes that have occurred over the years...JS

For Lyle and Lloyd, it's the road. "None of this was here of course," pointed out Lloyd as we rolled through the Entrance Station. "The paved road, the visitor center, all of it except Bates' house (former superintendent Bates Wilson who lived in the stone house now adjacent to the visitor center), was a part of Mission 66, the big nationwide construction project to improve the facilities at parks and monuments. Actually, the first section, where it switch-backs up the cliffs was begun by the C.C.C.s (Civilian Conservation Corps) in 1939 or 1940.["] Lloyd remembers that the first C.C.C. camp was set up on the site of the Atlas pond, "but they must not have been here long because they didn't get very much done." And for good reason. In December 1941, the United States entered the war and everything got put on hold for fifteen years.

"Before this road was finished, we had to go up the main highway several miles to a turnoff just beyond Seven Mile; then it was eight or nine miles up a dirt road over Courthouse Wash and past Willow Springs to the Wayside Exhibit, about the only interpretive visitor center we had."

The staff at Arches in the late 50's consisted of a superintendent, a chief ranger, an administrative officer and a maintenance foreman. In addition, the National Park Service hired two seasonal rangers each summer, one at Arches, the other to be stationed at Natural Bridges National Monument in San Juan County. The residential area at Arches looked something like a shanty town—a remnant Hooverville from the Depression. Lloyd and his wife Marian had two kids, and when the Jamisons showed up with their four, the housing problem became critical. To remedy Lyle's problem, the park managed to procure a couple of trailers from Coronado National Monument. They situated the trailers face to face and built a "lovely patio" as Lyle called it in between. Lloyd lived "in an old shack. Bates tied a dilapidated haybarn to the side of it as the kids' bedroom. It was adequate."

The work that employees at Arches National Monument performed thirty years ago has changed some. It would be unfair to say their responsibilities were specialized. In fact, it would be ridiculous to say that. "Each of us took our turn," recalls Lyle, "at patrolling the road, cleaning the outhouses, picking up garbage and talking to the tourists." Lloyd recalled the trail building projects that were one of Bates Wilson's specialties:

> Bates really had my tail dragging on that trail work. He was a wiry kind of guy and could work me right into the ground. I remember once, not long after I got here, Bates hauled me out to the Devils Garden to do some trail work. He said we wouldn't need to take water, that there'd be plenty of pothole water out there from the recent rains. Well, he was right, but the potholes were full of good stuff like deer turds and larvae, and algae, all kinds of interesting things floating in the water...real good drinking.

As for law enforcement responsibilities: "Law enforcement? What law enforcement?" Lloyd chuckled. "We had a gun, I think," speculated Lloyd. "I think that's right," agreed Lyle. "But I don't think I ever issued you guys any bullets." So much for crime.

When the uranium boom reached its peak, Lloyd and Lyle spent a lot of time chasing prospectors out of the park. "These guys never seemed to know where the boundary was," remembered Lyle. "They'd come out here with spray paint and little red flags, spraying the rocks and setting the flags to mark the claim. Sometimes, we'd be right behind them, pulling the little pennants and rolling over the spray-painted stones."

It almost sounded like something Ed Abbey would do. The question naturally arose; what was Abbey like?

> When I got here in August of 1956, Bates had already hired Ed for the season. He lived by himself up at the trailer near Balanced Rock. When he came back the next season, Ed had a beard. Bates took one look at those whiskers and pulled me aside, wondering what we should do. I checked the manual and there was nothing in there that said he couldn't grow a beard. Bates figured we'd just have to live with it, and then Ed came along and shaved it off himself.

But the beard wasn't nearly as much of a problem as the "subversive" risk Abbey apparently presented to more conservative elements of the Park Service. "In the spring, a memo came down to us from the Regional Office, saying before you hire this man, check with us. This was the McCarthy Era, and there was a whole list of organizations thought to be Communist or subversive by the House Un-American Activities Committee.

"Bates and I discussed it, and decided that when Abbey showed up, we'd show him the memo. When Ed saw it, he went straight to Santa Fe (the Regional Office) to set the record straight. I guess he did because he kept his job."

Lloyd also recalled the size of Abbey's head. "We couldn't find an official NPS Smoky hat to fit him and for a while he wore a black cowboy hat. But Bates didn't like the look of it and finally he made Ed start wearing a pith helmet with an NPS emblem. Abbey didn't think much of that pith helmet."

> Bates got into some trouble, because he had so much of this surplus stuff. He'd been poor for so long, that he just couldn't resist all this stuff. I think the epitome of Bates' habit of latching onto surplus, is when he came in one day with four or five sheets of quarter-inch thick stainless steel. He was going to make grills, until we found out that nobody knew how to weld stainless steel. That stuff was worth a small fortune, but I don't know what they ever did with it.

By 1958, Mission 66 funds started to roll in and the road and visitor center construction projects were underway. It was hard getting used to all that money after so many lean years.

According to Pierson, "Arches survived on surplus materials from World War II and later the A.E.C. (Atomic Energy Commission). That's how we finally got a jeep. Until then we'd use Tug's jeep (Bates' son) to get into rough country."

With the new construction came new problems, a taste of things to come. For starters, Bates, Lloyd and Lyle found themselves in the middle of a labor dispute. During the summer after work began on the visitor center, Bates and his son Tug were laying water line, when a large Cadillac rolled up. Dressed to the nines, the car's occupants asked to see these two guys' union card. Bates bristled—"I'm the superintendent of this park, this is my son, he's working for nothing and we'll do what we want." The union men retreated. Later the Cadillac made a second appearance. According to Lyle, "these guys looked like they came from the Mafia. They represented the Iron Workers Union from Salt Lake City. One of them was about six foot four and three hundred pounds. The contractors were using non-union labor to place the steel beams and the labor bosses weren't too happy."

By 1959, the first nine miles of paved road were completed to Balanced Rock, and a short time later, the new visitor center opened for business. Visitation began to climb and has never stopped. By 1961, over a hundred thousand tourists came to Arches. Today annual visitation approaches a million. With all that success, perhaps it was inevitable that bureaucratization of the park would follow. Still, both Lloyd and Lyle take a dim view of today's Park Service…

According to Jamison,

> the Park Service is bloated, overextended. Everybody has office jobs, and nobody is in the park. It's just a big bureaucracy, and that's a shame. It used to be we knew everybody in the Park Service; we were like a big family, and our paths crossed all the time. Now, it's a faceless organization.

Lloyd Pierson sees the day when the Park Service will have to split itself up into smaller units before it sinks under its own weight.

> They need to break it up into Natural Areas, Historic Areas, and then these damn Recreation Areas. And stop transferring people back and forth between them. Pick your field of interest and stay in it. None of us who wanted to be in a natural area felt that working in some horrible place like Lake Powell was anything like a National Park.
>
> The other problem with the Park Service is their management attitude. They want to manage everything, and sometimes the best way to manage is to leave it alone. Sometimes you've just got to sit on your butt and not do a damn thing. Let Nature take its course...the Park Service doesn't understand this. Mother Nature has been doing the job for four billion years. Sure, the Park Service can and should protect these places, but Nature really doesn't need a helping hand. Only Time.

By 1989, both Lyle and Lloyd had retired but were still actively connected to a place they both loved. Lyle Jamison died in 1991, but Lloyd at 91, is as ornery as ever. He gathers with his NPS peers each Wednesday at McDonald's...JS

27

Ken Sleight Remembers

Arches (2016)

Jim Stiles

Ken Sleight led raft and horseback trips throughout Utah and the West for decades. He may have gone down Glen Canyon more than any other person, leading Boy Scout troops and his own company's trips. He became a close friend of (and, briefly, co-owner of a Green River farm with) Ed Abbey, who transmogrified some of his friend's characteristics into the character Seldom Seen Smith in the comic novel The Monkey Wrench Gang. *In recent years he has been a grass-roots public lands activist and a sort of environmental sage. He and his wife Jane live at Pack Creek, formerly part of the M-4 Ranch owned by the Musselman family mentioned in the supervisors' reports. Here Sleight remembers Arches and proposes some radical changes in Jim Stiles's* Canyon Country Zephyr; *Stiles's editorial comments are in italics.*

EDITORS NOTE: Last year [2015], the enormous Memorial Day crowds trying to visit Arches National Park finally overwhelmed the place. Parking at the Devils Garden and at Delicate Arch overflowed—there was literally no place to park. Lines of vehicles outside the main entrance backed up for miles. Finally, the National Park Services [sic], for the first time in its history, CLOSED the park. There was simply no more room. In the weeks and months to follow, NPS and local officials and special interest groups have debated possible solutions. Should they make visitation to the park by reservation only? Will dramatically raising the entrance fees reduce demand? Does an equitable solution even exist? Here's what Ken Sleight was writing about Arches, its past and its future, back in 2004...JS

I became intrigued in Arches—even before visiting it—after reading Dale Morgan's 1945 edition of *Utah, A Guide to the State*. He told of the two thousand natural sandstone arches, including the magnificent Delicate Arch. Here is the greatest density of natural arches on earth. Indeed, he wrote glowingly of the great variety of unique geological resources and the redrock formations. Here were arches, balanced rocks, fins and pinnacles. Here rock layers revealed millions of years of deposition, faulting, erosion and other geologic events. He told of the striking environment of contrasting colors and curious landforms that highlighted the extraordinary features of the park. I longed to visit it. On my first visit there in 1953, I had joined with a group of college friends during spring break to search out these dazzlingly beautiful canyons. We pretty much followed, I suppose, the first wagon and auto dirt road into the Arches' area—a route named the Willow Springs trail. We drove to the Balanced Rock area and the Windows section and then down to Park Avenue and hiked therein. The present entrance road was still in the planning stage. In 1981, while I still lived in Green River, I began my horse trip concession activity in Arches after buying the Horsehead Pack Trip horses and assets from rancher Pete Steele of Monticello. On one of my favored trips, at the rim of Seven Mile canyon, we'd dismount and allow our horses free rein into the abrupt box canyon as we all hiked down the rough cattle trail of cut steps and rock walls. At the bottom we mused over an old hewn-out log-watering trough, shades of the Old West. Again mounting, we rode past dripping springs and huge cottonwood trees and then headed downstream along the sandy bottom of Courthouse Wash.

After our evening rides in Courthouse, we enjoyed evening cookouts near Abbey's old trailer site. Jane would have the small campfire glowing and her sumptuous Dutch oven pot-roast supper ready when we pulled in. As we ate we watched the colorful Arches sunset. And particularly, I remember my solo rides and hikes into my own secret and favorite places—pools and hanging gardens, canyons, caves, and arches. I remember our group rides down the old horrid natural-gas path to the enchanting Lost Spring Canyon and making camp at an old rancher line cabin. And the following days we would explore its varied red rock canyons. It was especially pleasurable, on one of the trips, in watching friend Tom Till taking pictures of a gigantic arch in a narrow side canyon. And memories linger too of my trips down Salt Creek until the Park Service introduced desert-bighorn sheep in that area. I chose to cease operations there to give the sheep a chance to get established.

Many of us were concerned about the environment of Arches, we showed up at a public hearing held in Dec 1967 at which the Park Service proposed the establishment of designated wilderness in Arches that would comprise 12,742 acres. Most of us agreed that the Park Service was on the right track. I remember speaking at the activist Earth First! Rendezvous in Arches—presenting Abbey's scribbled fighting words along with my own from the tailgate of Ken Sanders' old battered up junky truck.

Those were the days that many of us sprawled about on the sands and slick rock while watching outdoor musical concerts. Especially do I remember Abbey's and my impulsive visit with ranger friend Jim Stiles—at our banging on his trailer door late one night and lingering for a couple or so hours over beer, chatting about the whatever. Then on leaving Stiles' ugly trailer of sorts and his unexpected warm reception *(Editor's note: "Stiles' UNEXPECTED warm reception"???)* of us, Ed and I chugged down to one of our favorite sites and we camped on the slickrock under the night stars. A sudden rain squall drenched us—causing me to drag my bedroll under his truck where I resided till dawn. And in the morning we took an energizing and unforgettable jaunt out over the rising and falling slick rock to view the breaking sun and the beautiful canyons.

And on Abbey's tragic death, many of his cherished friends met at that same place to hold a memorable memorial to him—at which a number of us expressed ourselves, the best we could, in remembering him and his great contributions to the canyons and the environment. Then at the ending of that great era, I regretfully pulled my guiding operations out of Arches. It just wasn't the same no more.

Now today, I worry about the future of Arches. I fear that it may have already become a "sacrifice park." I suppose it was inevitable—because of the affinity between money and politics. Arches today is being deluged with more traffic and always more people. The extent to which Arches National Park should be accessible to the public is central to the concerns of many of us. I understand the laws and the declared purposes for establishing national parks. Providing public access to Arches National Park is one of its central purposes. But so is the protection of the Park's unique natural resources.

In 1916 Congress officially established an agency, the National Park Service, to manage the nation's parks. The Congress gave the Park Service its strong directive: "...shall promote and regulate the use of the Federal areas known as national parks, monuments...which purpose is to conserve the scenery and the natural and historic objects and the wild life therein and to provide for the enjoyment of the same in such manner and by such means as will leave them unimpaired for the enjoyment of future generations."

Clear isn't it? Years ago, local citizens spearheaded the drive in support of National Monument status. One of them was Loren L. (Bish) Taylor, editor and manager of Moab's *The Times Independent* and one of the most enthusiastic and successful boosters. Soon after, President Herbert Hoover issued his executive proclamation of April 12, 1929, creating the National Monument. On this subject, Taylor wrote in an editorial, that the touring public "...will soon become known the world over for the unique scenic wonders it contains. The Creation of the new national monument will prove a big boost in exploiting the scenic resources of southeastern Utah." So right Bish was. It did indeed exploit.

Now the Park Service must get its priorities in order. It's clearly a matter of development vs. protection. It's obvious on which side the Park Service has recently taken. Observe the increased new roads, parking areas, new-hardened trails, and a new tourist center. "Build it and they will come." Many people feel that access should be open for all people despite their recreational preferences or physical abilities. To them, restrictions that limit equal access clash with the mandate creating the parks. All Americans—tourists, the handicapped, the elderly, rock climbers, hikers and bikers—should be welcome in our parks, they reason, even if it requires new roads, trails, and other developments.

Look at the pressures. I was sitting on the Grand County Travel Council board in past years, and certain interests from Thompson Springs brought to the board their proposal for the federal construction of a paved highway that would access Arches from Interstate 70. They reasoned that the construction of such a road would serve the needs of the traveling tourist as well as further aid the local economy. Horrors be to that idea.

However in spite of the fierce opposition, there are many persons that would restrict this uncontrolled access. They cite crowding on trails and traffic jams and the destruction of native vegetation. Some of them advocate limits on the number of visitors in the park during peak periods. Others would support a reservation system or tourist quotas. Some would confine public access to designated portions of the park to give the park a chance to cleanse and restore itself—believing that the park has a natural healing ability. Arches ought to protect those areas that still remain wild and beautiful. Many travelers come, but many of them don't know just how to visit it. Ed Abbey has the answer in his advice to visitors in his book, *Desert Solitaire*:

> In the first place you can't see anything from a car; you've got to get out of the goddamned contraption and walk, better yet crawl, on hands and knees, over the sandstone and through the thornbush and cactus. When traces of blood begin to mark your trail you'll see something, maybe. Probably not." And then he added: "In the second place most of what I write about in this book is already gone or going under fast. This is not a travel guide but an elegy. A memorial. You're holding a tombstone in your hands.

Let me offer a few thoughts.

Let us not make Arches itself a memorial, a tombstone, a sacrifice area. Areas of greater ecological vulnerability must be protected with zoning that is more restrictive. This is a part of the plan of yesteryear.

For a starter, we need to remove the campground.

There may be a few areas that would withstand present levels of human use, but there are also other areas that could be easily spoiled. Targeted protective and restoration management is critically needed.

I'm aware that park officials recognize that visitors have a wide range of needs, desires, and expectations. How they are to accommodate such diversity is the difficulty.

However, we just can't meet all interests. We need to define the desires of the tourists and the desired resource conditions—to know what facilities would or would not be allowed in order to protect this natural environment. We need to look closely at the consequences of past actions and begin a restoration process.

Under present growth patterns, I feel that it is inevitable that many more people in the future will visit Arches. Nonetheless, the park officials must in the future, at some point, limit the number of people who visit it.

Limiting the number during the summer months would help solve over-crowding. Especially, visitation needs to be controlled during peak periods and holidays. To do this it may mean restricting personal vehicles and then instituting a public bus transport system.

Park officials must concede that the park cannot accommodate an endless number of visitors. It cannot even comfortably find room for the current population without constructing new roads, parking areas and other facilities.

Some areas need to be treated as wilderness areas, and in those areas no roads and few trails should be permitted. We need to go back and dust off past wilderness studies. In these reports, the Park Service said that the sandstone formations "provide numerous opportunities for solitude and removal from the activities of man. Each proposed wilderness can be effectively managed for the perpetuation of these values and the preservation of the scientific and outstanding geologic features found therein."

The Coalition of Concerned National Park Service Retirees has just issued a report, A Call to Action: Saving our National Park System that calls for an extensive overhaul of many national parks over the next 12 years. The group feels that actions are being undertaken that diminishes the values and purposes for which the national parks are established. I agree.

And the Red Rock Wilderness Group is calling for the protection of wilderness values in federally administered areas outside the park—which the exploitation of such areas do in fact have a damaging effect on the park's very integrity.

We must now see that the National Park Service does indeed "...conserve [the resources] and provide for the enjoyment of the same in such manner and by such means as will leave them unimpaired for the enjoyment of future generations."

28

Life Comes to Arches
Josef Muench's 1953 Photograph of Delicate Arch, Utah (2022)

James Swensen

James Swensen is an associate professor of art history and the history of photography at Brigham Young University. He is the author of Picturing Migrants: The Grapes of Wrath and New Deal Documentary Photography; In a Rugged Land: Ansel Adams, Dorothea Lange, and the Three Mormon Towns Collaboration, 1953–1954; *and coauthor of* Returning Home: Diné Creative Works from the Intermountain Indian School. *He also helped edit the photographs for this volume.*

On any given week in the 1950s tens of millions of Americans, or an estimated one quarter of the total U.S. population over ten years of age, read, or at least looked, at *Life* magazine.[1] Never before or since had an American magazine had such reach. In an age before widespread adoption of the television and cheap airfare, the photo-magazine was one of the key ways Americans knew their world. And that world was different after *Life* began publication in 1936.

When the latest issue arrived in homes across the nation on April 13, 1953, it must have made people look, and look again. On the cover, the most coveted space of the magazine, was a ring of red sandstone that most Americans had never seen. (Plate 3). Despite the fact that it had been featured in previous publications like *National Geographic*, this was the great debut of Delicate Arch.[2] Captured by the seasoned landscape photographer Josef

Muench, the cover featured the arch famously standing before the rugged Colorado River Country and the snow-capped, cloud-lined La Sal Mountains. It was one of the few times that a landscape was featured on top, and the first time in the magazine's history that a natural landmark was printed on the cover in color. Presented in an array of soft reds, grays, and blues, this photograph must have been a revelation, a shock, and a surprise.[3]

Muench's image did more than capture the stunning beauty of Delicate Arch. Published twenty-four years after Arches was named a national monument and nearly twenty years before it became a national park in 1971, it provided a window into an important period of change and expansion for Arches. Coming at a time when more and more Americans had the means to travel, Muench's dramatic photograph helped lure an increasing number of camera-toting visitors to eastern Utah. Yet the photograph does more than show a distinctive landscape. It also gives insight into the experience and uniqueness of the park and what would become its most important feature, Delicate Arch.

Muench's cover shot was not an isolated glimpse into the West. Rather, it was the lead image to an informative essay on the earth's varied geology and the ever-changing, restless "face of the land." Written by Lincoln Barnett and accompanied by illustrations and photographs of North American landscapes by Muench, Andreas Feininger, Loomis Dean and others, the article discussed the formation of mountain ranges, plains, and deserts. Sandstone arches, the article informed, were the product of erosion—an admixture of wind, water, and time. Weakened by water seepage and cut, "grain by grain," by moving air, the author instructed, holes and tunnels were gouged into standing rock over thousands of years.[4] Muench's photograph of Delicate Arch's unique silhouette, however, made slow-moving, natural processes seem exciting and new.

Delicate Arch has always had a certain gravitational pull. It was a photograph of the arch that drew photographer Tom Till away from the Midwestern landscape of his youth to canyon country and Moab.[5] Another transplant, Edward Abbey, understood its allure. "Delicate Arch has the curious ability to remind us," he wrote "that *out there* is a different world, older and greater and deeper by far than ours, a world which surrounds and sustains the little world of men." It provides, Abbey believed, "the shock of the real."[6] For those who experienced this *Life* cover, it must have provided an impetus for unmooring oneself from little worlds to see the big world, the world out there, anew.

Despite its promise, the photograph did not produce waves of tourists flooding westward in search of the national monument. Rather, less than five hundred people traveled to the park from the previous year. This was not too surprising. In the 1940s visitors came by the hundreds. In 1941, for example, it was reported that 200 visitors came to the monument.[7] By the 1950s, the numbers were in the thousands and yet, as Abbey reported, Arches was still quiet and undeveloped.[8] However, Muench's shot—the most famous photograph in America during that early spring week in 1953—may not have propelled thousands to immediately jump into their car, but it undoubtedly would have resonated, becoming a silent motivation for future pilgrims.

When these arrivals did come, they found a natural preserve that felt new and different. They found a twentieth-century park. Unlike other older western parks with longer legacies like Yellowstone, Yosemite, or Zion, it did not follow the same evolution and bypassed many of their traditions. It did not attract Teddy Roosevelt or women resembling Gibson Girls riding in mule-trains. It did not feature a famous lodge, nor did it have the same pretensions. Arches never conformed to the same hierarchies. In other words, it was *never* a pony, tweed, or petticoat park. Rather, it is a people's park where one is more likely to encounter hikers and tourists in cut-off jeans or Day-Glo nylon, never too far from their cars.

The first automobile entered Arches less than twenty years before it was featured on the cover of *Life*. When Muench reached the trailhead of Delicate Arch, he traveled along rough dirt roads. Modern paved roads were soon to follow, changing the monument forever. Asphalt pulled together Arches' most valuable scenery and brought most visitors within reach of its key monuments. For Abbey this was too much and he decried the arrival of "industrial tourism" and the "wheelchair explorer."[9] Yet, no protest could halt the increasing "serpentine streams of baroque automobiles pouring in and out."[10]

The accessibility of Arches also made it one of the nation's most photographed places. Cars brought Arches within reach and mass-marketed cameras helped visitors feel that it could be captured and possessed. As nature's own window, natural stone arches and bridges have always been popular subject matter for artists and photographers. Not only are they natural wonders, but they create near-perfect compositions that fit and fill the frame. There is more, however, that makes these geological oddities appealing to the lens. Unlike a mountain range or ocean, even the largest stone spans, like spindly Landscape Arch, are understandable on a human scale. They are still extraordinary, but one can see and experience them in their entirety. They are sublime, yet manageable. Two weeks after Muench's photograph appeared in *Life*, one letter reprimanded the editors for not including a figure "to give an idea of its size."[11] The writer, a Salt Lake City high school teacher, included his own, which the magazine published.

There is another reason why arches are relatable. With the unfathomable vastness of geological time, stone arches have a lifespan that seems more manageable. Temporarily (in geological terms), they defy gravity, becoming gloriously ephemeral. Their temporality propels artists and photographers with a muted urgency to capture their form before the inevitable collapse which viewers seem to feel, or dread, may or may not happen within their lifespan. This is particularly true of Delicate Arch, the "fragile ring of stone," which many already lament will pass.[12] No delicate "masterpiece of beauty" will be around forever.[13] This urgency has always motivated people to visit and photograph these beautiful "freaks" of nature before they crack, crumble, and fall.[14]

Despite the various desires to capture stone arches, Arches, as a subject, possesses a rather short and shallow photographic legacy. Unlike other geological wonderlands in the West, it was not recorded by the topographic photographers of the sweeping nineteenth-century western surveys. Timothy O'Sullivan, William Henry Jackson, or John Hillers never wandered among its rocky fins. Likewise, it was not presented in albums or captured in stereographs, the technology that vicariously introduced the world to other national parks a generation earlier. As far as we know, no one photographed any part of Arches prior to 1898.[15]

Tellingly, the first person to photograph Delicate Arch was probably a woman, Flora Stanley, who lived with her father and family at Wolfe Ranch, not far from the landmark. To help his daughter overcome her homesick-

Delicate Arch, Flora Stanley. Photo courtesy of Arches NP.

ness and the desolation of their surroundings, John Wesley Wolfe mail-ordered a camera and kit from Sears.[16] She taught herself how to develop her photographs that she sent home to relatives in Ohio. Stanley photographed the arch around 1908 with members of her family, sometimes including her children Ferol and Esther, for scale.

Already it was described as a "wonder to look at" and Stanley recorded that the stark surroundings in her photograph gave "a good idea of the appearance of the country thereabout."[17] Over the decades that followed other photographers returned to the spot including George A. Grant, the official photographer of the National Parks; Frank Beckwith; and Hal Rumel, an important, if largely forgotten, chronicler of the Utah landscape.

By 1954 there were probably hundreds of others who photographed the La Sal Mountains through the aperture of Delicate Arch. It was not a unique view and already bordered on cliché. Muench did not mind, confessing that he was not in search of the bizarre or off-beat. "I have never subscribed to the theory that once you have seen one area, all others become mere facsimiles. Far from it!," he professed.[18] Bigger-name photographers of the

West, however, were wary of creating a copy. Phillip Hyde took a Delicate Arch shot, but when Eliot Porter came to the monument, he avoided the "veritable galaxy of natural wonders," choosing instead to photograph a gnarled juniper against a redrock backdrop.[19] Surprisingly, Ansel Adams, the most important and famous photographer of America's national parks, never photographed Delicate Arch. He never worked in Arches. Adams's absence is telling; the future park's rise co-existed with the photographer's slow decline. And yet, one wonders what photographs he would have made if he had worked in Arches.

As good as Josef Muench was, he did not possess the gravitas of Ansel Adams. Few, if any, have. Credit for his *Life* cover did not appear until page twenty-five in small print. As frequently happens, this gives the erroneous impression that a photograph is anonymous and that anyone in the right place could make a similar shot. It is never that easy. Since it was not steeped in photographic history, the "avid shutter bugs" who came to Arches could feel that they were among the first to capture its forms, which only added to its popularity.[20] By 1967, it was acknowledged that "photography is probably the largest sport enjoyed" in the area.[21]

Over the decades millions of tourists have made the 1.5-mile hike to Delicate Arch, one of the most perfect hikes in the national park system, to stand, more or less, where Muench made his photograph decades ago. Most make their own updated versions. The absence of a master photograph of Delicate Arch has opened the way for numerous photographers with a little confidence or more expensive equipment to profess, somewhat ironically, to have made their own "Ansel Adams" of the famous feature. Indeed, on any given day it is possible to be stuck between snapshooters wanting to have their children photographed under the 85-foot span of rock and "serious" photographers, with tripod and camera poised for perfect light, yelling at everyone to clear their path.

In the decades following Muench's photograph, travelers continued to make "millions of square yards of photographs" of Arches.[22] In the digital age, the same sites are now recorded in millions upon millions of pixels. Nearly all of these photographs are quickly forgotten, but Delicate Arch, Arches' most famous landmark, is still the star. However, the qualities that made it alluring and approachable have also spread it thin. In the mid-1950s

Delicate Arch was a vision that forced people to look and see. Decades later its ubiquity has made it almost invisible. Indeed, the world's most famous natural arch is everywhere, featured on license plates, t-shirts, posters, and even in snow globes. It has become a form of lazy shorthand for Utah, the national parks, and nature itself. Particularly for those living along Utah's Wasatch Range, it is nearly impossible to count the number of times its silhouette is seen and experienced on a daily basis. With each representation, it seems, Delicate Arch is remembered less and less.

It may be difficult to renew the shock and surprise of Delicate Arch, but through new eyes it is possible to see it anew. In 2013–14, the artist-photographer Millee Tibbs stood more or less where Muench created his earlier photograph for *Life*. Her work in the national park was part of a larger series that aimed at "interpret[ing] and confront[ing] cultural myths surrounding the representation" of the American West.[23] Instead of making the now-trite view of this famous place, she forced the perception of the viewer by manipulating the scene. In one example she created two slightly different versions of the site and linked the stacked images with concentric circles that do more than echo the circular pattern of the arch. (Plate 4).

Together the forms unite the work, add a pulse, and produce a nearly audible shockwave extending toward the viewer. Her alterations also remind viewers of her presence and interrupts the fantasy of an "untouched and untouchable vista."[24] In another version she used a needle and colored thread to stitch orbiting circles around Delicate Arch's width and length. (Plate 5).

This act of physically manipulating a photograph would have been dismissed by purists like Muench, Adams, and their generation. For Tibbs, however, the creative act is not limited by medium. Her new forms, which weave in and out of the arch's features, highlight its beauty, its balanced asymmetry, and its delicate ridges and lines. Her artistic act focuses one's gaze and by so doing reiterates the strange and yet miraculous existence of Delicate Arch. In all, these works succeed in helping viewers linger on the image and the arch.

One of the problems with quick tours of natural wonders is that we do not take the opportunity to stop and look. "They do not stay long enough," Bernard DeVoto wrote of visitors to the national parks. "The deeper evocations of spectacle and beauty require time and tranquility of mind; they do not come at a glance."[25] The same is true with photographs. Few, in fact, invest the time needed to fully appreciate what one is experiencing, whether in person or through a photographic image. It is still possible, however, to reexperience the shock and surprise that readers experienced in 1953 when they saw Delicate Arch for the first time. It is possible, *but* it may take more time, more patience, and a lot more creativity to be reminded of a world full of marvels. For, as Abbey wrote, "if this ring of stone is marvelous then all which shaped it is marvelous."[26]

Notes

1 For more on the popularity of *Life* see Erika Doss, "Looking at Life: Rethinking America's Favorite Magazine, 1936–1972," in *Looking at Life Magazine* (Washington and London: Smithsonian Institution Press, 2001), 2–3. See also James L. Baughman, "Who Read *Life*?" in *Looking at Life Magazine*, 42.

2 See Jack Breed, "Utah's Arches of Stone," *National Geographic* 92, no. 2 (August 1947), 175–192.

3 Edward Abbey, *Desert Solitaire* (New York: Ballantine Books, 1971), 45.

4 Lincoln Barnett, "The Face of the Land," *Life* 34, no. 15 (April 13, 1953), 98.

5 Tom Till, "Touched by Angel Arch," *In the Land of Moab: Photographs of a Canyon Wilderness* (Moab, UT: Fable Valley Publishers, 2001).

6 Abbey, 45.

7 Richard A. Firmage, *A History of Grand County* (Salt Lake City: Utah State Historical Society, 1996), 291.

8 Abbey, 10.

9 Abbey, 54–64.

10 Abbey, 54.

11 George P. Unseld, "Letters to Editor," *Life* 34, no. 19 (May 11, 1953), 12. See also Writers' Program (WPA), *Utah: A Guide to the State* (New York: Hastings House, 1941), 453.

12 Abbey, 44.

13 Hoffman, *Arches National Park*, 78.

14 *Grand Memories* (Grand County, Utah: Daughters of Utah Pioneers, 1973), 177; Abbey, 44.

15 See "A Natural Bridge in Utah" earlier in this volume.

16 Maxine Newell, *A Story of Life at Wolfe Ranch* (Moab, UT: Canyonlands Natural History Association, 1980), 20–21; Hoffman, vi. See also "Wolfe Ranch Memories" earlier in this volume.

17 Edward H. Anderson, "Events and Comments," *Improvement Era* (July 1909), 757; Edward H. Anderson, "Events and Comments," *Improvement Era* (October 1909), 1004–1005.

18 *The Southwest of Josef Muench* (Phoenix: Arizona Highways, 1974).
19 Breed, 173.
20 W. Lohman, "The Geologic Story of Arches National Park," *Geological Survey Bulletin* 1393 (Washington, DC: U.S. Government Printing Office, 1975), 51.
21 *Grand Memories*, 174.
22 Abbey, 63.
23 Millee Tibbs, "Mountains + Valleys," https://www.milleetibbs.com/in-the-american-west/mountains-valleys/statement.
24 Tibbs, "Mountains + Valleys."
25 Bernard DeVoto, "The National Parks," *Fortune* 36, no. 6 (1947), 120.
26 DeVoto, 45.

29

Tom Till's Arches (2022)

Tom Till

Tom Till is a renowned landscape photographer who has published over thirty books. His photographs have also been featured in a variety of environmental campaigns. He lives in Moab, and his Tom Till Gallery has been a Main Street mainstay for two decades.

I remember seeing an image of Delicate Arch in a book called *The World We Live In*. I was about eight and someone had bought it for me for my birthday. I marveled that such a thing could exist in the world, let alone in my country, even though I had seen some great topography in trips from my home in Iowa to Yellowstone, the Tetons, and the Black Hills. I couldn't understand how the mountains could be so snow-covered and how it could be that there were apparently no roads, no houses, and no cornfields. Later at the age of 17, I hiked into Havasu Canyon with my cousin. After that stunning trip, I schemed throughout college about how I could explore the canyons, and in 1968 I went to the Grand Canyon on a winter break and hiked to the bottom. Besides the beauty that surrounded me, a storm was rolling into the canyon and alpenglow light bathed the walls above in a kind of transcendent radiance that touched my soul. On the way home from the trip, I drove through Moab just at sunset and the same scene I see every night from my house unfolded in an equally fantastic tableau. You can actually live where this light lives?, I thought to myself.

My timing was perfect. I arrived in the early 70's and for the most part I had Arches and Canyonlands National Park and the surrounding infinity of canyons to myself. A number of memories linger from that early period. I remember standing at Plateau Point in Arches and thinking to myself, "I want to know and understand in my head how all these mesas and canyons fit together." I climbed high up into Double Arch without a soul anywhere around or a car in the parking lot but mine. I went to Delicate Arch day after day and each visit was different. Sometimes a few people would be there, but mostly I was alone. I also recall driving along the road near Wilson Arch and dedicating myself to exploring the Colorado Plateau—an endless task I had no chance of completing. I also pledged to myself that I would somehow become a professional landscape photographer, which was much easier than I had thought.

I had grown interested in landscape photography in college because bookstores were selling lots of outdoor photography books. While heading to a gig with one of the half dozen bands I played with in college, I bought a copy of *Arizona Highways* magazine featuring a huge portfolio of the photos of David Muench, the best color landscape photographer of the late 20th century. I bought a Yashica camera and David's first Utah book and began trying to take photos. A year or so after that, I came West, I bought a 4x5 camera and one lens. I had no idea how to use it. Ansel Adams books were pretty useless, classes in photography from Utah State extension were helpful, but a workshop with my hero Philip Hyde was cancelled—no takers. The idea of a mentor was laughable in tiny, isolated Moab.

I also wanted to do something different with my work. Whenever possible I eschewed the standard scenes, but also emulated my heroes. From David Muench I learned about shooting in bad weather and how great that can be, from Eliot Porter I learned the power of intimate landscapes, and from Philip Hyde I learned about making my images available to environmental groups. I even proclaimed that I wouldn't shoot Delicate Arch because it had already been done enough (I later learned this was wrongheaded and career destructive). I tried whenever possible, though, to get something different by finding new locations in the Park (many of which have still not been discovered by other photographers) and trying to work under unusual weather conditions: heavy snow, fog, flash floods, rainbows, stormlight and reflections in water pools, to name a few. In time, I moved away from copying my heroes as most artists do, and I learned about and found places in Arches I had never dreamed of.

Essentially, I had the place to myself photographically and most of the time literally, but after 25 years, Moab's period of innocence was coming to an end. I thought many times that Moab had the physical attributes to be another Jackson Hole, Telluride, or Sedona, but I never saw it coming. Also, it happened gradually at first, and then took off like a rocket. We now have many of the social problems of a big city. For the first time in my life, after visiting perhaps a thousand or more National Parks worldwide, I was attacked by two drunk people in the Devil's Garden last year. By pretending to call a ranger and by the appearance of some strangers who would be witnesses, I was able to escape. I also had a problem with what is now called "trail rage" this year in the Broken Arch area, and at Corona Arch, which is outside the Park.

The environment of Arches has seen some of the worst problems of Moab's growing notoriety. Popular areas like the Windows, Delicate Arch, and Devils Garden are in grave danger, but I am a little comforted by the fact that much of the park away from these spots is pretty much still trackless and unvisited. Perhaps the proposed new rules such as ones in Rocky Mountain National Park may limit visitors and allow the Park to recover. I often wonder how saddened and angry Edward Abbey would be. I remember his elegy at the end of *Desert Solitaire* about not hurrying to see the beauty he had described because it was already gone. That was in the 1950's. Sometimes I feel the same. However, we now have many people in Moab working hard to save the beauty that surrounds us, and a lot of them are young and full of energy and ideas.

These changes can't come fast enough. There is a race between overvisitation and destruction. Climate change is also a major factor. I still guide people into the park on photo tours. We take one or two at a time. We stay on trails. We try to communicate our love of the place to our clients, and explain its tenuous fragility. I think this is the best way to introduce people to the wonder that is Arches National Park, and I hope and pray for its survival.

30

Visitors on the Trail (1953, 2008, 2010)

Visitors to the park are strongly encouraged to register at trailheads before they hike into rough terrain, especially when it's particularly hot or cold. But visitors go well beyond leaving their names and the number in their party, as this selection from the Elephant Butte Trail Registry makes clear. (Names have been removed.)

Protect your park
don't bust the crust
stay on slickrock
and in sandy
          washes
or your
going to hell
and hell is hotter than here

Farewell to Arches N.P. after five rewarding, tedious, hot, frustrating, joyful, freezing, windy, sandy, sad, wonderful, painful, sublime, confusing, transcendent, and absolutely amazing years. Take care.

Arches N.P.
Park Ranger
2005–2010

4th annual Chic-Fest

A poem:

> Here we are at chic-fest,
> canyoneering with the best!
> Cute and fuzzy in the dirt,
> chocolate brownies ease the hurt
> Hiking, rapping, working hard,
> pot luck feast is our reward
> Chatter, gossip, having fun,
> raucous laughter everyone!
> No men aloud
> cause we are proud!
> They'd only fear
> our special gear!
> Growing closer by the hour,
> we embrace our chic power!

31

Commendations and Complaints (1978, 1987)

Some of the millions of people who visit national parks are not shy about sharing their written opinions about the experience, and the National Park Service archives those opinions.

I have been visiting this area for 35 years and always enjoyed the incredible natural aspects of "Arches"—After an absence of a few years returned and discovered that an asphalt merry-go-round had been established within the major arch complex replete with outhouses. It was a hard pill to take and it went down dry and rough. Wherever I turned, an R. V.—or irate parker (honking) polluted the visual and auditory aspects of this phenomenal natural wonder. This is no improvement, but a catastrophe that found a place and you allowed it to happen. Remove the circle and allow people to again walk in to the liturgy of the greatest cathedral of them all. (1978)

Beautiful, awesome, spectacular! Surely Arches is one of the most gorgeous parks in the system. The campground is the most beautiful we have ever seen. The campground host is to be commended. He is visible.

Now for my complaint. There were far too many teenagers in the campground. They monopolized the restrooms, washing and drying their hair, applying makeup and using the stalls as dressing rooms. I had to walk the full length of the campground to use a restroom. Even the facility at the campfire circle was full of girls. If these young people are to be allowed to come to this wonderful place, they must be told to leave their selfish, inconsiderate habits at home. Just because they monopolize the bathroom at home gives them no right to do it in a national park.

My suggestion would be to get rid of the electrical outlets in the women's restrooms. (1987)

32

Reactions to the Expansion of Arches (1969)

Just before he left office in January 1969, President Lyndon B. Johnson, along with his Secretary of the Interior Stewart Udall, signed an executive order that more than doubled the size of Arches National Monument. A month later, a town meeting in Moab allowed local citizens, elected officials, and National Park Service staff to discuss the move.

SPEAKERS

SENATOR [WALLACE] BENNETT:

When this withdrawal was made we were as stunned and surprised as you were. This is our first opportunity to get out of Washington since Mr. Udall and President Johnson's order, made 1–1/2 hour before Johnson's term expired. We are here to have you tell us your reaction—give us as much information as you can about the effect the change will have on the economy of this part of the country, and tell us how you feel. A formal hearing will be held later on. We should tell you the status of the land after the action by President Johnson. It is now a part of the National Monument, just as though Congress had voted it in. The President has the power to do this, and used it. We, in Congress, can change the boundaries as far back as they were before the land withdrawal. We cannot refute the action of the President. President Nixon has the power to recind [*sic*] it, but I am sure he will not. He will leave it to Congress to make any changes. Since we have the power to change the boundaries, we can—we can increase them, we can change the shape of the Park by changing the boundaries, and leave it the same size, if Congress should decide to do it. We have the vehicle on which to act. I have introduced bills to raise the status of the previous monuments, and turn them into Parks. Senator Moss has introduced a bill to make the new area into a Park. With those bills, we have the necessary bill to operate—to hold hearings and discussions, and finally, to vote. I am not a member of the Interior Committee in the Senate. Congressman Burton is a high ranking representative of that Committee in the House.

CONGRESSMAN [LAURENCE] BURTON

We have had a beautiful day, as I always do when I get down in this country with Bates and other experienced people. Tomorrow we are going to explore more country, then head for Capitol Reef, going over the proposed additions. We were called on Thursday night before the Inauguration and invited to Udall's office the next morning. We went down, and with other members of Utah delegates, sworn to secrecy. It did leak out in the press. Monday the President hadn't signed the order. He did at 10:30. The area was added. The magnitude can best be demonstrated by comparison with Canyonlands. We labored four to six years to bring forth a bill people would be satisfied with. Everyone was heard who wanted to be heard. We finally brought forth the 257,000 acre Canyonlands National Park. This executive order added 264,000 acres—bigger than Canyonlands, without a hearing. There are many complaints. People don't like what was done. There is no way to recind [*sic*] an executive order of this type. We are here to spend three days to learn what you have to say. One of the specialists with us is Dr. [William] Hewitt, Utah Geological Survey Director. He is here to explain to all of us some maps....

HEWITT

...At Arches, we have done more than study fringes of the added area. The potash and magnesium extends underneath the area in the new boundaries. We recognize there has been drilling to the North, but there is very little information on this. We suspect most of Salt Valley may be underlined with magnesium and potash beds. We don't know the depth or potential when it comes to finding oil and gas beds. What we see at the surface is not a reflection of what we have at depth. At the present time I wouldn't want to stand here and swear what there was, but we are reasonably sure these items exist.

DARYL YOUNG—Young Machine Company—Monticello

In as much as we have seen from a geologist the loss of potential economic value, I would like the best qualified expert on what this transfer of land to the Park Service might result in economic benefit to the area. Maybe Mr. Wilson could tell us what the value could be when we don't even have over-crowded parks in the area at this time.

ROBERT RUGGERI—ATTORNEY

The Park Service ought to tell us what they expect.

BATES WILSON—Supt. Canyonlands National Park

With the enlargement of Arches, it can now qualify as a National Park, with criteria to qualify. One is scenic value and its protection. With the enlargement of the boundary it gives us the protection of the scenic value of Arches, and qualifies it as a National Park. We have learned the trend of travel of the visitor is from park to park. He takes in the Monuments enroute, but for some reason he feels Parks are superior to Monuments. The size doesn't matter. The largest area in the Park Service is a monument. We have new scenic value in the criteria for establishing a Park. As to economic value, we have East of us Mesa Verde, West and South, Bryce and Zion, and the actual value of getting Arches in as a National Park will mean we will get more travel in this area. The economists of the University of Utah, prior to the establishment, did an economic study of the impact of Canyonlands on the community. It so happens in that period we entered into an undeclared war in Viet Nam which took a great deal of money. The first agency to feel the pinch, and rightly so, is the National Park Service, which is not essential to the war effort. Development came to a screeching halt. When the area is developed—and Canyonlands will be—we will have the greatest center for tourist business in the entire state of Utah. I can't say exactly what a tourist spends a day—the last figures were $30 per day per car for 3-1/2 people per car. Arches at the moment is drawing over 130,000 people. A little bit of simple arithmetic will give you some idea of the economic benefit.

LLOYD HATT—MAYOR OF GREEN RIVER

I am a representative of the Eastern Utah Cattle Growers Association. Even though my cattle operation is not affected, I cannot remain silent and watch livestock operators pushed aside with attempts to dislodge in a few moments work that took a lifetime to build. There is no way to justify this move. Many in important government positions have spent a lot of money and time to fill the people with the idea that cattlemen have benefitted from free range. The stockmen are willing to work out an agreement. Many livestockmen spend more money trying to utilize BLM and Grazing Service Land than it would cost for private land, because the government range is close to their own lands. Suddenly we have to ask, do we have a future, or can we be pushed aside to make way for a Park without even having a public hearing. The past president pushed aside many individuals with the stroke of a pen. "It may hurt a few, but will benefit many", is a ridiculous statement. We should not be talking of hurting anyone. It is not necessary, to create Parks. We have heard so much that the withdrawal will not hurt anyone because it will be phased in. If in the 10th year a water hole needs fencing, livestock men will do it, and they will leave the range in good effect because they know they cannot starve livestock. Just 10 years to get used to the idea of being forced out of 18 years of business. I know why you are concerned. During those 18 years we have witnessed several recessions. We will witness some more. During recessions tourist trade slows down; people sit on their money. If it hadn't have been for oil, mining and side work, communities would have been hurt. Our community needs a multi-use Park to complete the business opportunity. I suggest to solve an injustice—the stroke of a pen placed this area in a park without consulting our people. It is not fair, and un-democratic. With another stroke of a pen we can put the boundaries back where they were, then let's do it right. Meet with leaders and establish boundaries that will benefit all. Make all new parks multi-use. If we place complete confidence in President Nixon we can work together, maybe. This is the time for the President and the Secretary of Interior to show they can work together. If old park boundaries must be extended, make them multi-use. When you go back to Washington, we ask you to explain to the President and Secretary, we are drifting away from a government by the people, and becomming [*sic*] a government for the government. We hope Mr. Nixon and Mr. Hinckle will give you this opportunity.

D. L. TAYLOR—LIVESTOCKMAN

We lose 1,834 AUM's, or 1 cow per 1 month, 156 cows per 5 months, during the winter season; 1,052 sheep. These animals taxed pay $432 taxes, get an average gross income of $1,015 dollars grossed and spent in this community. We personally lost 96 AUM's; we paid $100 per head for this permit a few years ago. It does amount to a little loss to us. I have some figures on the mineral value. There are 6,337 acres of state owned land, nearly all leased, which grosses $281 to the State school fund; 6,032 acres leased oil land at $1 per acre, besides minerals and potash, on the addition. There are up to over $10,000 we know we will be getting. I wasn't able to get figures on Federal land, some 42,000 acres. Nearly all is staked for various claims, most is under oil gas and mineral leases. 37–1/2 percent of money from oil and gas leases, and 37–1/2 percent of minerals found, are returned to the state of Utah, which recently received over a million dollars from the BLM for this type of land. Over 80—in some areas as much as 90 percent, of Utah land, is government owned, under BLM multiple use. If you will think back, about 15 years ago no one had heard of potash, Lisbon, Aneth oil... The thing I would like to have you think about, once land is put in a Park, you cannot get it back out. If it is kept in the BLM, if you don't find minerals, then you can put it in a Park. The new acreage comprises over 2,000 acres of private land, which would support ______ sheep—Paxton wasn't asked if he wanted to donate that land. I am not in favor of what was done, even if it had been done in the most orderly way I could think of. As to Bates' argument that we need more protection, I would like to suggest if they need this buffer zone, call it a recreation area, which leaves it open to multiple use.

HANK RUGGERI

If you don't fight it all the way, you lose.

CARL TANGREN—CITIZEN

They will sell us down the river like they did with Canyonlands.

SENATOR BENNETT

We would like to have these figures. I would be interested in knowing what percentage or proportion of the cattle or sheep industry in the county is involved in these lands—interested in dollars. I have an active curiosity about what percentage of Grand county is Federal land. The average of the State is 74%. Down here is it about 90%? Find out what percentage is federal land.

LEE HOWLAND—GREEN RIVER

I would like for someone to project this potential of dollars and cents in a county like Grand which hasn't been one tenth explored. There are over 7,023 million acres of land in the USA controlled by the Federal Government. If this land was vital, we would be willing to share our wealth and beauty, which is supposed to be the greatest in the USA, great for potential in mining, and cattle. We are willing to share, but we would like our share to pay our taxes. Someone in this part of Grand County shares 72%. Udall says private property is outmoded. Land owned by the Federal Government in the USA is greater than a combination of (lists foreign countries). How many acres have <u>we</u> got left?

MAX IRISH—Moab Sportsman Club

Economically I do oppose the last act of President Johnson in which he extended the boundaries of Arches. I do not feel it is in good taste. I feel it is more beneficial to more people by remaining as multi-use land. We feel these citizens will be deprived of the right to these lands and want multiple use.

PETE BYRD—Businessman

I have here the new Grand County Master Plan. The Federal Government owns 71% of land in Grand County, and the BLM 68%.

BATES WILSON

What percentage does the National Park Service hold?

MAYOR WINFORD BUNCE

I think this is going around the wrong direction to start with. I'm sure if they had come in here and sat down with people, they could have gotten some land. There is some area on the North side and West that should be taken into the National Park or Monument. In Salt Valley, I've never seen much that looks like Park status. It's good mining or ranching. The BLM had some hearings and part of Big Dry Mesa area there was taken into Wilderness area by the people of Moab. On the area they are taking, I had question if there was any mining there anyway. I know there is stock raising. I am strictly a believer in Parks and Monuments, and I think we need these things. I am sure the people of Moab would be willing to sit down and try to figure this out and put it in a Park where it wouldn't be a detriment to livestock owners and others. I am a firm believer in multiple use in the first place. I think they got carried away with the Dry Mesa area, and question the Court House wash section. I've been in there; it's practically inaccessible. I question it would be a buffer. No one can crowd in there because they can't get there. If we have to have a Park, and the Monument can't qualify for a Park, do we have to take in that large an area to make a Park? I think we better stay with the National Monument and forget the national Park.

CITIZEN

How much is needed to make a national park?

BATES WILSON

As I said before, there is no size requirement for a National Park. The criteria is its scenic value, superb scenic value, and protection for that. The reason for the protection—once Bob Norman drew a picture which showed a potash plant in the middle of Salt Valley, with smoke blowing smoke rings through Delicate Arch. It's not so funny. It could happen. But there is no size—larger areas than parks can be monuments.

CITIZEN

In other words, it is very possible that the size could be changed in certain areas involved.

BATES WILSON

This was not done in 90 minutes—we have been working on this for several years. I have talked to Bennett and Moss about it.

SENATOR BENNETT

I have had a bill to make a National Park, but not to change the boundary.

BATES WILSON

Salt Valley is the remains of a salt anticline. In the process of erosion, joints eroded into thin fins, making arches, which is why such a concentration of arches. The interpretative story is Salt Valley—and the collapsed anticline. The size doesn't make any difference.

CITIZEN

I think we went over this thing back in May of this part year—the U.S. BLM.

BERT SWINK

On April 5, 1968, the BLM published in the Federal Register a proposal for multiuse of 1 million acres of land in Grand and San Juan counties. At that time public hearings were held in Moab—on May 7—for the purpose of explaining multiple use and receiving suggestions. Several comments were received, most favorable to the classification. All comments were carefully considered. As a result they have eliminated the proposal to eliminate 40 acres from Arches to the river. I believe people at that meeting were real open minded in getting this particular area classified around Green river, Cisco, Thompson. I believe we are open minded in getting results of the May meeting.

JOHN EWING

A little earlier it was suggested Nixon recind [*sic*] the bill. Could you discuss the legality.

CONGRESSMAN BURTON

It could be, but it wouldn't be done. There has never been a precedent. The chance is nill [*sic*].

EWING

Why, if he could recind [*sic*] the Trans Pacific Airlines, could he not recind [*sic*] the enlargement of the Arches bill?

SENATOR BENNETT

He has the power under law to control Trans Pacific Airlines. Due to power under this law he could do this, but Congress has no power to effect allocation of airline routes. However, Congress does have the power to modify boundaries, and he would rather for us to act.

KEN SUMMERS

I have listened with interest and would like to point out a few things. Maybe we become emotional sometimes, maybe it is good sometimes. There is the secrecy with which this was put together. I don't think we have anyone denying that here tonight. We have Burton, and Bennett, pledged to secrecy; we also have had Wilson who has been working on this thing for several years. Those are interesting comments. We here in Utah are primarily back of the government because they own our land. We are fastened to those things. Our economy, well being and traditions, all tied to these things, and when we see by the stroke of a pen—the President said he wouldn't do all Udall was asking, because he thought it would go past his authority. You can't deny those facts. We have a compilation of agencies putting together a package for the people of Utah without their knowledge, and when our representatives were told about it they were sworn to secrecy. It is coming to a pretty past. This is un-American, un-christian, and not in the traditions of the Government of the United States to do this. I think we better take another look at it, go back and start over. Do the thing Laurence Burton suggested here—let the people have a say....

CALVIN BLACK [SAN JUAN COUNTY COMMISSIONER]

I would like to mention one thing. There is no question in the minds of all of us, all facets of economy are important, and we don't want to lose any of it. It has been referred to as multi-use property. One statement I doubt, that we are short on Parks, either in numbers or acreage. What we lack is development. I would like for all persons to use our resources for development so they can be useable. Another point can be made, we have probably one of the greatest attractions in the state in the Bingham Copper Mine, which attracts more people than all Parks and Monuments. All these areas can have mining and livestock, and still be beautiful for tourists. We don't have to look up and see only one thing. Any area with one phase is a sick area. Every business is diversifying now. Another thing is that we have Glen Canyon National Recreation area. As near as I know, except in certain areas, it would be amenable. This type of area can have all these things, with a recreation area it would be far more productive. One other point, personally I am involved in mining and tourists. I think one thing, on the disputes and controversy of establishing the Park, virtually all acreage came out of San Juan. When the Park was created we were promised roads were going to be—has it all on film. Now we are told this was not a promise, just a projection. The University of Utah projection was that by 1966 a million visitors would come to Canyonlands. There have been 30 or 40,000. I think we can take with a big grain of salt any projections. Now the Park Service, in spite of local feelings—Parks are for people and should be developed—now we can't put a road through Canyonlands because it would ruin it. I think this is a bunch of hog wash. I think we better be careful of letting any Federal agency gain control or we will soon have nothing to say about it....

CONGRESSMAN PEACOCK

I am very impressed with this day's activities. First, I feel real confident and proud that I have been able to be with a Senator and Representative willing to take three days of time to come in and get a first hand picture. I am very impressed with all I have seen. I was privileged to fly over the area, and to travel into the area in a jeep. Now, as I have listened, I am most impressed. This is the American way we intended things to be resolved. Government was created for the people. We are here debating—an inquest of basic honesty and morality, people who should have been consulted herein. Statements of people here all in a way expressed the same thing. They are hurt deeply that they did not have the chance to give voice. We are here trying to shut the barn door after the horse has fled. If it can be corrected, I am sure the many here can do it. It is a pleasure to come into your area and see things first hand. I teach kids the very heart and soul of conservation is wise use of the land. I am sure this can be used in terms of multiple use of the lands in question, they can be used and be useful to all....

GLEN RUBY, SALT LAKE CITY

I would like to make a few observations. Bates is accused of being a bureaucrat, but he is just a stooge for them. There was no hearing, the people here were not consulted about boundaries or anything else by guys who have them under their thumb. They are the ones planning it for the benefit of boys over them. I want to colaborate [*sic*] what Dr. Hewett said about mining and oil potential. First, I came to Utah in 1916, then came back the next year, and have been working in the State off and on ever since. As far as scenery, it's some of the most spectacular, for those who see any scenery. But there are those who see a rock with a hole in it and make it into a National Monument, then a National Park.

As far as the National Parks in Utah, hardly a one doesn't have potential mineral value. There is grazing value. I don't know why scenery can't be just as good in a monument than in a National Park. What we need is more bureaucrats with monuments on top of them. The concept of multiple use has been settled by the example of the immense area of scenic wonderland around Wayne. It is different, much less spectacular than that area outlined as Canyonlands, but some of the most diversified scenery in the state. These things are managed by people we cannot see—they manipulate the puppets. The thing we have to bear in mind is the public is influenced by columnists and everything they read. We are influenced by that, as we don't read between the lines.

We are fighting air pollution—we have had it ever since man knew how to build fires. I love the smog of smelters; they produce metal better than free air, that does not produce anything. The basic thing is the people; they are all individuals—they visit parks, throw beer cans and postum tins, then we hire men with stiff plummed [*sic*] hats to tell them to pick it up. It is growing all the time. If we build these parks, make Parks out of Monuments, then we make a highway—like Green River to Cove Fork. That is a lot of 4-lane highway. Some places construction hasn't even started, but they have built a barb wire Berlin Wall all the way. You cannot get off to trail claims, unless you carry pincers, which I do...

33

Where There's a Will, There's a Way (2015)

Jim Webster

Jim Webster was chief ranger at Arches for fourteen years, while his wife Vicki worked as the park archivist. Their children, including Sam (see his story earlier in this volume), grew up in the park. Webster participated in many rescues and told this story about two resourceful young brothers at Utah State University's Moab campus commencement in 2015.

I come from a background of both community service and emergency service. Because of that, you'd better believe that I have a lot of good stories to tell. Here's one that might strike a chord with you.

My guess is that most, if not all, of you have spent at least a little time at Arches National Park. Back in the day, when I was the Chief Ranger there, we had lots of search and rescue missions, just like today. One morning, by about 1100, it was already well over 90 degrees. Spring Break in Moab—you can picture that—pretty busy. I was in my tiny, cluttered office, with all sorts of "important" piles of paper on the desk, floor and available chairs when my ears perked up—a radio call from the Devils Garden Campground—something about a missing child, young boy of about 10. The campground host was calling—an ex-Marine who didn't get too excited about much. But, he sounded concerned. I knew that one of the rangers would head up there right away to assess the situation. I didn't need to do anything at the moment, but I did prepare to respond in case they needed me.

Let me tell you about protocols for missing people. The ranger makes contact with the reporting party—in this case, a single mom out camping with her two sons and daughter. Name, age, description, what was he wearing? Shoe track description? What did he have with him? Where was he last seen, and by whom?

Let me tell you about the area. DGCG is a kid's paradise—lots of easy-to-climb slickrock. Tall red sandstone fins that you can easily walk on, but have steep edges leading to sheer drops of 50–100.' At the base of the fins, sandy and rocky bottoms that lead into a maze of trails. A perfect and fun place to wander around in, but an easy place to get lost.

We had several people out looking for the child in short order in what's called a "hasty search." We sent out a crew of 3 people from the point last seen with whistles, covering areas most likely to find him.

By the time I get there, Mom is beside herself—NOW, she doesn't know where the younger 8 year old brother Bobby is either!! Bobby told her that he was going to look for his big brother Billy, and then he got away from her. GREAT. Now we've got two kids lost, and about 10 people working. We are definitely gearing up. It's been a few hours, and IT…IS…HOT.

I get a radio call from one of the rangers who has found the younger brother Bobby. YAY! Yep, on top of a 100 foot tall fin, a mile from camp, Ranger Galen has found Bobby, and he says that he knows where his brother is. Bobby says that he saw a signal from his big brother. A signal?

Bobby is pointing. Galen looks across the 50' gap to the next fin over, and then down the fin quite a ways to where Bobby is pointing. Galen sees something odd—a "white object" popping up from the top of the adjacent fin, and disappearing again. Galen quiets Bobby down, blows his shrill whistle, shouts Billy's name. Nothing in response. Yet, this "white object" keeps randomly popping up and disappearing. Time…and…again.

Remember, the next fin is only 50' away as a raven flies, but to get to it, Galen needs to walk ¼ mile down the fin he's on, climb down off of it, and find a way to get on top of that next fin. So, with Bobby carefully in tow, Galen heads off to investigate the mysterious "white object." Everybody else is still carrying out their respective search assignments.

15 minutes later, I get another radio call from Galen. He's found Billy and he is unhurt and in good spirits. DOUBLE YAY! However, Galen needs

a couple more rangers, along with some technical rescue gear—rope, drill, rock bolts, hammer, harness—in order to rescue Billy from his current location. When I arrive with the gear, I see Billy 15' down a hole—a circular natural pothole some 25' across—on top of the fin. Smooth walls, not a single foothold or handhold to help him climb out. The sloping top of the hole wasn't too steep, but it quickly turned into a sheer drop to the flat bottom of the dry hole.

It seems that Billy, in his exploration of a child's fantasy world of rocks, sand, and freedom, came across "the coolest hole ever." He shinnied down the sloping top part of the pothole, and then jumped in to get to the bottom. Only after fully exploring the fun at the bottom of the pothole, did he realize that he was stuck, and maybe stuck for good. WHOA, what to do? After he got hoarse shouting and screaming with no results, he thought about his situation...and thought...and thought.

Finally, Billy took his shoes off. He removed a sock and filled it with sand from the floor of the pothole. He started tossing that white cotton sock into the air above the rim of the pothole. Billy had created the "flare" that attracted Bobby's attention...which Galen saw...that lead to his ultimate rescue.

WOW. Where there's a will, there's a way. I've often wondered where Billy is now, what he has done for himself. He was cool, calm and collected during and after his episode in the pothole. Does he carry that trait with him today?

Billy was at the beginning of his life when I met him. Whether he knew it or not, he was at a defining moment. In his case, he approached his problem in a creative way. He used what he had at hand, using his skills and mind to help himself out of that situation.

Today, all of you are at a defining moment in your life. You obviously, and thankfully, are not in the bottom of a hole like Billy, but more like at the top of a hill or mountain, or at a major fork in the trail. If you turn around and look back, you should be able to see the route you have taken to get here today. There might be a pretty direct path to this point, or you may see behind you false starts, sudden stops and dramatic changes in direction. You might have been stuck in a rut at one time, like being in the bottom of a pothole. But, like Billy, every one of you had the will to persevere, working hard to achieve the goal we recognize here this evening. And I congratulate you on that accomplishment.

Clearly, Billy had a will and he found his way. He used what he had to help himself. After today, you will have something new that you can use to help you move forward. Another arrow in your quiver. Take stock in what you have, but don't waste time and energy worrying about what you don't have. So, here's my first bit of advice—like Billy and his sock, see the potential in yourself to solve your problems.

Second, the road less traveled may be the best way for you. Those routes may present you with opportunities you never imagined, so learn to recognize and seize an opportunity when it is in front of you. Sometimes those opportunities don't seem obvious in the beginning, but dare to try them. When we search for a missing person, we look in the obvious places first. But, we always consider UN-likely areas as well.

Third, your word is your bond. Honor and follow through on commitments you've made. You will become known as reliable and dependable. Looking for Billy, our several search teams had their assignments, and I was confident that they would thoroughly cover their areas, as they had in previous searches. I knew I could count on them.

Fourth, learn from people you admire and respect. Find your own role models and learn from them. Hear their lessons and listen to their stories. I've taken many a lesson from my own mentors to develop leadership and life skills. In managing the search for Billy, I used lessons and strategies learned from those I worked with in the past.

One of the best skills you can develop is the ability to really listen to others. Galen listened to Bobby when he said "I've found my brother." Many people might have ignored words from an 8-year old, but Galen heard!

Finally, look at your connection to others. By your very presence here today, you've proven that you don't give up on yourself. But remember, you're here today with the support of family and friends, teachers and mentors. As you continue the journey that you are now on, remember them, bring them along, keep them in the loop because they need you, and you need them. No one succeeds without the help of others. Bobby may have located his big brother, but it took a team to bring him to safety. Find your team.

So, back to Billy. Where there is a will, there IS a way. Each of you has achieved something today, and you should be proud. Remember from where you've come and use your background to inform your future. Honor and thank those in this audience, and those who couldn't be here today—those who have supported you and cheered you and loved you.

Congratulations, and carry on, graduates! Thank you.

34

Dealing with Cremains (2016)

Noel Poe

Noel Poe served as superintendent of Arches National Park from 1990 to 1995, a period of continued rapid growth in visitation. Like all superintendents, he was faced with a variety of challenges, but this one was particularly unusual.

As Arches superintendent, my office was in the Rock House—a Civilian Conservation Corps project in the 1930s where the CCC crew cut sandstone blocks and built the stone house for Superintendent Bates Wilson and his family to live. One day I was doing obligatory paperwork when the phone rang. The Chief Ranger asked if I could come over to the visitor center as a visitor wanted to talk to me about getting a permit for cremains.

The Chief told me the visitor did not think it was right to require a permit to scatter his uncle's ashes in the park. He wanted to tell me "to my face" that he was going to scatter the ashes without a permit and there was nothing I or the park rangers could do about it.

Such a position on a specific issue is not unusual. I experienced numerous such topics as I learned how to be a field ranger, supervisory ranger and now a superintendent. Americans for the most part love their parks; they think of the park as their own; they are taxpayers that pay my salary; and what wrong would this little issue cause. It didn't matter what the specific issue was, the discussion went something like the above—sometimes a lot more heated than other times and sometimes "little" issues are elevated to my supervisor, the regional director or a congressman.

As I walked from the Rock House to the Visitor Center, I knew telling him "It is a law that you need a permit and I have to enforce the law!" was not the way to address this issue. Enroute an idea popped in my brain that might help solve the problem.

In the visitor center, I introduced myself to the visitor and handed him my business card. If he ended up taking this issue to the U.S. Congress, I wanted my name, title and address spelled correctly. I started the conversation with "small talk," and invited him to come into a vacant office where he, the Chief Ranger and I could talk about potential ways to resolve the problem.

The issue I heard over the phone from the Chief Ranger was correct. His uncle thought Arches was the best park in the world and had asked his nephew to scatter his ashes in some remote place in the park. I asked if the rest of the family knew about the request and were they along on this journey. The whole family knew and "No, he came by himself to do the job and he promised his Uncle he would do it." I asked if the family is going to quiz him on where he scattered the ashes when he got back home and what evidence he would have that the Uncle's request was obeyed.

I explained that the permit to scatter ashes signed by the park superintendent could be the genealogical validation he would need. I suggested that he write a short description of the location on the margins of the permit or maybe in this situation write a more lengthy statement on a separate paper stapled to the permit. When he got home he should give photocopies of the permit to the family elders. Particularly give a copy to whoever in the family has the genealogical records and be sure that person got it recorded and filed in a permanent place. The Chief picked up on the solution and told him this recording was not for the immediate time frame but think 50 years from now someone doing genealogical research would want to know what happened to the Uncle's body and where it was buried. The permit from Arches National Park would provide evidence to these questions.

That approach solved the problem. The Chief went and got a permit, we filled it out "*right then and there*" and I signed it. This also gave us the opportunity to talk about avoiding environmental impacts such as, "Take the cremains to an isolated place away from trails, please don't bury the cremains in an archaeological site or in an overhang, don't put them in a spring or a pothole that fills with water, if he wanted to bury them as opposed to scattering them don't dig a big hole in the cryptobiotic soil crust and by all means take photos of the general area where your Uncle's cremains will spend eternity."

We shook hands, walked him outside towards the parking lot and wished him a good day. The Chief and I went to the break room for a cup of coffee and wondered whether someday the nephew would be making a request of his family to bury ashes in Arches National Park. While this approach "popped in my head" walking to the visitor center, I have told the story to numerous other rangers so they will know an approach that might work when a visitor refuses to get a permit for burying or scattering ashes.

35

The Very Original Arch Hunter (1969)

Doug Travers

Jim Stiles calls Doug Travers "the very original arch hunter." For thirty-five years the Texas native and his sons visited the park and scoured its backcountry for uncatalogued arches.[1] *Travers and other "arch hunters" are memorialized with a sign in the visitors' center. Here, he writes the park superintendent in 1969.*

Dear Sir:

Since first visiting Arches in 1964 I have returned once or twice a year with one or more of my four sons, and have found the park increasingly interesting each time. About two years ago I began to photograph the arches in a systematic manner, hoping eventually to obtain pictures of all 89 (or 95 or whatever is the accepted number now). I began to realize this past year what a formidable but nevertheless highly rewarding experience this task can be.

In order to maintain some degree of rigor in my records I photograph each arch in both color and black and white and from a variety of viewpoints and times. During this past year I obtained photographs of a number of openings, some off the main trails, which may or may not be among the classified arches. Your help in providing the names, if any, of these and indication as to whether they are among the ones officially counted is now requested.

Note

1 Jim Stiles, "Reuben Scolnik—The Original Arch Hunter (1917–2015)," *Canyon Country Zephyr* (August/September 2017), https://www.canyoncountryzephyr.com/2017/08/04/reuben-scolnik-the-original-arch-hunter-1917-2015-by-jim-stiles/.

36

The "Stabilization" of Delicate Arch (2015)

Jim Stiles

The National Park Service organic act of 1916 famously directs the Service "to conserve the scenery and the natural and historic objects and... to provide for the enjoyment of the same in such manner and by such means as will leave them unimpaired for the enjoyment of future generations."[1] At Arches, no object is more beloved, or seems more fragile, than Delicate Arch. In the 1950s, some possibly overzealous NPS officials decided that Delicate needed help to remain unimpaired for the future. Jim Stiles tells the story.

> There have been some, even in the Park Service, who advocate spraying Delicate Arch with a fixative of some sort—Elmer's Glue perhaps or Lady Clairol Spray-Net.
>
> —E. Abbey, *Desert Solitaire*

When I first read that passage by Abbey, I thought he was kidding; I learned, over the years, to take some of Cactus Ed's "facts" with a grain of salt. The idea of spraying Delicate Arch with a fixative was too ridiculous to be taken seriously. This, of course, was before my decade of employment with the federal government.

During my first winter at Arches, when the tourists were few and far between, I spent much of my day rummaging through file cabinets reading old monthly reports and looking at the black & white photo collection.

One day, a labeled folder caught my eye. It read: Delicate Arch Stabilization Project. I remembered the remark in Desert Solitaire but still couldn't quite believe my eyes.

What I found inside was a decade's worth of memorandums, letters, and reports, all dedicated to the question—should the Park Service save Delicate Arch from imminent collapse?

The issue was first raised by Arches Custodian Russ Mahan on August 28, 1947 in a memo to the Regional Director. On a recent hike, Russ had observed

> The eroded condition of the east leg of Delicate Arch . . . It is my opinion that some measures should be taken to prevent further erosion and to stabilize this particular point. If we lost this arch we would be losing one of the most important features of Arches National Monument.

Mahan was convinced apparently that the collapse of Delicate Arch might very well take away any incentive to visit the park at all. If that were true, I'd go out there with a load of dynamite tomorrow.

In any case, the letter got the ball rolling, but just barely. The acting Regional director sent Mahan's concerns to the Director in Washington. "There was," he added, "the possibility that (the) condition of the formation may endanger visitors there." But the threat of an arch squashing innocent tourists was not enough to elicit much interest. The next memorandum, dated September 13, 1951 said only that, "with specific data, previously lacking, the matter can be discussed again to determine what action, if any, this office is willing to recommend."

Obviously, there was not a great deal of enthusiasm for this project. But 18 months later, interest was re-kindled when Southwest Regional Assistant Director Hugh Miller visited the arch and threw his support behind the plan:

> I have decided to join, as a result of this trip, those who believe that stabilization of Delicate Arch is warranted. I would favor the proposal only with the understanding that a very simple plaster jacket could be placed over the weak point in the arch at which erosion threatens to

> topple it, sufficient only to arrest further erosion at that point. Careful staining would suffice to make such minor support unobjectionable in appearance and it seems to me that it might reasonably be effective. From my own point of view, the Delicate Arch is so outstandingly unique a formation as to merit the adoption of stabilization methods.

The general superintendent in Globe, Arizona was delighted. "It is encouraging indeed," he said, "to know that Mr. Miller is in accord with our view." Although the NPS Advisory Board opposed the stabilization of geological formations in National parks, [Southwestern Monuments Superintendent John M.] Davis insisted that Delicate Arch should be an exception. On December 22, 1952 he wrote:

> I believe we are all agreed that one use of our Parks and Monuments is as great outdoor museums and, as such, Arches National Monument has perhaps its most effective exhibit in Delicate Arch. To allow this unique formation to fall without making some effort to prolong its existence would be to lose forever an integral part of the story justifying the existence of Arches National Monument.

Within months, memorandums no longer asked if the arch should be stabilized but "where and what method should be used." By the spring of 1954, the memorandums were flying at a fever pitch. A meeting was proposed for March 3, 1954 and were [*sic*] to include representatives from the Engineering Division and the Landscape Architectural Division. They were to "discuss the stabilization of Delicate Arch and to make arrangements for the execution of the proposed work."

And then came landscape architect David Van Pelt. Obviously not caught up in the stabilization fever that had affected others, Van Pelt met with Bates Wilson at Arches, discussed the question of stabilization and filed his report. He was the first to see that meddling with Mother Nature might very well backfire. "It should be realized," he wrote, "that the wisdom and success of whatever action may or may not be taken to stabilize the arch can never be accurately appraised."

Van Pelt proposed two alternatives:

1. To take no measures toward stabilization. This view arises not out of indifference nor apathy, but from a consideration of the uncertain benefits of stabilization, of the very real possibility that more harm than benefit may be done, and in the knowledge that Delicate Arch is "in extremis," its collapse only deferred by the efforts of man. The stabilization of ruins does not offer a precedent in the analysis of the weaknesses of the arch, nor in procedures for strengthening it. The collapse of ruins follows definite patterns according to their methods of construction, such methods being few in number and not fully understood. They are restored by proven techniques, based on known forces, strength of materials, etc.

   A complete stabilization, using methods common to ruins stabilization, of Delicate Arch would involve uncertain results, not inconsiderable danger to arch and workmen, and great expense. The arch is in a relatively inaccessible location, to which all materials and equipment would have to be hauled by pack-animal or small tractor. It is poised on the edge of a deep canyon, necessitating extra safety precautions. No one can say that it would not partially or wholly collapse while work was in progress.
2. The contention that nothing should be done is prey to the equally defensible argument that, since the patient is doomed anyway, we are justified in making some attempt to prolong his life.

If the project was to proceed, the most efficient technique seemed to call for the spraying of the weak leg with a silicone epoxy. Another option, proposed by engineer J.R. Lasstic, was "to ring the weak point of the weaker leg with a concrete collar, making an attempt to color and form the concrete to blend as well as possible with the natural structure."

Superintendent Davis in Globe, Arizona bubbled with enthusiasm. Despite Van Pelt's warnings, Davis felt that "the trial use of a silicone preparation can certainly do no damage and it may well afford some protection from weathering." The Regional office seemed to be in contact with every silicone manufacturer in the country requesting free samples. And Davis added, "I suggest that all of these be field tested at Arches." Meanwhile, the staff at Arches appeared to be hiding as best it could from the entire project. Arches superintendent Bates Wilson's signature is conspicuously absent from all correspondence. General Superintendent Davis, concerned that the silicone had not been tested, inquired as to whether they needed more. A few weeks later, Davis sent another memo to Bates Wilson, asking him to estimate needed additional funds to complete the job. No reply from Arches. On October 13, 1954 the acting General Superintendent sent Bates one more memo. "Will you please," he pleaded, "make a special report on this project at your very earliest convenience?"

Acting Arches Superintendent Bob Morris finally responded. Well, it seems they mixed the ethyl silicate solution back in February and it was supposed to be applied within 90 days. Now, with winter closing in, Morris asked Davis, "To get the proper results, should we not order a new mixture?"

A tense memo came back from Davis. Write the manufacturer, he suggested, if they thought the silicone had gone bad. "A tabulation of the dates of treatment and a complete record of your observations should be made and forwarded to this office." Arches appeared to have worn the general superintendent down. The memos petered out and the issue died for almost two years. Then in 1956 Mr. Cutler, a visitor to Arches, sent a letter to the NPS Director, concerned with preserving Delicate Arch "for millions yet unborn." Incredibly, he suggested "that a clear, erosion-resistant material could be sprayed on."

The Acting Regional Director, Harthon Bill replied to the letter and advised the concerned citizen of the March 1954 study. "This office," Mr. Bill advised,

> is not currently aware of the immediate status of the work at stabilizing Delicate Arch. We can, however, assure you that this is an active project and every effort is being made to slow down natural processes of weathering with the objective of lengthening the life of this natural feature to the greatest possible extent.

Finally, on April 27, 1956, Mr. Cutler received another letter from the Park Service Regional office. "During a recent visit to this office," the letter stated, "Superintendent Wilson stated that several of the chemicals had proven unsatisfactory, because exposure to the weather had caused them to turn white, or scale off, or both." Wilson also felt that it would require "several more years of experimentation" before the process could be implemented on the arch.

With that, the idea finally collapsed. Bates Wilson, it appeared, simply outlasted the Regional bureaucrats. No one loved Delicate Arch more than Bates, but the idea of sealing silicone on it with an orchard sprayer never appealed to his common sense. He continued to worry about Delicate Arch, but not from the standpoint of its collapse. In a monthly report filed not long after the Cutler letter, Bates wrote: "the increasing desire of fools to carve their names in public places has reached the highest level possible in Arches at Delicate Arch." Thirty five years later, the wind and the rain continue to sculpt the arch, picking away at it grain by grain, and idiots with big egos and no brains still come to the arch to scratch their names on it.

Continuity.

Note

1 National Park Service Organic Act of 1916, Public Law 64–235, U.S. Statutes at Large 39 (1916): 535.

37

New Arches Opposed (?) (1977)

Tom Sloan

The National Park Service, the federal government in general, and environmentalists are not universally beloved in southern Utah. This article appeared in the San Juan Record *in 1977.*

The recent announcement of plans to expand Arches National Monument, with the construction of seven new arches, came under immediate fire from several citizens groups this week.

Leading the opposition is Mr. N. Viron Mintle, President of the "See Error Club," who stated that the building of these new arches and the concomitant increase of visitors would damage the habitats of several species of wildlife including the neotoma Cinerea (packrat) and the formididae [*sic*] (red ants). He further stated:

"We cannot become complacent now that we have stopped Kapairowitz [*sic*] and have the Central Utah Project in trouble; we must continue to see errors in all proposed projects and fight to save the earth's treasures and resources for the natural inhabitants!"

Mr. Mintle listed several deficiencies in the plans for this project and some of these Mintle deficiencies are as follows:

1. This project would benefit the area with increased tourism:

   "This is a fallacy; everyone knows that tourists represent an undesirable transient element in a community!"

2. This project would provide employment to local residents:
   "Wrong again—this introduction of work is an erosion of an individuals natural right to public assistance payments!"
3. This project should be completed so that more people could view these scenic wonders.
   "This is ridiculous, only those who are willing and able to hike twenty-five miles and sleep on rocky ground should see these scenic wonders! We don't want those 'sickees' with bad hearts or physical handicaps out there. We'll sell them colored slides if they want to see the arches!"

The "See Error Club" has been joined by the "Friends of Animals and Trees" group in the vociferous protestations to the planned construction project. The F.A.T. head, Ms. Kay Ohtie, stated:

> "This project is an insidious attempt to increase the motor traffic, and therefore, the carbon monoxide levels of the air, to poison the coyotes in the area!"

In response to Mr. Rayne's charge that the original contractor must have used inferior materials, Mr. Billie Gram, who claims to be the sole representative of the original contractor, offered this rebuttal:

> "Although the original contractor put up the masonry, the firm of Wynde and Wahter sub-contracted the arches construction and they bear total responsibility for any present defects."

Mr. Rayne answered cirtics' [*sic*] contentions that the arches should be natural and not man-made by stating that St. Louis and Paris have done well with their man-made arches, so why should we be limited to the vagaries of nature?

(A little late for April Fool, maybe, but it's the thought that counts. —Editor)

38

Arched Entrance Arches Eyebrows (1987)

Correspondent Todd

The Stinking Desert Gazette *was a satirical newspaper published in Moab from 1986 to 1989. In 1987, "Correspondent Todd" took on the National Park Service bureaucracy, local business boosters, and the often-convoluted attempts to protect or exploit Arches' features.*

A consortium of local developers have resurrected a plan to span the North entrance of town with Delicate Arch, the most beautiful and well-known arch in nearby Arches Park.

The bold proposal, set forth in the group's recent application for federal development money, is truly awesome in scope, and would employ some of the most sophisticated mock-up construction technology ever attempted.

The idea is a variation of the plan put forth by the now-defunct Moab Underground Chamber of Karma.

That group dropped the scheme after "lengthy and deep consideration" of the feelings of the arch. They concluded that its pride would probably have been hurt by the construction of a copy of it, no matter how skillfully it was done.

They later re-organized as the Black Pantheists, and are presently the loudest critics of the current proposal.

The prime movers of the massive project are forging ahead with the design and funding groundwork, and have hired a team of lawyers to begin securing the necessary permits. Despite massive and well-funded opposition, the plan seems well on its way to becoming a reality.

"We expected the environmentalists to squeal like a bunch of stuck pigs! But I for one don't know why they are so upset about it," chuckled group spokesman Harold Gaynurd.

"We've got a workable design, an eager work force of unemployed miners, and the engineering know-how to construct a perfect imitation, accurate to the last detail."

"We've got to stop giving in to these damned obstructionists. We have studied this whole thing and you can quote me on this: any environmental damage that might result has been judged to be negligible."

Reporters for the *Stinking Desert Gazette*, however, learned that strong opposition is also likely to come from the National Park Service.

Park officials deny rumors that a decision against the project has already been arrived at, and stress their willingness to cooperate with the town in any venture that might help relieve the economic slump that has characterized this county since the demise of the uranium industry.

They maintain, however, that nothing of this breadth and scope has ever been requested of them, in the entire history of National Parks administration.

Contacted by telephone, Arches Park Superintendent Trustin Parry reiterated his desire to reach a solution that "best serves the interests of all concerned."

"If it isn't one thing, it's another," lamented Parry.

"As you already know, our legal and technical people have been working for months on the 'Hide the Weenie' Project."

"Then came the flap over our 500% increase in park entrance fees, which are scheduled to go into effect this year. And now this!"

"All I can tell you is that we are proceeding with an open mind and that a final decision will be made only after all of the facts have been made available to us. Nothing is as of yet 'cast in stone.'"

"We'll try to work with these guys. But, all this controversy is enough to make a man consider an early retirement!"

Public reaction to the mammouth [*sic*] endeavor is mixed. Many Moabites have strong reservations regarding the ethical ramifications of the project, although most admit that it would bring more tourists than anything done thus far along those lines.

But Black Pantheist President Cherty Biohern denounced the idea as but "another in long series of attempts to unfairly exploit one of our most beautiful natural attractions."

"Let me make one thing perfectly clear," insisted Biohern. "We are not, as some have insinuated, angry about the fact that they have 'stolen' our idea."

"This monstrous scheme is nothing at all like our proposal!"

While some final details have yet to be worked out, the preliminary plan has been thoroughly outlined in the engineering proposals accompanying the development funding request on file in Washington.

The project involves the insertion of a massive 10 foot eyebolt into the top of the arch and, with the aid of drills and shims, loosening the structure from its natural pedestal.

Once detached, a team of giant cargo helicopters will airlift the structure the 10 miles or so to a prepared masonry base at the north end of Moab. There it will be permanently mounted, straddling the highway, advertising Moab as the "arch capitol of the world."

In its place in Arches Park, a full-scale model will be constructed, perfect in detail and, according to the developers, "better than the original."

"This would enable every red-blooded American to see the real thing!" insisted Gaynurd.

"Hell, the way it sits now, you have to walk nearly two miles to see the thing from the nearest parking place."

"Nobody I know can walk that far. It's just a waste of a perfectly good arch."

39

Edward Abbey
Druid of the Arches (1976)

Bruce Hamilton

> *By the 1970s Edward Abbey and* Desert Solitaire *were icons of the environmental movement. In this Bruce Hamilton profile, originally published in 1976 and reprinted in the* High Country News *at the time of Abbey's death in 1989, Abbey talks about development, Arches, and writing.*

People picture him, at least I did, as the latter day John Muir in the land of the Latter Day Saints. What Muir was to the Sierras in California, Edward Abbey is to the canyon country of Utah. [Both men] achieved in their writing an integration of language and the wilderness experience. Abbey's frequent forays against Glen Canyon Dam are reminiscent of Muir's fight to save Hetch Hetchy from inundation.

Muir knew Yosemite in all weather, all seasons, all moods. He scaled its highest granite peaks, climbed towering pines to experience its wild storms, washed in its glacier-fed streams, rode out its avalanches, slept on its peaceful valley floor.

Abbey's base is the parched colorful canyon country in and around Arches National Park. An area he describes in *Slickrock* as the

> least inhabited, least inhibited, least developed, least improved, least civilized, least governed, least priest-ridden, most arid, most hostile, most lonesome, most grim bleak barren desolute [*sic*] and savage quarter of the state of Utah—the best part by far. So far.

He walks the dry washes, bathes in potholes, runs from flash floods, floats its remaining wild rivers, and sleeps under the clear desert sky.

But the comparison, if carried further, is hard to complete and grossly unfair. Muir, posthumously, appears heroic, legendary, prophetic, wise beyond words. Abbey, available for personal inspection and interview, appears all too human.

In *Slickrock*, Abbey recalls climbing out of Coyote Gulch in the Escalante to have a look at the world that lay above and between the canyons. When attempting to return to the canyon floor he discovers: "All the sandstone hills look dismayingly alike, at least when you're lost..." He becomes "rimmed up" and backtracks and circles once, twice, three times until he chances upon the one and only route down. Safe at the bottom he reflects: "If I were the John Muir I'd like to be I would have spent the night up there."

I imagined Abbey as the desert hermit. Abbey imagines Abbey as the desert hermit:

> Someday, I thought, I shall make the experiment, become an ancient baldheaded troglodyte with a dirty white beard tucked in my belt, be a shaman, a wizard, a witch doctor crazy with solitude, starving on locusts and lizards, feasting from time to time upon lost straggler boy scout.

Abbey says he lives near Wolf Hole, a ghost town on the Arizona Strip. Where does he really live? It doesn't matter. Suffice it to say he and his family live in a semi-modern, comfortable house on the outskirts of a small city in the canyonlands. On the bulletin board in his study is a photo of a weary-looking friend beside a weathered sign which says Wolf Hole. The friend came to visit Abbey the hermit. He found only dust.

There are other photos on the walls. A photo of a clean cut, dark-haired, park ranger riding a power boat on Lake Powell—Ed Abbey in 1967. An aerial view of Glen Canyon Dam with spray paint graffiti across the roadway: "Bomb the dam, not Cambodia." A color poster of a buxom woman advertising chainsaws. A photo of him and Renee being married in the shadow of a cactus.

The ranch-style house is served by electricity which is probably generated by a dam blocking Abbey's beloved Colorado River or by a coal-fired power plant which pollutes the clear desert air. The yard is slowly being invaded by weeds and transforming back into a desert ecosystem. In the meantime, there is tumbleweed—Russian thistle—an introduced species which has become the quintessential symbol of the Old West. Alas, poor Abbey, he's allergic to the omnipresent weed.

The Volkswagen in the driveway bears the bumper sticker: "Eat more gophers and mice, 20,000 coyotes can't be wrong." A beer cooler in the back seat serves as the car's odometer. Five six-packs from Arches to Lander, Wyo. A slight tell-tale paunch protruding from his otherwise sturdy six-foot-plus profile reveals the consequence of a lifetime trying to get drunk on 3.2 beer, one of the hazards of living in Mormon Country.

"It's always somewhat of a letdown to meet an author," Abbey tells me. "I put the best part of me in my books. I keep the scummy side secret."

Wild Preservative

Abbey is not a conservation group leader like Muir. In fact, he's an anarchist. He is a writer, leading from behind. What he offers environmentalists is spiritual leadership—a quality many desk-bound, environmental leaders lack.

Abbey doesn't limit himself to conservation themes, but he is best known and best loved for his writing in defense of the land. He says he "tumbled into" environmentalism many years ago, "and the more I try to dig myself out, the deeper I get."

Unlike Muir and other conservation leaders that followed in his footsteps, Abbey claims he doesn't know "a megawatt from a gigawatt, a syncline from an anticline."

He says he's "too ignorant to be a true environmentalist or conservationist." Instead, he classifies himself as "simply, a wild preservative." That means "I prefer to save something no matter how worthless and let other things go to hell," he tells me.

Abbey was born in 1927 in Home, Pa., where he was raised on a farm. In 1944, while hitchhiking back East from California, Abbey got his first glimpse of the canyon country from an open boxcar door. He was pressed into the infantry in 1945, and was released two years later—still a private.

"The Army made an anarchist out of me and what with one thing and another I've been living off the government ever since," he says.

Abbey attended Indiana Teachers College (one year), University of New Mexico (six years), Edinburgh (one year), and Yale (two weeks). He has been a fire lookout, a university teacher, a park ranger, a social worker in and around Nelson's Marine Bar in Hoboken, N.J., a desert rat, a guest lecturer, and all this time, a writer.

His books include *Desert Solitaire*, *The Monkey Wrench Gang*, *Slickrock*, *Black Sun*, *Fire on the Mountain*, *Cactus Country*, *Jonathan Troy*, *Appalachia* and *The Brave Cowboy* (on which the film *Lonely Are the Brave* was based).

Abbey says he flunked journalism in high school not once, but twice. "I couldn't get basketball scores right." His biggest problem has always been that he "was not interested in facts; only in truth," he says.

"I think I could have been a great writer if I'd stayed in Hoboken," Abbey says as he strokes his salt-and-pepper beard. "It was easy to write there. It's hard to write in the West. Hard to stay indoors. Hard to carry your typewriter in your backpack."

Twist of Fate

Abbey disavows being a regional writer, even though his most famous books are set in the Southwest. Abbey explains his venture into writing about the West as a twist of fate. He was merely following the writer's first rule of thumb—"reject all rejections." He tells me the story this way:

> One New York publisher's editor once had the gall, brass and temerity to return a novel to me saying, "This here book, Mr. Abbey, has no form, no content, no style, no point, no meaning, no nothing. It's not even obscene. It has no redeeming social value whatsoever. I advise you to destroy it before it multiplies."
>
> He was right, of course, and that book has never been published—thank Gawd—but at the time I was rather hurt by his remarks. And astonished: how could any one man be that stupid? Takes team work to be that dumb. So I replied at once by return mail. My letter began: 'Dear Sir, In simple justice I must inform you that I am saving your letter for the laughter and ridicule of posterity. You have committed the greatest literary blunder

since Simon and Schuster rejected the *New Testament.* Beethoven's early work, too, was scorned by the academic critics of his time,' etc., etc., in that vein.

Well, a few days later this same publisher's editor invited me to lunch. I was living across the Hudson River, in Hoboken, at the time. (Hoboken is in New Jersey. New Jersey is in hell.) So I put on my galoshes and walked across the river—the sewage gets thick on the Hudson—and we had lunch.

He said, 'Why don't you write about something you know about?' I said, 'Well, I don't know.' And he said, 'Write about Hoboken. Write a book about the Wasteland.' I said, 'I don't really know much about it.' And he said, 'Make up something.'

I said, 'OK,' and went home and wrote a book about the desert, which made me rich and popular—and ruined the desert...

Ever since I wrote the desert book I've been tagged and banded as a regional writer—Southwest—which I resent. If I'm a regional writer I want it understood that I claim not only the Southwest, but also Hoboken and Naples and Edinburgh and the human heart and the human reproductive organs and Moab, Utah, and Wolf Hole, Ariz., and Diamond Street, San Francisco, etc., etc.

I am not a writer of westerns. I refuse to be put in that paper bag—just because my bag is paper.

Abbey also resents being labeled a travel writer. "I had a letter from some landscape photographer who wanted me to help him 'do' a book about Cape Cod," says Abbey. "Cape Cod! Good God! What do I know about Cape Cod? Good God! I ain't no caption writer. I'm an artist. A serious artist. As I've told Eliot Porter, Ansel Adams, and Phil Hyde: 'One picture is worth two, three, words. Maybe.'"

Arches Revisited

We're traveling together through Arches National Park, the setting for *Desert Solitaire*. "In the center of the world, God's navel, the red wasteland—Abbey's country." At least it was.

The arches are about the same as they were when Ranger Abbey scouted the trails, but much of the park has yielded to the inroads of "industrial tourism." The desert persists, but the solitaire has been invaded.

The old sign at Courthouse Wash which read "WARNING: QUICKSAND. DO NOT CROSS WASH WHEN WATER IS RUNNING" is gone—replaced by a bridge. Most of the dirt jeep trails have been paved. Ranger Abbey's late night hikes to remove roadcrew survey stakes were ineffective. (Abbey notes that the statute of limitations on this "crime" is up.) The campground is crowded with Winnebagos and campers trailing dune buggies and dirt bikes. In the evening, bats soar in and out of the persistent glaring lights at the modern comfort stations.

The seasonal ranger, Jim Stiles, complains about the insensitive tourists. He toys with the idea of blowing up the arches so people won't be interested in entering the park. Hopefully, they would all stay in the visitors center and watch the park movie. Then the area would be saved. In his spare time, Stiles draws and markets "exploded views" posters and note cards. His most popular one is a view of Glen Canyon Dam in a pile of rubble. The caption: "To Edward Abbey, wherever you are." On his house trailer at the campground is a sign which tells inquisitive tourists, no, this is not Edward Abbey's trailer.

"I went through some heartbreak 20 years ago when I saw Arches changing," laments Abbey. "I suppose the paved roads haven't destroyed too much. But it takes away the adventure for some."

But Abbey refuses to forgive and forget the construction of the Glen Canyon Dam and the death of the free-flowing Colorado River which ran through the temples of slickrock that he loved so well.

> Let all the Faithful living down-river from this dam take warning. There are thousands of us who never forget, during our bedtime prayers, to ask God for one little precision earthquake in the immediate vicinity of Glen Canyon Dam.... We are devout; we have faith; and someday soon our prayers shall be answered.

Abbey's latest book, *The Monkey Wrench Gang*, details the exploits of a band of eco-saboteurs in the Southwest. They blow up bridges and heavy construction equipment, but their ultimate goal is to blow up the dam.

"Living out here in the West I find plenty to get mad about," says Abbey. "I long ago had the idea of blowing up the dams, but it took awhile to materialize it into a book."

Asked if he condones the type of sabotage plotted by the Monkey Wrench Gang, Abbey says he is "opposed to all forms of illegality—except at night."

Home on the Rocks

We start hiking down one of the trails in Arches. The heat is torturous, but the scenery makes it tolerable. Abbey wears a tiny Army surplus backpack filled with a water bottle and a lunch. On his head he wears a drugstore straw hat—so old the top has fallen off and only the brim remains.

He walks slowly. No sense working up a sweat. Sweat comes freely without any work. Stop frequently. Drink often, or you'll desiccate.

I feel vulnerable. I carry sun screen cream, Chap-stick, Gatorade, and salt tablets.

We stop at a muddy pothole. Abbey takes off his shirt, soaks it and puts it back on. I do the same.

We pass through a wonderland of grotesque, startling, spellbinding rock forms. Sandstone shaven into finely sculpted shapes by winter. Fins, arches, bridges, balanced rocks. If you sit still enough, you can feel the magic of the place.

The rocks have names as well as spirits. The petrified sand dunes are Navajo sandstone. The arch-forming layers are Entrada sandstone. Abbey follows the trail up a rock face made safer by Park Service cement steps. Portland formation, says Abbey.

He scrambles up a nearby rock tower and sits down to soak in the desert. He pulls what is left of his hat down over his eyes to block the sun. Chews on a piece of dried grass. (What? Picking grass in a national park?)

Abbey says his highest ambition is to pick out a good spot and just sit there, not moving, for about a year. Keep your eyeballs peeled and just sit there, through the hours, through the days, through the nights, through the seasons—the freeze of winter, the stunning glare and heat of summer, the grace and glory of the spring and fall and watch what happens, he wrote in *Slickrock*.

One evening, we walk the trail to Delicate Arch. I marvel at the way the trail follows a level ledge along a sandstone cliff to reach the arch. I ask Abbey if he thinks the trail was worn so evenly just by weather and frequent human use. Abbey replies no, he blasted out the trail with dynamite when he was in the Park Service. "The Park Service spawned my interest in using explosives in southern Utah," he says.

I laugh, and look up at the precariously balanced Delicate Arch nearby.

As the sun sets, Abbey walks over to the thin foot of Delicate Arch and pretends to pry the supporting boulder foundation away. The night is clear and still. All that can be heard is the sound of a distant coyote and the nearby grunts and groans of Abbey struggling at the base of the arch trying in jest to topple it into the Colorado River.

Fat Masterpiece

Another evening, Abbey talks to a group of writers and students about writing. The occasion is casual—a seminar held in Arches. Abbey sits on a sand dune, beer in hand. He claims he can't speak extemporaneously so he reads something he's written and departs from the text to tell jokes.

"Why write?" he asks. "Especially in view of the fact that ever since God first spoke The Word (what word *was* that?) the world has been flooded with words, words, words...

> We live on a great leaning tower of babble, assaulted on all sides, outside and inside, by a constant hail of messages, a rain of books, a deluge of paper and print...
>
> We are deforesting a continent in order to suffocate ourselves beneath a flood of print. Why? I think of those joyous young pines, with who knows what aspirations of their own, cut down in the flower of their youth and ground to pulp, for the sake of paper paper paper. Muchas papeles. Why?

Abbey then reveals the reason behind the question: He feels guilty. He feels there are too many books, and yet, his ambition is to write a great fat book.

"Or, if not great then at least fat," he says. "A monstrous tome, or tomb—of exactly 1,000 fine-print pages. When I get to page 1,000 I'll quit.

Right in the middle, and resign myself from the writing business. That's a promise. Retire to my stone hut in the desert and spend the rest of my life contemplating...my novel."

The title of his fat masterpiece will be *Fat Masterpiece*.

Abbey concludes in the course of his speech and his six-pack that there are several good reasons for writing: money, fame, women, easy life, alcoholism, early death and ecstasy. "Never mind the flood of books. Throw another in the river," he advises.

"I'll tell you why I have to write. Because nobody, nobody, has yet written the book that I want to write...

"Why climb Everest? Mallory said, 'Because it's there.' Why do I want to write that one more book—and then maybe one more? Because it's *not* there, yet."

Later, members of the group ask Abbey questions.

"How much time do you devote to writing?"

"As little as I possibly can."

"What's your sign?"

"Get out of Cambodia."

Then self-proclaimed anarchist Abbey offers his disciples some political advice: "I've always been reluctant to join any organization. But if we are going to defend the American West against industrial exploitation, we will have to cooperate with one another in some kind of political, social and legal action."

Abbey suggests supporting candidates for public office "who will put the public interest before corporate-business interests. The two are seldom the same." He regrets that in Utah there are no such candidates. "We'll have to find some, or invent some," he says.

He tells the group we are all "obliged to join or work or at least contribute money to a citizen conservation organization." Having little time or effort to offer such groups, Abbey says, "I appease my guilty conscience by giving a tithe of my income—like a good Mormon should—to several environmental organizations.

"Devoted though we must be to the conservation cause, I do not believe that any of us should give it *all* of our time or effort or heart," he warns. "Give what you can, but do not burn yourselves out—or break your hearts." He continues,

Let us save at least half of our lives for the enjoyment of this wonderful world which still exists. Leave your dens, abandon your cars and walk out into the mountains, the deserts, the forests, the seashores. Those treasures still belong to all of us. Enjoy them to the full, stretch your legs, expand your lungs, enliven your hearts—and we will outlive the greedy swine who want to destroy it all in the name of what they call GROWTH.

God bless America. Let's save some of it. Long live the weeds and the wilderness yet!

Druid of the Arches

An hour before sunrise, I get up to take a morning bird walk. Abbey is still asleep in the back of his VW wagon.

It is a good morning for bird watching. In the pinyon-juniper forest of the Devil's Garden in Arches I find a rock wren, scrub jay, plain titmouse, blue-gray gnatcatcher, sage thrasher, common bushtit and hairy woodpecker. A porcupine waddles across my path. In the sand, tracks of kangaroo rats, dune beetles and cottontails can be found.

The sky lightens. There is a faint glow over the Sierra La Sal to the east. I flush a Cooper's hawk. Then a strange noise catches my ear. Not a bird call. More like a faint elk bugle. No, I must be hearing things.

There it is again. And then a series of notes. Why, it's flute music!

I follow the sound and there, perched high on a fin of sandstone, facing the rising sun, flute in hand, is Abbey. The druid of the arches.

He plays a wide variety of tunes. Softly. Clearly. Some he starts, but stops abruptly. Half the concert is silence. Listening to the accompaniment of the natural world.

He plays "A gift to be simple." Two does and their fawns walk by between Abbey and me. He plays "Greensleeves." Silence.

The sun appears behind the mountaintops. Its pale yellow light strikes the deep wine-red sandstone and makes it glow. Abbey makes a shrill long whistle with his flute. Then another. Silence.

He repeats the call. And from somewhere in the east a chorus of coyotes answer. They yodel for several minutes. I look back at Abbey to see if he'll repeat his coyote call. He is gone.

Muir-like? No, just like Abbey.

40

The Pasty White Shellfish Comes to Arches National Park (2022)

Ken Sanders

Ken Sanders co-founded Cosmic Aeroplane Books and Records and founded both Dream Garden Press and Ken Sanders Rare Books. He has been in the book business for fifty-plus years and is frequently seen as a rare book expert on Antiques Roadshow. *Here he describes some 1980s Earth First! activism.*

Q. How many watts does it take to screw up the environment?
A. One James Watt

In 1980, Ronald Reagan became the 40th president of the United States and the upstart radical environmental group, Earth First! (always with the exclamation point), launched their first action: a commemoration of Pancho Villa's invasion of the United States at Columbus, New Mexico in 1916.

The then-little known radical right wing Mountain States Legal Foundation, largely funded by the Coors Brewing Company of Golden, Colorado (aka the "Coors Mafia"), would be amply rewarded for their loyalty. As a direct political payoff to the "Coors Mafia," Reagan appointed James Watt as Secretary of the Interior, Anne Gorsuch as the head of the EPA, and Robert Burford as the director of the BLM. All three individuals were associated with the Mountain States Legal Foundation. After their tour of duty in the Reagan administration, Gorsuch and Burford would marry.[1] No word on whether James Watt was their best man.

An evangelical Christian from Wyoming, Watt would become a lightning rod as the Secretary of the Interior, in charge of public lands, including

BLM lands and the National Parks. During the 80s, Watt was a poster boy recruitment ad for national environmental and conservation groups like The Sierra Club, The Wilderness Society, The Grand Canyon Trust, and here in Utah, the newly formed Southern Utah Wilderness Association (SUWA).

These two actions—the election of Ronald Reagan as President and his appointment of James Watt and the Coors Mafia to rape and pillage America's public lands, coupled with the birth of the radical environmental group, Earth First!—would lead to four years of environmental mayhem, chaos, and destruction played out upon these self-same public lands in the American West. In which myself, Edward Abbey, and the legions comprising Earth First! would play a small role. Or at least my alter ego, Spurs Jackson, would.

A Sidebar on Spurs Jackson and EF! Aliases and Nicknames

Dave Foreman went by Digger Dave, Ed Abbey became Cactus Ed, EF! co-founder Bart Koehler was the troubadour, Johnny Sagebrush, and his girlfriend became Wildcat Annie. I soon began to feel naked without a moniker, so Spurs Jackson was born. Truth be told, I stole the name from a WWII-era comic book that featured one Spurs Jackson and his Space Vigilantes, who beat up Nazis on Mars. Ah, the good old days. It seemed somehow fitting.

The late author Edward Abbey published his first three novels in the span of eight years, from 1954–1962. His fourth book, *Desert Solitaire*, was published in 1968. In 1975, his fourth novel *The Monkey Wrench Gang* came out. Both *Desert Solitaire* and *The Monkey Wrench Gang* have become classics in their field (a term Ed always dreaded) and have gone on to sell millions of copies. I devoured them both, and met their author at my old Cosmic Aeroplane bookstore in SLC, not long after the publication of *MWG*. Abbey was still living in Moab at the time and happened to wander into the Cosmic. I led him into my rare book room and asked him to sign copies of first editions of his books, meanwhile lecturing him on the atrocious (to my mind) habit of Hayduke and Co. in *MWG* to litter beer cans up and down western highways. In spite of this, shall we say, awkward, clueless beginning, Ed Abbey and I became friends and would have many adventures together in what would become the last decade and a half of his life.

In 1980, I founded my publishing company Dream Garden Press, and I was eager to do an Edward Abbey publishing project. In the spring of 1981, Ed called me and invited me to what he referred to as some kind of "spring rites" down at Glen Canyon Dam(n), at a place called Lone Rock on the shores of Lake (reservoir) Powell. He said we could talk about my "silly" calendar if I wished. The "silly calendar" came from an idea to publish a literary calendar devoted to Abbey's works. It evolved into a lavish full color photographic calendar with Abbey quotations, "The Edward Abbey Western Wilderness Calendars," along with a slew of other national park and wilderness books which I would go on to publish for ten more years.

In the spring of 1981 I had been planning a backpack into the heart of the Maze, in Canyonlands National Park, and thought what the hell, "spring rites" aside, I would journey down to the Lone Rock Campground so I could convince Ed to let me go ahead with my publishing schemes. These included what would become the "Edward Abbey Western Wilderness Calendars" and the R. Crumb illustrated edition of *The Monkey Wrench Gang* in hardbound, which would come out a few years later in 1985.

I left SLC a few days early and headed down to the lonely wind-swept rocky shores of Lake Powell, and the so-called Lone Rock campground. There was a lone rock there, a drowned element of the old Glen Canyon, but no sign of what any civilized human being would call a "campground." Yes, there was ground there and I would camp upon it, but nothing else. As I traveled down the lonely track, my way was impeded by a VW bus, with a large lump of what appeared to be plastic, larger than the bus, bulging over its sides. Outside of the VW were 3 or 4 large burly men in cowboy hats, arms folded across their chests, and unfriendly scowls on their faces. They inquired as to whom "the fuck I was" and "what the fuck" I might be doing there. I didn't care for their demeanor or their manners and the last thing I was going to let them know was that I was a friend of Ed Abbey's. Besides, who were these scowling cowboys and what the fuck were *they* doing there? I backed up Alphonse (my trusty 54' Chevy flat black pickup truck) and drove around the scowling cowboys and camped at the end of the road. Things were a bit tense between the two camps until later that evening, when another pickup truck arrived, disgorging Cactus Ed himself and a girlfriend.

The black plastic cowboys introduced themselves to Abbey, whom they had invited, and in turn Ed introduced me to the cowboys. They were a then-unheard of radical environmental group, Earth First!, who would become nationally famous a day later after dropping a three-hundred-foot plastic crack down the face of Glen Canyon Dam as a symbolic protest. Yes, the scowling cowboys turned out to be three of the founding members of Earth First!: Dave Foreman, Bart Koehler, and Howie Wolke. The other two founders, Mike Roselle and Ron Kezar, would join us later, along with Louisa Willcox. Once Foreman and company learned that I was a friend of Abbey's, they gleefully confided to me their plans for the next day, i.e. the cracking of the dam; sounded good to me. I was in. That fateful day would go down as the day that both Ed Abbey and I met EF!

This is a tale of Arches, however, so the real story of "the Cracking of Glen Canyon Dam" will remain untold. You'll have to settle for the video that was made on March 24th (John Wesley Powell's birthday) in the interim. But that memorable meeting with the founders and friends of Earth First! would set the stage for years of environmental mayhem in and out of the national parks and public lands and would prime the pump for another encounter with Glen Canyon Dam and the forces that be, exactly two years later.

In the early spring of 1983, the National Park Service decreed there would be a 20th anniversary birthday celebration for Lake Powell & Glen Canyon Dam. A birthday party to celebrate a drowned river and about 10,000 known archaeological sites, Indian rock art panels, dwellings, gravesites, countless natural wonders like Gregory Natural Bridge, Music Temple, and Hidden Canyon? I thought not. Through my emerging role as Spurs Jackson, the minister of Information of EF!, we organized and declared a funeral party to be held at the same time.

The Park Service was rolling out James Watt, the secretary of the interior. Two huge new ships with the governors of Utah (Scott Matheson) and Arizona (Bruce Babbitt) launched from Wahweap on Lake Powell with many other official dignitaries. I cannot begin to tell this story either, replete as it is with James Watt, the then-governors of Utah and Arizona, the Page High School Marching Band, the launch of the big ships, the launching of the EF! pirate ship, the big storm, Ken Sleight aka Seldom Seen Smith, the FBI film crew, the SWAT teams, the infrared rifles, the agents provocateurs, the airplane, the counterdemonstrations by EARTH LAST! and Mutants For Watt, the sheriff's departments of Utah and Arizona, Glen Canyon NRA law enforcement and the Coast Guard, the men in suits who were never introduced, Willie's Waterdog Saloon in Glen Canyon City and the son of famed Mormon polygamist Alex Joseph, Johnny Sagebrush's impromptu concert that blew our cover as bass fishermen, meeting Charles Bowden for the first time, and most importantly (at least for the purpose of this story) the James Watt dummy. That story will have to wait. This story is about James Watt's unexpected journey (both in person and as the mannequin) to Arches National Park. It really is.

Suffice to say, high atop the Earth First! pirate ship (née Lake Powell houseboat) from Wahweap to Lone Rock the mannequin secretary sailed, surrounded by the Beach Boys (who he banned from the White House) and on his knees praying for helicopters to rescue him from the boredom of a river trip down the Grand Canyon. This is where the James Watt dummy was born, and how his unexpected journey to the Arches began.

Hoping for a few days of r&r after days of FBI videos, SWAT team surveillance, law enforcement types of all stripes and agents provocateurs, my female companion and I loaded up the detritus of the Lake Fowell Funeral into Alphonse and headed up to Moab via Monument Valley for a few days of hiking and relaxation. Or so we thought.

Arriving in the valley of Moab, we were greeted by the news of the arrival at Arches National Park the very next morning of the same secretary of the interior that we had been chasing around Lake Powell! It seems the pasty white shellfish had at the last minute agreed to make a stop for a photo-op at Arches and had actually agreed to get out of the vehicle and walk, presumably unaided except by his horde of security forces, on his own two feet, some fifty yards or more to The North Window, a massive arch near Balanced Rock in Arches National Park.

This was an opportunity that we could not afford to let slip by, tired and exhausted as we were. Especially after the secretary had proclaimed that he was unaware of any demonstration back at Glen Canyon Dam! Really? He never saw the pirate ship with his dummy on top, chased by the Coast Guard? Despite being on one of the two big ships, he never saw our funeral and our demonstration, and he failed to hear or see the airplane that buzzed

Page, Arizona, the dam itself and flew over our heads hauling a large banner that said: FREE THE COLORADO. EARTH FIRST!? Well, he was going to notice something at Arches the next morning. So much for our time off.

Later that same evening at a friend's, another friend offered to loan us his vehicle. My old truck, after having been the stage at the Glen Canyon rally and after having been videotaped by the FBI, was too high profile for the nightwork we had in mind. By 2:00 am we found ourselves pulled over at the side of the road by Balanced Rock, deep in a heated discussion over exactly where to place our James Watt dummy that we had smuggled into the park. Louisa argued for free climbing Balanced Rock and hanging the dummy from a noose to greet the James Watt motorcade the next morning. I argued against leaving something so profane atop a rock so sacred.

I won the argument and we drove onto the side road that led into The Windows. The windows section of Arches is dominated by two large monolithic arches, and many smaller ones. The two large stone openings are The North & South Windows and that is where we had been leaked information that Watt would step out of his vehicle for a photo-op the next day.

The James Watt dummy was placed, in his suit, down on his knees, his upraised hands crushing a pair of Coors Beer cans while beseeching the heavens, 666 painted on his forehead. The pasty white shellfish (or at least his dummy) had arrived. A few hastily spraypainted greetings were left as a sort of a "welcome" to the secretary, and satisfied with our work, we departed the park.

It was now 3:00 am and as we arrived back at the T intersection with the main Arches road, the hairs literally stood up on the backs of our heads! There before us, in gigantic letters in white spray paint sprawled across both sides of the road, were the words:

JAMES WATT
A
NATIONAL
DISGRACE

Needless to say, this message had not been painted across the highway just an hour before. Someone else was out there creepy crawling in the park that night! They had certainly been as aware of our presence as we were oblivious to theirs! Feelings ran very strong towards James Watt. The following day on national TV, his face red and contorted with rage after confronting his doppleganger dummy at the North Window, Watt spewed and sputtered against "these vandals who would destroy our national parks." Oddly, he was talking about himself and the Coors Mafia Reagan had appointed to rape America's public lands. The television cameras, of course, never once showed the Watt dummy with his crushed cans of Coors praying to his god unknown. I will leave to the reader to decide who were the real vandals destroying America's National Parks and wilderness areas back in the 1980s.

Longtime seasonal Park ranger Jim Stiles was tasked with the investigation of the park vandalism, and after the Watt dummy was dusted for fingerprints, he took possession of it. We never heard what became of that investigation.

Some time later, the James Watt dummy turned up at the loop road at Devil's Garden, just before the turn into the Devil's Garden campground, not far from where the ranger residence trailer used to be. The Watt dummy was buried in the sand with only its legs sticking up in the air. For a season or two, it became a very popular photo op at the park. Occasionally, puzzled tourists, especially Japanese and German visitors, would query Ranger Stiles about the dummy. In his NPS uniform and hat and with a straight face, he would reply: "That's the secretary of the Interior, ma'am, searching for oil and gas."

POSTSCRIPT

The head ranger of Arches at that time was Joan Swanson, who at age 26 became the first female head ranger at Arches National Park and the youngest female head ranger in the National Park system. I have it on good authority that Ms. Swanson was our fellow monkey wrencher that evening, out there creepy crawling with Louisa and I in the dead of the night. It was with her help and the spirit of Edward Abbey that we gave such a heartfelt welcome to James Watt back in the spring of 1983.

The current whereabouts of the James Watt dummy are unknown.

Note

1 Gorsuch's son Neil became an associate justice of the U.S. Supreme Court in 2017.

41

Tourists in the Vortex (2007)

Jim Stiles

Parks are for people, the old saying goes. But are people good for parks? Are they good for gateway towns like Moab? Jim Stiles isn't so sure, as this excerpt from his 2007 book Brave New West: Morphing Moab at the Speed of Greed *suggests.*

Sitting helplessly and innocently in the center of this ugly debate about the future of the rural West is the hapless tourist himself. Maligned and beloved, praised and condemned, urged to stay longer and encouraged to leave sooner, he stands at the Moab Information Center, bewildered, confused, and wanting the answer to the one pressing question that matters most, driven by the most painful of all agonies, the distended bladder and a place to relieve it.

Most tourists are oblivious to the uproar, divisiveness, and controversy their mere presence creates. It never occurs to them that, in fact, a tourist town is ultimately designed and constructed to appeal to *them*, not the residents who live there, those who work, raise children, and pay taxes. They roll into town, check into a motel, wander the streets in search of trinkets and T-shirts. They schedule a river trip on the Colorado for the following day or a drive to Arches and Canyonlands. Then they return in the evening for a hot meal and a beer or two, stumble back wearily to the motel, and rise early the next morning for the next long driving segment of their marathon two-week journey to do the West.

There was a time when tourists in Moab seldom thought to even venture off Main Street to see what lies beyond the shops and stores. For many, it was like a no man's land.

"What's back there, Daddy?"

"Nothing, honey. We don't want to go in there. People live there."

In Moab, of course, that indifference changed in the late 1980s when affluent out-of-town visitors discovered the incredible real estate bargains to be gobbled up for peanuts. Moab's subsequent ascendancy to Brave New West Yupstertown made real estate shopping as essential a part of the trip for some tourists as "doing the daily" float trip on the Colorado River.

It feels at times as if the world wants to move to Moab. In truth, though, the vast majority just want to get in and out as quickly as possible, with as little difficulty as possible, and with the hope that they'll see some lovely scenery and have experiences they can share later with their friends back home. Most Americans rarely take the time or find the opportunity to do anything memorable and unique. These days vacations are intended to convince the traveler that he still lives an interesting life, even if the experience he seeks is not at all spontaneous. Tourists seem to assume that since they're on vacation, they'll escape the cruel realities of the life they left back home. It never occurs to them that cruel reality lurks everywhere.

Because being a tourist is only a part-time job, he never has an opportunity to develop any real tourist skills. Practice really is everything. So, imagine millions of humans out there on the highway, total novices at the tourist game, and they've all chosen to leave their coping mechanisms at home. It's a recipe for chaos, for disaster.

It took a long time to reach the current frenzied state of tourism gone bonkers. For most of Moab's history, tourism was merely a sideline. From Ringhoffer's discovery of Tower Arch in the early 1920s and the creation of Arches National Park in 1929 until a decade past the close of World War II, most rural Utahns regarded tourism as a tolerable way to make a few extra bucks. Though farming, ranching, and mining still dominated the local economy, there were a few notable exceptions. The *Times-Independent* editor, Bish Taylor, and longtime tourism booster J. W. "Doc" Williams were both fervent supporters of expansions at Arches National Park. As active members of the Moab Lion's Club, Taylor and Williams actively embraced subsequent promotions they both hoped would bring more tourism to this remote corner of America. But the Depression and World War II did little to create a tourist boom. In the early 1940s, most of the rangers enlisted and left their park assignments behind. The CCC crews that began construction on an Arches entrance road in 1940 left, too. Hardly anyone in America was sightseeing in the early 1940s. With war's end and a booming peacetime economy, however, change came rapidly—too rapidly for some.

New Mexico native Bates Wilson came to Arches in 1949 and stayed until his retirement in 1972. He saw visitation at Arches grow from just a few thousand when he arrived to almost a quarter million when he left to take up ranching in Professor Valley. Wilson's tireless campaigning led to the creation of Canyonlands as a new national park. His expansive personality was destined to make him a legend in his own time.

When we weigh the polarization that exists between special interest groups now, it's difficult to imagine one man managing to bridge the animosities that existed fifty years ago, but nobody didn't like Bates Wilson. He repeatedly found common ground, simply because he chose it for himself. He never thought too highly of himself, despite the way he introduced himself to strangers, "I'm so glad you got to meet me." Wilson didn't think much of hierarchy, and he was known to show up unannounced at a work site simply to get familiar with new rangers and maintenance men alike. If a trail crew was doing maintenance, he'd grab a shovel and help out, and he'd often reward the crew later with one of his famous Dutch oven dinners.

Wilson was as tolerant a man as any of us could hope to find or try to be, but he did not suffer fools gladly. His exasperation with graffiti scribblers made its way into the old monthly reports in May 1956, when he wrote, "The increasing desire by fools to carve their names in public places has reached the highest level possible in Arches at Delicate Arch." Later, graffiti vandalism got worse.

Another entry in the monthly reports conceals the frustration and grief with green, inexperienced tourists that Wilson must have felt, particularly in this case. In June 1959 Leroy Black, a sixty-seven year old from Bethlehem, Pennsylvania, was hiking at Natural Bridges National Monument, 100 miles south of Moab, and failed to return to his car. Wilson organized a search and determined that Black had missed the trail to Kachina Bridge. Black had instead continued downstream through White Canyon. He hiked fourteen miles and for three days before search parties caught up with him. It was June, so water was plentiful in potholes and the stream itself, but apparently

Black was concerned with issues of water quality and would not drink from it. His dog meanwhile was having a grand time and probably [never] failed to miss an opportunity for a swim and a drink. When Wilson found Leroy Black he was suffering from severe dehydration.

Wilson reported,

> He was found on June 28 at 3:00 p.m. still alive, but in very poor condition. As there was not sufficient time to remove him from the canyon, he was made as comfortable as possible in a sleeping bag and fed small quantities of water and broth. By 10:30 p.m. he appeared to be much stronger, but around midnight he died.

Most tourist fatalities are particularly difficult to accept because they're often so senseless and easily avoided.

Bates Wilson played an integral role in the creation of Canyonlands National Park. He was once on a reconnoitering trip, one of his celebrated horse pack trips into the Great Red Unknown with Secretary of the Interior Stuart Udall. Bates hoped to persuade Udall that the magnificent Canyonlands needed federal protection. If anybody could convince Udall, it was Bates Wilson. Joining them was another park service administrator, Bill Briggle, and one of Bates's dearest friends, Arches heavy equipment operator Dutch Gerhardt. Gerhardt wasn't schooled to be a diplomat. He was a man who said what was on his mind, clearly, succinctly, and bluntly, qualities that Wilson admired. It was the reason they were such good pals. But not all park service managers appreciated candor, and Briggle was one of them.

They had been riding all day, and as the sun dipped below the canyon rim, the group decided to make camp. As Wilson unsaddled his horse, he turned to his old friend and said, "Gather up some firewood, Dutch. I'm going to be needing it pretty soon for supper."

Gerhardt squinted at Bates for a moment with icy disdain and said, "Go to hell, Bates. I'm off the clock now. Go get your own goddamned wood."

Briggle sprang to his feet, bristling with officious indignation, stepped between the horses, and practically bumped noses with Gerhardt. Gerhardt didn't move. With a man just six inches away and breathing heavily, you'd think Gerhardt didn't even see him. He looked bored.

"Mr. Gerhardt!" Briggle sputtered. "Mr. Wilson is the superintendent of this park, and he is your supervisor. When Mr. Wilson tells you to do something, you don't question his instructions, you don't ignore them, and you certainly don't act like this! You *do* it! Do I make myself clear?"

Briggle's face was the color of a crimson sunset. The veins bulged at his neck and temple.

Gerhardt looked deeply into his eyes. "Fuck you, Briggle," he said. He turned to his supervisor, "Fuck you, Bates." And then he turned to the secretary of the interior of the United States of America and said, "And fuck you, too, Udall, and the mules you rode in on."

Gerhardt spit softly on the ground, gave Bates a wink, and lumbered off to take a nap. Some say that Briggle was never the same man again. But a year later, Udall announced his unconditional support for the creation of Canyonlands National Park. Congress approved the legislation in 1964.

Forty years later, many of us aren't sure if the park creation was such a good idea after all, but in those days, park status seemed to be the only and best way to protect the land. In order to sell the idea of a park to local politicians and the citizens they represented, the National Park Service promised much more in the way of new roads and developments than anyone should ever have committed to. It left a bad taste in rural Utahns' mouths for many years.

But road building did come to the parks, even if the scale wasn't as grand as some had hoped for. The old Arches entrance road near Seven Mile Canyon was abandoned in the late 1950s, when a new paved highway was completed. By 1963 more than twenty-three miles of pavement were laid, and at one end of the park workers put the finishing touches on a Visitor center. At the far end of the road, the Devils Garden campground opened. It was part of a federal spending program called Mission 66. The idea was to upgrade the parks to provide for the ever-increasing numbers of tourists. But what the National Park Service did, by building thousands of miles of new park roads nationwide, was to provide far easier access to them. As a result, tourists came to the parks in numbers that exceeded anything they ever dreamed possible. The park service has been playing catch up ever since.

Abbey was there, of course, to disapprove of everything he saw. He wrote in his journal, "The tourists drift in and out of here like turds floating through a sewer. The simile could be extended in several directions. And I? I am a watcher of turds."

He lived in a trailer near Balanced Rock for two seasons. I was one of the last people to see Abbey's trailer intact before it was taken from the old park service boneyard and sold to the Mesa County Road Department in Grand Junction, Colorado, for salvage. It was later junked for the axles. Before they hauled it away, I stole the "#1" sign from his front door. Today, I could sell it on eBay and retire. Ed and I had revisited his trailer site years before and discovered that the old septic tank cover was still there along with some of the leach field lines. We contemplated taking the pipes, cutting them into three-inch sections, and mounting them on cheap wooden plaques with the message, "Edward Abbey's Shit Passed Through This Pipe." Abbey would autograph and authenticate it, I'd handle the marketing, and we'd both be rich. Somehow we never got around to it, but there was money to be made.

Of course, making money is what tourism is all about, but it's more complicated than that. Embracing a tourist economy means being willing to tolerate, accommodate, even grovel to the most insipid, helpless human specimens ever to point at a map and say, "Where are we?" Bless their pointy little heads.

Years ago, I met a woman from New York at Moab's old Westerner Grill. She looked fatigued, worn out, defeated.

I asked her what was wrong, and she replied, "You people around here really hate tourists, don't you?"

"What?" I exclaimed. "Certainly not! Tourists are the life blood of the community," I schmoozed.

> Well then, explain this. First they got mad at me out at that Arches Park because I told them they should really provide toiletry kits to visitors using the rest rooms. Then, at the post office, I suggested that tourists should be able to go ahead of other people because we're in more of a hurry. And, finally, at the gas station, I'd meant to buy the unleaded regular but put the supreme in my car instead. When I asked them to pump the expensive gas out and replace it with what I wanted in the first place, the man just stood there and stared at me. I mean, what was *his* problem?

I just stood there and stared at her.

"Well, say something, young man."

"You're right. You are absolutely right. We do hate you. You'll be lucky if you get out of town alive. In fact, I have a good mind to throttle you myself."

She fled for the door and was never seen again.

This little story illustrates that, while tourists fear being bitten by rattlesnakes and scorpions, tourist towns have a bite all their own. And there's no bite like a Moabite's. It's a defense mechanism, for we must strike or be struck. The residents of tourist towns, "locals" we like to call ourselves, feel as if our towns are occupied by people who don't live here. As the occupied, our resentment doesn't come from any seriously imposed oppression by our brightly dressed invaders. No, instead, our resentment comes from a long-held attitude by locals, a bias if you will, that most tourists are genetically and environmentally inferior. It's shameful and unfair, it's bigotry at its worst.

Having been a tourist myself in places where *I* felt like a floundering fish out of water, I realize that tourists simply need a helping hand. A recent trip of my own to New York City reminded me just how stupid I could be when away from my native stomping ground. To be sure, we all need some guidance occasionally, and tourists are no different.

So a few years ago, I tried to reach out to the tourists and offer a few subtle hints that might keep visitors from making total fools of themselves. I wanted to help. I wanted to impress upon my tourist cousins that, in order to survive, they must not only learn how to deal with Mother Nature, but how to deal with *us* as well. I prepared a survival guide of sorts for tourists, which I published in the *Zephyr*.

After years of first-hand analysis, I thought I'd found the key. I realized that the difficulties tourists encounter are often related to the methods they've chosen to convey themselves. What I mean is, the ways a tourist can incur the wrath of a local when driving a thirty-eight-foot motor home are very different from the ways that riding a bicycle can annoy us, for instance. Consider some possibilities.

The Mega Motor Home

Mocking the Winnebago is almost a cliché now, but clichés are wrapped in truth. Tourists who travel in large mechanical monsters have public opinion working against them at the outset, because size *does* matter. Some locals despise motor homes.

Many of the wheeled palaces I've seen are bigger and certainly more ostentatious than the modest homes we common folk live in all the time. I recently saw a diesel-powered, deluxe forty-five-foot motor home that I learned had a sticker price of $300,000. The opulent owners towed a Mercedes-Benz SUV behind it. It made me nostalgic for a vintage Airstream trailer.

So, to you wealthy weasels in mechanical, high-tech mansions, all I can advise is that you not make things any worse than they already are. If you can, try not to draw attention to yourselves. When you pull into a crowded grocery parking lot, don't park your rig diagonally across eight or nine parking spaces, forcing the rest of us to park at the back of the lot. *You* park at the back of the lot. The walk will do you good.

If you're in a national park campground, don't fire up your Briggs & Stratton generator and ask the ranger to help align your satellite dish. Rangers are now heavily armed. Many of them are extremely unstable and on medication or are very bored with their jobs and on medication. The two conditions are interchangeable.

Do not twist off and get crazy just because a campground doesn't have a dumping station. Never aim your raw sewage hose at the ranger. It won't change the situation, and he has a limited clothing allowance.

Do not activate the loudspeaker system on your motor home and broadcast, from one end of town to the other, Lawrence Welk's greatest hits.

If you and your wife are the proud owners of a large RV, and you, like many other large recreational vehicle owners, prefer to wear matching royal blue Mickey and Minnie Mouse jump suits when traveling, and you want to take a drive into the La Sal Mountains in the autumn to look at the colors, *don't* do it. Hunters in the area may see the flash of royal blue, mistake you for Lycra-clad mountain bikers, and shoot you with highpowered rifles. Play it safe. Show off your outfits in the relative safety of a KOA.

Finally, be humble.

Europeans Who Tour America in 1975 Ford Station Wagons

For some reason, many European visitors have recently taken to buying beat-up old station wagons when they arrive in New York or Los Angeles and use them to tour the country or until they blow up. But the station wagon is how I've learned to spot our European friends. In any case, the foreign tourist offers a completely different set of challenges to the intolerant local. If you are from a foreign land and you are concerned about international relations, here is what you can do to improve them.

If you are at the grocery store and you're ready to pay for your goods, remember, you have to go to the back of the line. It's a silly custom we have here, but you can't go to the front of the line when there are already people *in* the line. If you violate this custom, it's called "butting in line," and Americans despise a line-butter.

If someone points out your error to you and suggests you do something about it, like move to the back, don't excuse yourself by saying, "It is alright, vee are German." Don't do that. As the former assistant superintendent of Canyonlands National Park and one of my early heroes, Tom Hartman, once said, "We whupped you twice, and we'll whup you again."

Der Kampingplatz ist voll! Ubernachten ist verboten! That's all the German I know; it means, "The campground is full! To stay overnight is forbidden!"

If you are a guy and you intend to mingle with other people in public places, put some clothes on, please. Most of you gentlemen don't have the physique for it anyway. You look ridiculous walking around town with nothing on but a Speedo, a gold chain, a scrubby goatee, and a cowboy hat. Most of you don't even have a tan. Have a heart.

Thank you, and be humble.

The Yupster/Boomer Couple with the Obnoxious Kids in the Back of a BMW

Well, you waited to have kids until you were financially secure. First came the Beemer, then Beavis and Butthead. Now you want to show them the American West, recreating the great trip you remember taking with *your* parents almost thirty years ago.

But you spoiled the little buggers rotten, and now they rarely look up from their Gameboys and PlayStations to check out the scenery. When they do, they articulate the experience as best they can, "This sucks."

Sure, you'd like to kill them. So would we. Even if you think it's the best thing for yourselves, for us, and the future of civilization, you cannot take them down to our world famous Colorado River, put them in a pillowcase, and throw them in the water, the way some Moabites have been disposing of their excess cats for decades. Well, you *could*, but as Richard Nixon once said, "It would be wrong." Besides, you parents spoiled the little greedy monsters in the first place. If anyone should "do the daily" in a pillowcase, it's you.

I am not a parent, but you all must surely agree with me that some of these kids need to be conscripted into military service. If you've brought the kids on vacation, take away their electronic games. Remove from their clutches the personal cell phones. Make them get out of the car and look around. But don't turn them loose on our streets, because we have enough of a gang problem already.

At night, when you've gone down to McStiff's for a wheat ale, don't leave them in the motel room to watch cable television. Get them a copy of *Desert Solitaire* and tell them if they don't read it, you'll bring them over to my house and I'll read *to* them. In fact, I'll read the complete works of Edward Abbey over and over and over until they get it.

Teach your children (and yourselves) humility.

"Our Economic Salvation," the Mountain Biker

If you're a mountain biker, do not tell us you're Moab's economic salvation. You may get a response from some locals like, "Salvation *this*, you bubble-headed Spandex freak!" Some of the old uranium miners carry grudges for many years.

Please keep in mind that, although Moab has been designated the "Mountain Bike Capital of the World," probably less than 20 percent of Grand County's population actually ride a bicycle. Some of us still ride pickup trucks, dip snuff, and spit out the window. A few of our elected officials still think wilderness is a commie trick.

Yet, on any given day in our town half the men seen on the street are wearing brightly colored tights. If you ever feel the desire to blend in, slip a pair of Levis over your Lycra, complain about all those damn espresso shops, and say ugly things about Hillary Clinton or something. The old locals will embrace you and invite you home for supper.

Here's another tip: When you're sitting around the campfire on a Friday night up on the Sand Flats and some of our local boys drive by in their pickups and shout thoughtless epithets at you, don't respond by giving them the finger or mooning them. If you perform such gestures, you need to remember we have some teenage boys in this county who are almost as stupid as you are, and life is cheap out here in the wooly West. The things they'd like to do to your titanium frame bikes defy description.

Like our Speedo-clad European friends, don't wear Lycra if you don't have the body for it. This is true for men and women alike, although men are by far the greater offenders, especially when they have no butt. Have you ever seen a guy with no ass wearing Lycra, with his drawers all droopy in the back? Yes, I am a heterosexual male, and I try not to notice, but it's like police photos of a bad car wreck—you're disgusted, but your morbid curiosity gets the better of you. If you are a buttock-free person, try overalls.

Finally, don't tell us you saved our economy. Be humble.

Miscellaneous Tips

Try to avoid asking stupid questions. Actually, there's one question you should always ask *yourself* before you pose another one to someone else, "Can I figure this out on my own?"

For example, before you ask for directions to the bathroom at the Arches Visitor Center, did you actually make an attempt to look yourself? Did you rotate your head from side to side and look for the international symbols? If you didn't and asked the ranger anyway and she glared coldly, you have no one to blame but yourself.

Have you ever asked, "What time does the wind stop?" There is not a meteorological table that provides that kind of information. It's not like the sunrise and sunset or the tides, Okay?

Unless you want to die an early and painful death, don't ask Pat at the post office if she's posted tomorrow's mail yet. It's doubtful if she'll post tomorrow's mail today. She'll probably post it *tomorrow*. Get it?

Here's another one: Don't go into a Moab restaurant, take over a table or two, and then tell the waitress you don't want to order anything because you brought your own food and merely came inside to get out of the weather. "You know, we're having our picnic inside. It's not *our* fault. No one would tell us when the wind would stop."

Be Humble

This is the key to everything. If I have sounded harsh or somewhat intolerant of tourists, you've misunderstood my intentions. I know how dopey tourists can be because I become a dopey tourist every time I leave home. I've humiliated myself from one end of this country to the other and beyond, in ways I didn't think were possible. I'm only now beginning to appreciate the true value of groveling. Practical experience has taught me that humility is a beautiful thing, and it takes the sting out of stupidity. Humans will forgive damn near anybody for being stupid, if they'll just admit it. It's *arrogant* stupid people, the deadliest combination of all, that make my blood boil.

So the next time you invoke the ire of a Moabite simply because you were confused or just because you've put your brain on hold during summer vacation, do what I did when my own confusion angered a cab driver in New York City. He was about to toss me out the door, when I said, "Look I'm screwed. I'm an idiot. I'm from *Utah*!" His mood changed, his eyes almost glowed with compassion, and he never uttered another harsh word.

With a few modifications, you can save your butt, too. That is, if you have one.

42

Tourists Bite Back: Posts to Arches National Park's Facebook Page, Memorial Day (2015)

Just getting through the park entrance gate during peak times had become a problem by the twenty-first century, and tourists weren't happy about it.

"Got here at 8:05 am just to be told that the park was closed, even though there was a line of cars in the park. Was told they weren't sure if it would reopen at all, if it did it would be late today. Took our chances and just kept driving back and forth on the highway, about 10 minutes later they opened it again and allowed cars in. After 5 minutes the line was long and they closed the entrance again. They definitely need a better system in place, this system is not informative at all for visitors being turned away. Seems to just be causing more traffic problems on the highway with people flipping around back and forth hoping for a chance to get in."

"Thanks for not posting anything about your closure on the highways leading to the park. Drove hours out of our way and the only arches we get to see are the Golden Arches of McDonalds. Run some shuttles. Shitheads!"

PART IV

IMAGINING ARCHES

43

Near Delicate Arch (1979)

José Knighton

José Knighton managed a Moab bookstore and spent years exploring Arches.

Time is indelicate and restless.
Each grain abrades the days of life.
Each sun-borne breeze creases foreheads
or carves its path thru martyred stone.
This stone we name Delicate by kindred fear!
which is the most frail—the most fantastic,
this single seeming weakness of immortal stone
or the mind that wanders Entrada canyons
close to the edge, waiting for thunder
not of sky,
but dying rock?
There is a murmuring deep in the earth,
but the truly wise will never listen.
It is the constant Siren of the soil
calling us back.
Some run along the rim
like lizards—taunting the abyss,
others remain like willows trembling in the shadows.
Both hear the call too loudly.
Here is wisdom!
(something much more delicate)
look,

this sandstone pool
not big enough to drown in
two days away from dust
filled with tadpoles ten days immature
that continue to swim.

44

A Picture is Worth, Maybe, 25 Cents (2011)

David Feela

David Feela is a poet, essayist, newspaper columnist, book collector, and retired teacher. He has traveled and written widely about the Colorado Plateau.

We'd packed everything in the truck and headed out for a fall trip to the Utah canyon country. Usually I forget some back country necessity, so I pulled out of the driveway with that chronic, partially digested feeling, knowing that a few miles down the highway I'd figure out what I'd forgotten. For 20 miles I ticked each item off my mental checklist: Boots, socks, water bottles, maps, sun hats, binoculars, sunblock, pocket knife, two thick comfy towels, and our slick, new national parks pass.

For the first time in our natural history as a couple, my wife and I coughed up the cash to purchase an annual park pass. No more sneaking into our public lands at midnight after the tollbooth has drawn its shades, and no more sneaking out before sunrise while the tollbooth is still dreaming about collecting revenue. Middle age has turned us into staunch supporters of our national parks, and we carry our shiny plastic card everywhere, just in case we come within fifty miles of a national park entrance where we might quickly pull through the gate, flash our card, and congratulate ourselves on saving another ten bucks.

Thirty miles out of town, with the Dove Creek grain elevator punctuating the horizon like an enormous exclamation point, our 10-minute conversation abruptly ended when Pam announced, "I didn't bring the camera."

Damn, I thought, but I didn't say it.

And then I thought, why am I mentally kicking myself? We rarely bring our camera, no matter where we travel, and when we do we forget to use it. In our household the invention of the camera ranks right up there with a shipment of winter clothing to a nudist colony. I mention clothing because the weather was rather chilly, and we'd left home, wearing shorts and t-shirts, hoping to find a quiet niche in the rocks to pretend it was still summer.

I finally admitted to the windshield by way of a reply to Pam's observation, "Neither did I."

We drove a few more miles in silence, crossing the State line into Utah, and our conversation started up again, each of us trying to account for the discomfort we always feel posing before a camera. I could report the entire conversation, but really, that's the business of a tape recorder, and I didn't have one of those either. Let's just say that both of us distrust the way photos fabricate the illusion of a fixed, unchanging world, and we share a sense of diminution when it comes to photographing the landscape around us. I mean, if a picture is really worth a thousand words, why won't people shut up while flipping through their photo albums?

Our drive ended at Arches National Park, and we decided to hike in magnificent weather along a primitive trail that wanders away from the main thoroughfare to Landscape Arch. I still think Delicate Arch is my favorite formation in the entire park, but that image, sadly, is chosen to appear in so many brochures, I figured, what's the use of going there. I can get the same view just by visiting any tourist information stop.

Okay, seriously, I know it's not the same thing, but I swear to much of the camera-toting public we encountered on the trail there's not a lot of difference between experiencing the natural world and appearing with some feature of it prominently displayed behind them. The tendency to pose strikes me as a way to avoid the effort of holding the image in the mind, a means of reducing what inspires us to a convenient postcard.

If primitive people were correct in fearing that cameras steal the soul, then perhaps we've stolen nature's soul carte blanche. We have carved it up into Kodak-sized pieces and sold it to America like Hollywood sells its newest film. Yosemite conjures the image of El Capitan with the moon still visible, only the geyser of Yellowstone rises forever in our minds, and Mesa Verde hangs on to its niche with an endless string of nationally syndicated glossies that appeal to our collective, cliff dwelling memory. We rush out to meet these pictures we remember by RV, camper, and bus, pilgrimage to the site of each photographic shrine, and move on to the next. We seek the truth through our viewfinders and if we get the chance to take the picture, we remain convinced that those fools who cry about a vanishing wilderness have merely run out of film.

Like everyone else, we climbed out of the truck with all the others who parked their cars at the trail head to Landscape Arch. Photo naturalists milled about the parking area, near the restrooms, and formed a short line beside the drinking fountain. Some of them were already pointing their cameras, digitally encrypting massive slabs of rock onto their memory cards so they could carry home a few billion tons of sandstone and load it all effortlessly onto their computers. Clearly, the traditionalists were present, too, with incredibly obscene zoom lenses, tripods, filters, and puffy black bags to pack it all down the trail.

Three groups of hikers in two short miles asked us if we'd take their picture. And please, don't get me wrong: We were happy to help out, but our aim to find a quiet spot and soak up the sun became more and more misdirected. Finally we left the main trail, seeking the less populated primitive route, and wouldn't you know it, another couple waited for us to catch up at the next bend.

"Would you mind..." one of them started to ask, but I interrupted by saying, "There's nothing I'd like better than to take your picture." And I smiled. And they smiled. And I pointed and pushed the little blue button that promptly caused the camera to buzz and whir and shrink its telescoped lens back into the camera.

"I think you just turned it off," the nice gentleman observed.

"Yup," I replied.

The sun was climbing toward noon when the heat would radiate from the rocks in a delicious intensity, so we pushed off. To a photographer, noon light means encountering seriously reduced photographic opportunities, when all those artistic shadows slip under the rocks and the world looks, well...overexposed. To us, though, the world was just coming into focus.

45

Wall Arch (2016)

Rebecca Bailey

Rebecca Bailey is a former NPS ranger, outdoor educator, poet, novelist, and columnist. She has lived and worked in Canyonlands and elsewhere on the Colorado Plateau.

Who knew Entrada Sandstone was detachable?
Only hours before, tourists claimed the shade
to eat chicken sandwiches, Clif bars,
and potato chips, drink Gatorade and H2O.
Now not even a spindle or rib remains
of Wall Arch, just rusty red rock bookending
a deep aquamarine summer sky,
The sudden space feels incomprehensible.
I would like for there to have been a witness,
a ceremony, a Maori bagpiper, perhaps,
or a feathered sturgeon, a female ranger in a top hat,
something as incongruous as the shock
of geologic time collapsed into a few
seconds of thunder on a clear night.
Wall Arch is now merely a fractured picture
of boulder with pine needles;
yet the tree survived. Did a flying nightbird's
eye witness this, or only the solitary pine?
Some night I will go down the closed trail,
lantern in hand, to watch. And listen.
This new place has opened in the universe.
Surely something will come through.

46

Adventure Highway (2012)

Erica Olsen

Erica Olsen does archival and curation work for archaeological museums in the Four Corners region. Her fiction and essays have been widely published.

The approach to Moab from the south: the gigantic earth was Gulliver, strapped down by the grid of roadways and power lines. The mighty red rock suddenly hamstrung, all knees and knuckles. Tyler Swanson was driving in high dudgeon. Lately, dudgeon had become Swanson's mode of being, though he tried to keep it at a low-to-moderate level. Not today. What had happened to Moab? It seemed all motels. On the north side of town, on the way up to Arches, he noticed people pedaling their bikes earnestly on a path that paralleled the highway on the east. If the path had been there before, and he didn't think it had been, it certainly didn't used to be paved. What had happened to dirt?

That ribbon of asphalt—it symbolized all that was wrong with the world. An ever-expanding list that included, among recent items:

- Having been passed over for a job that should by rights have been his
- Having to go on this trip without his girlfriend, Courtney

Swanson had a feeling that things in general had been made easier for people in general, but not for him. Regarding the latter item: Courtney had canceled literally at the last minute, as he was loading gear into the car. One moment he was cheerfully wrangling tarps and lawn chairs, the next her voice was buzzing into his ear the excuse that work was "crazy busy."

He should go, she'd said—of course he should go.

And so he did, resolving to make the best of it. This time, this gift, this Swanson solitaire.

For solitude, Moab in April was, it seemed, exactly the wrong place. The presence of so many determined fun-havers was giving Swanson a jaundiced view of canyon country. Sweating in his vehicle, he waited his turn through the Arches entrance station. Through his lenses (amber, polarized) the heaps of rock looked like so much hamburger. He parked next to a planted island, which a spindly cottonwood shared with some bravely blooming globemallow. On the other side of the parking lot some people were taking photos of the cliffs adjacent to their RV. Maybe this was as far as they were planning to go. To the west, the cliff wall amplified the sound of traffic where the highway climbed out of town. Swanson heard the other inescapable sound, the confirming horn-honk of a car door locking, and groaned.

He'd wanted an adventure, or at least a getaway from the Bay Area winter of endless rain, but he struggled through the new visitor center. The building was very nice, depressingly nice, with its displays of faux sandstone, its lessons on the Entrada and Chinle formations and all the rest. A video screen set into an indoor cliff told Swanson *Congratulations!* He didn't want to know what for. He missed old visitor centers with their quaint dioramas, their dusty specimens of taxidermy and such. The high-gloss treatment here was like a billboard for the real world, which needed no advertisement. It was right there! Out the window! Through the glass, the red cliffs shimmered, a little paler than they were in reality. Inside was a scaled-down version of Delicate Arch that Swanson didn't want to walk through and yet there he was, walking through it. If the outside was hamburger, this sandstone mockup was pink slime, the processed beef that had been so much in the news lately. An indictment of our culture, Swanson thought.

What worried him most was just how many things seemed to him, these days, to be an indictment of our culture. He understood this for what it was, a sign he was middle-aged. Moab, at this time of year, was a veritable slide show of past and present fun he'd inexplicably missed out on.

For him there was the parking lot ordeal of sun block and sun hat and sun shirt.

He drove up the switchbacks of the escarpment, passing the *Gather No Wood in Park* road sign, whose medieval diction he used to alter to *Gather Ye*, then rhetorically inquire, *What about wool? Is wool-gathering allowed?* He passed it with a morose acknowledgment; there was something that used to make him smile.

At the trailhead Swanson overheard a vacation dad lecturing his vacation son, who was maybe nine years old: *When are you going to start acting appropriately?* Which, in context, may well have been a reasonable question, but Swanson glared at the dad, felt for the kid.

He felt for himself, having planned this trip buoyantly for months. But to face facts: Courtney had been questioning the travel arrangements. He'd proposed car camping—air mattresses and bathrooms, with plumbing whenever possible. Her reaction had been less than enthusiastic. He had to admit, now, she'd been giving him signals that she didn't want to go. She was really more of a hotel girl.

He passed a geology class trip from somewhere ridiculously far away, Texas or Tennessee, giving a group thumbs-up to some roadside rock formation.

Spring break.

Swanson headed down the Park Avenue trail then ducked off it at Courthouse Wash. The academic year had not been good to him. He'd put in the time as an adjunct—freshman English, American Studies. Swanson had always been flexible, accommodating—and he had not been selected for an interview. That was a blow. He suspected his colleagues of looking askance at his methodology. His ecocriticism. Swanson had not published, not enough and not well enough; he'd put himself on the fast track to perishing. But he wasn't dead yet! He wanted—he wanted—what? Utah, the geologic opera that used to make what he called (for lack of a better word) his soul feel as big and light as a balloon, wasn't working for him this time. He looked at nature, and he felt nothing. Maybe it happened to everyone. Up the wash, where he'd hoped for tranquility, some boorish idiots, or idiotic boors—no doubt the same ones who'd let their kids scratch their names and the date across the rock of the main trail—were hallooing for the echo.

He hadn't seen her for a few weeks, between his grading and her work schedule. That might mean something. Or nothing—people were busy sometimes. There had been a fight, though. He remembered her angry tears, the queasy feeling that still came over him when he recalled her revelation that she didn't want to settle. He hated that word, settle.

"Settle down?" he'd asked.

"Settle." She added, "It's not fair to *you*."

Yelling and clapping. Were they playing Marco Polo back there?

Swanson slunk away, continued on to the next pullout.

Where, next to an interpretive sign, a ranger was lecturing someone about hiking off trail. The trail itself was quilted with footprints. In his sun-blocking armor, Swanson plodded past a plethora of petrified hoopla.

And then, just like that, he'd had enough.

Enough! he said to himself.

He stuffed the hated nylon sombrero into a trash can and marched himself back to the car.

Before getting on the road he checked for a signal, checked for messages (he had none), then speeddialed Courtney. He got voicemail. "Hey. It's Tyler," he said. "I was just. I was just wondering." He laughed a little laugh. "When are you going to start acting appropriately?"

South of Moab, he was back in starkly empty country, the sage plain interrupted here and there by reefs and fins of exposed rock. Back before it was paved, this road was one of the country's last adventure highways. He'd read that somewhere. That was before his time, of course, but adventure highway was what he wanted. Spaced out on open space, miles and miles of it, he almost missed the turn lane. He braked hard and without signaling swung right onto the turnoff to Newspaper Rock. The RV behind him sounded a bitchy toot of the horn. Swanson wished his fellow humans a fuck-you-very-much. This was exhilarating. Up ahead was a good pullout, with a sturdy pinyon-juniper grove for shade. He set off cross-country in a tonic rage—the ranger the trail the rules—then headed up a pink sand wash.

Out here, he could begin to face facts. What mattered here was life and death, rock and rainfall, the weird-looking cryptogamic crust that Swanson stepped considerately around. Not the romantic travails of a forty-year-old, the humiliation of another middle-aged breakup. Courtney was a few years older than he was, and in the back of his mind he'd assumed that when things went south it would be his doing. (A pretty grad student, a conference fling.) He'd been wrong about that. In her forties, Courtney had started to turn heads. And she was likely not to be there when he returned. She'd said as much the last time they got together, after the holidays. He just hadn't wanted to hear it. The thousand-mile drive had given him ample time to turn her words into something ambiguous, something he could reasonably interpret in his favor.

He hiked hard, feet plowing the thick hot sand, until the voice in his mind quieted and he started to see what was around him, the beautiful world. A phalanx of cliffs glittering through his sunglasses, some unassuming low-growing yellow flowers. *Goosefoot*, he thought; the name came unbidden from some store of knowledge he'd forgotten he had. Feeling heavy, weary, he paused for water and a snack, then gave in to the gravitational tug of the earth. He sat himself down on some Late Triassic. (In relation to Swanson's ability to identify strata, the visitor center had done its work.) A weatherbeaten juniper extended its limbs in fellowship. Some Mormon tea was growing in its shadow, gaunt yet luxuriant.

He stretched himself out on a bench of warm rock for a nap a collared lizard would envy.

He woke up in near-dark, shivering, and the water bottle had rolled away somewhere, and Swanson, who had wanted an adventure, cursed his stupidity.

How far in had he hiked? An hour or two, surely no more than that. Though there may have been some wandering near the end, some wandering concurrent with poetic musings and observings, during which time he may not have paid strict attention to his surroundings. During the time he took to assess the situation the last light vanished from the sky. He was in his technical shorts with the mesh vented panels, and the breeze rattled him. Why hadn't he worn pants? He blinked against the confusing darkness.

His headlamp, of course, was in his car. (He remembered how this trip began, his pride in packing the gear just so. Once he'd gotten on the road it was a mess, of course, his good work undone. Why had he tried so hard in the first place?) The car was at the trailhead, and the trailhead—he did not know where it was.

He fumbled for his cell phone. He could use it to light his way.

He scanned the ground, gray and indistinct, for his own footprints, instructing himself: Don't fall. That was the first rule of hiking, day or night. Swanson set his feet deliberately. Why had he worn sandals? They were like huge flopping rafts, ill-fitting, a stupid choice. His feet chafed, and almost certainly he had blisters. No, the first rule of hiking was Be Not Stupid, and he was violating it by hiking in the dark instead of waiting for daylight. Or waiting for rescue. Not that he needed rescuing. And if he did, how embarrassing would it be to be rescued while wearing technical shorts? He should never have let himself buy them.

Swanson trod stone and sand and cobbles, watchful, mindful of his limitations.

Soon enough, his eyes grew accustomed to the night. The bare rock reflected starlight. The night was full of strangeness. He heard a bird he didn't know. Once he jumped at the appearance of a huge beetle that hovered in the air at knee level, clacking and swaying like some miniature robot drone. He had no idea where in the sky the moon would appear or in what phase it would be, but maybe if the world could pave a bike path from Moab to Arches it could give Swanson the moon. Swanson was not one acquainted with the night but it was remarkably freeing to stride along like this, unhoused. If he'd thought to stick a fleece into his daypack he was sure he could have ridden out the night in comfort. Why had he never taken up backpacking? This was the West, the wild and the free, the unfettered and confident. "You make a left turn at Albuquerque," he proclaimed in the voice of Bugs Bunny.

Swanson fell.

Climbing up a small ledge he was pretty sure he'd descended on his way in, his sandaled foot slipped. He lost his balance and sat back in the air, landing awkwardly on his shoulders on the downslope, legs pedaling. *Bassackwards* was the word for it. It took a few tries before he succeeded in righting himself. Sand and juniper bits in his hair and down his shirt collar. He brushed himself off hurriedly, as if there were an audience to witness his ineptitude and discomfiture and so on. He felt for blood, found his phone, calmed his racing heart.

It was not the end of Swanson.

And then the moon, the kindly moon, came up and saved him, kept him from continuing up the ledge into God knows where. In the moonlight he could see his footprints waffling down the sandy wash—the sandals were new and the tread was clear. He followed them. After an easy walk, he saw the glint of moon on metal: his car.

How long until the car would have been noticed—until he was missed? Swanson felt weepy and indignant. Nobody cared where he was. He drove too fast, crossing the center line on the curves. Once he almost hit a rabbit as it raced in furred desperation across the roadway.

Single and forty, survivor of various ordeals, he turned back onto 191.

Monticello was a scatter of lights, the promise of a meal and a motel, civilization. Swanson felt suddenly, absurdly at home. He'd been there before. Monti*cello* as in cellophane, he thought; not *cello* like the instrument or Thomas Jefferson's house. He could see lights high up on the mountain road, someone else making the long drive into town. Hart's Draw Road, it was called. The bloom of memory seemed wondrous to Swanson, as transient and lovely as spring itself. He slowed to forty-five, and saw the Maverik station on the north side of town.

Where the heck did that *come from?* he thought. It had not been there on his way up just two days before. Lights and angels and restrooms.

He pulled in across an admirably smooth curb cut, parked next to a full-size pickup with Arizona plates. The Maverik was obviously brand new, its expanses of red and black graphic and unspoiled. It was like a child's toy just out of the package, life-size and dazzling. The asphalt was unmarked with wads of gum or sticky pools of spilled diesel. The pumps were a remarkable lineup, newly extruded from the plastic Eden machine and barely touched by human hands.

Swanson went in and found the restroom. He had never imagined that a gas station bathroom could be so pristine. It was a wonder.

In the mirror over the sink he found that he looked no better and no worse than anyone else.

The pickup pulled out while he was in the restroom, leaving Swanson the only customer in the store. He wandered the aisles. He admired the photo murals of mountains and canyons and the disembodied portion of spruce tree and the dummy kayaker suspended in midair. He admired the taxidermy. At the sandwich trough, the choice between turkey and Black Forest ham brought tears to his eyes. He picked up one of each. He picked up potato chips and tortilla chips and honey-roasted cashew nuts and a pickle in a vacuum-sealed bag with a picture of a cartoon pickle on it. He did not stumble, and no one knew what he'd been through.

At the register, he ventured a mild flirtation with the checkout girl. Jolted out of her reverie, she blinked at him in astonishment and wished him a nice day.

Swanson went out to pump his gas. From where he was standing, under the canopy, he could just make out the poster on the video rental kiosk—some movie in which attractive people met, then fell in love. All eyes and lips and hair, and a title whose lettering, at this distance, he couldn't read. He made up his own title. *Maverik: A Love Story*. For the first time in a long time he felt that it wouldn't hurt him to watch something like that.

47

a meeting (2016)

Natasha Sajé

Natasha Sajé is emerita professor of English at Westminster College and a widely published and award-winning poet, cook, food writer, and memoirist.

a meeting
Arches National Park

here where the river flooded and wore
through Jurassic rock a channel
we reconsider empty
from Old English *aemettig* (at leisure)
the "p" a euphonic addition
language and leisure filled
to help us make sense of our senses
as now when in red sand with a dusting of snow
I see the print of my boots
hear the thrum of salt thousands of feet thick
smell sunlight like carbonation in the air
empty of smog
where the stream doesn't have to be here
to be felt

48

The Coyote Clan (1989)

Terry Tempest Williams

Terry Tempest Williams ends this book with thoughts about the nature of Utah's canyon country and the people who love the place.

When traveling to southern Utah for the first time, it is fair to ask if the redrocks were cut would they bleed. And when traveling to Utah's desert for the second or third time, it is fair to assume that they do, that the blood of the rocks gives life to the country. And then after having made enough pilgrimages to the slickrock to warrant sufficient separation from society's oughts and shoulds, look again for the novice you once were, who asks if sandstone bleeds.

Pull out your pocketknife, open the blade, and run it across your burnished arm. If you draw blood, you are human. If you draw wet sand that dries quickly, then you will know you have become part of the desert. Not until then can you claim ownership.

This is Coyote's country—a landscape of the imagination, where nothing is as it appears. The buttes, mesas, and redrock spires beckon you to see them as something other: a cathedral, a tabletop, bears' ears, or nuns. Windows and arches ask you to recall what is no longer there, to taste the wind for the sandstone it carries. These astonishing formations invite a new mythology for desert goers, one that acknowledges the power of story and ritual, yet lies within the integrity of our own cultures. The stories rooted in experience become beads to trade. It is the story, always the story, that precedes and follows the journey.

Just when you begin to believe in your own sense of place, plan on getting lost. It's not your fault—blame it on Coyote. The terror of the country you thought you knew bears gifts of humility. The landscape that makes you vulnerable also makes you strong. This is the bedrock of southern Utah's beauty: its chameleon nature according to light and weather and season encourages us to make peace with our own contradictory nature. The trickster quality of the canyons is Coyote's cachet.

When the Navajos speak of Coyote, they do so hesitantly, looking over their shoulders, checking the time of year so they won't be heard. They know his stories are told only after the first frost and never after the last thaw. Their culture has been informed by Coyote. He is profane and sacred, a bumbler and a hero. He straddles the canyon walls with wild oats in his belly. And they know him by name—Ma'ii, the one never to be taken for granted. They understand his fickle nature, how he seduces fools into believing their own myths, that they matter to the life of the desert.

Coyote knows we do not matter. He knows rocks care nothing for those who wander through them; and yet he also knows that those same individuals who care for the rocks will find openings—large openings—that become passageways into the unseen world, where music is heard through doves' wings and wisdom is gleaned from the tails of lizards. Coyote is always nearby, but remains hidden. He is an ally because he cares enough to stay wary. He teaches us how to survive.

It is Coyote who wanders naked in the desert and leaves his skin on the highway, allowing us to believe he is dead. He knows sunburned flesh is better than a tanned hide, that days spent in the desert are days soaking up strength. He can retrieve his coat and fluff up his fur after a wild day in the wilderness and meet any man, woman, or child on the streets of Moab and seduce them for dinner. Coyote knows it is the proportion of days spent in wildness that counts in urbane savvy.

Coyote's howl above the canyon says the desert may not depend on his life, but his life depends on the desert.

We would do well to listen.

The canyons of southern Utah are giving birth to a Coyote Clan—hundreds, maybe even thousands, of individuals who are quietly subversive on behalf of the land. And they are infiltrating our neighborhoods in the most respectable ways, with their long, bushy tails tucked discreetly inside their pants or beneath their skirts.

Members of the Clan are not easily identified, but there are clues. You can see it in their eyes. They are joyful and they are fierce. They can cry louder and laugh harder than anyone on the planet. And they have enormous range.

The Coyote Clan is a raucous bunch: they have drunk from desert potholes and belched forth toads. They tell stories with such virtuosity that you'll swear you have been in the presence of preachers.

The Coyote Clan is also serene. They can float on their backs down the length of any river or lose entire afternoons in the contemplation of stone.

Members of the Clan court risk and will dance on slickrock as flash floods erode the ground beneath their feet. It doesn't matter. They understand the earth re-creates itself day after day....

ACKNOWLEDGMENTS

Editing an anthology (especially one that takes as long as this did to complete) requires a lot of help: suggestions for writers and pieces, contact information, obtaining permissions, writing pieces from scratch, and more. I am indebted to all those below.

Thanks to those currently or formerly part of the National Park Service at Arches, especially archivist Paula (Peekay) Briggs, who spent hours fetching materials and answering dozens of emails, Diane Allen, Melanie Armstrong, Kate Cannon, Walt Dabney, Nick Eason, Lee Ferguson, Karen Garthwait, Chris Goetz, Paul Henderson, Laura Martin, Mark Miller, the late Lloyd Pierson, Noel Poe, Kaitlyn Thomas, Jim Webster, Sam Webster, Vicki Webster, Mary Wilson, Chris Wonderly, and Christian Wright.

Thanks to the present or former staff at the Moab Museum, including Tara Beresh, John Foster, and Mary Langworthy.

Thanks to the many people of the book who offered contacts, suggestions, and more, including Kirsten Johanna Allen, Charles Finn, José Knighton, Andy Nettell, Ken Sanders, and Ken Wright.

Thanks to Adrian, Tom, and Zane Taylor and Lisa Church at the Moab *Times-Independent,* and Rudy Herndon at the *Moab Sun News.*

Thanks to Clarke Abbey, Wade Allinson, Rebecca Bailey, Jane Beckwith, David Brandt-Erichsen, Gerald Callahan, Gerald Elias, Heila Ershadi, David Feela, Bill Hedden, Kaki Hunter, Eleanor Inskip, Amy Irvine, Len Jenshel, Leslie Kobinsky, Joette Langianese, QT Luong, Tom McCourt, Jeremy Miller, Gary Nabhan, Erica Olsen, David Petersen, the John Pfahl estate, Alice Allred Pottmyer, Raye Ringholz, Jed Rogers, Natasha Sajé, Dave Sakrison, Jim Stiles, Millee Tibbs, Tom Till, Stephen Trimble, Linda Warren, John Weisheit, Brooke Williams, John Williams, Louis Williams, Terry

Tempest Williams, Alan Wilson, and Caroline Wilson, for contacts and also for letting me use their words and images.

Thanks to librarians and archivists at the Delta City Library and the University of Utah's Marriott Library.

Thanks to Betsy Chapoose, Dorena Martineau, and Gideon Two Crow.

Thanks to John Alley, Glenda Cotter, Tom Krause, Steve Mecham, and Jed Rogers at the University of Utah Press.

Thanks to my student research assistants, Sean Lambourne, Walker Sorlie, and Maddie Peters.

Thanks especially to my friends and colleagues, the series editors of these readers, Lance Newman (who I outlasted) and David Stanley, for their sharp editorial eyes and otherworldly patience.

Special thanks to James Swensen, who did yeoman work on the photographs as well as his own fine essay.

And thanks as always to Cheryl Henley, for all the ways she makes my life better.

ARCHES TIMELINE

ca. 323–299 million years ago (MYA): Pennsylvanian period; oldest rocks visible today in Arches. Faulting and subsidence create the Paradox Basin in eastern Utah and western Colorado.

ca. 252–66 MYA: Mesozoic era; seas fill and empty the Paradox, eventually depositing about five thousand feet of salt. Surrounding mountains erode, burying salt under layers of sandstone, including Entrada; fossils are deposited at hundreds of sites in and around Arches.

ca. 70–35 MYA: Laramide Orogeny creates mountains, warps geologic column in Arches, creates anticlines and synclines, makes joints in sandstone layers. Under pressure salt flows, anticlines collapse, and salt partly dissolves, creating Salt Valley and fracturing rock layers above.

ca. 30 MYA: Colorado Plateau begins to rise, water (including the Colorado River) and wind erosion of sedimentary layers above Entrada Sandstone create most features.

ca. 12,000 before the present (BP): First humans, later named Paleo-Indians, arrive in the region.

ca. 8,000–3,000 BP: Hunters and gatherers, later named Archaic people, live in region.

ca. 100–1300 common era (CE): Ancestral Puebloans and Fremont live in region.

ca. 1000 CE: Shoshoneans (including Utes and Paiutes) and Diné begin to live in region.

1765: Juan María Antonio Rivera leads an *entrada* to the south bank of the Colorado River.

1844: Fur trapper Denis Julien carves his name and date, June 9, 1844, in Devil's Garden.

June 1855: The Church of Jesus Christ of Latter-day Saints sends the "Elk

Mountain Mission" to the Spanish Valley south of the Colorado; in September, Indigenous people drive them out.

1870s: Ranchers begin to settle the Spanish Valley and find William Grandstaff and "Frenchie" living in the old Elk Mountain Mission.

1880: Moab post office opens.

1881: William Grandstaff leaves Moab.

1890: Grand County incorporated with Moab as county seat.

1896: Justus Corbin establishes the *Grand Valley Times* newspaper, which becomes today's *Times-Independent.*

1897: Corbin recruits Dr. John Williams as Moab's first doctor.

1898: John Wesley Wolfe and son Fred homestead near Delicate Arch.

1903: Moab is incorporated.

1906–1908: Wolfe's daughter Flora Stanley and her family live with Wolfe.

1906: John and Fred Wolfe build the cabin that still stands.

1910: Wolfes leave arches, sell cabin and land to Thomas Larsen.

1911: Loren L. "Bish" Taylor begins forty-two years of editing *Grand Valley Times*; his descendants run the *Times-Independent* today.

1916: Larsen sells Wolfe cabin and land to J. Marvin Turnbow.

1922: Alexander Ringhoffer and sons explore "Devil's Garden," today called Klondike Bluffs.

Ringhoffer writes Frank Wadleigh of DRGWRR about tourist potential of region.

1923: Wadleigh and photographer George Beam visit "Devil's Garden."

Wadleigh writes NPS Director Steven Mather to suggest the area be made a national park.

1920s: Dr. Laurence M. Gould, geologist, and Dr. Frank Oastler, surgeon and photographer, explore arches and lobby for a park.

1929: President Herbert Hoover designates 4,520 acres as Arches National Monument, in two non-contiguous pieces: the Devil's Garden and The Windows.

J. Marvin Turnbow made first custodian.

An estimated five hundred people visit Arches in 1929.

1930: Moab Lions Club is founded and becomes major booster of Arches.

1933–34: Frank Beckwith leads Arches National Monument Scientific Expedition.

1935: Dalton Wells CCC camp established.

June 15, 1936: Harry Goulding, owner of trading post in Monument Valley, drives first automobile into Arches since it was made a monument.

November 25, 1938: President Franklin D. Roosevelt issues proclamation enlarging Arches National Monument by about thirty thousand acres, including Klondike Bluffs.

1939: The first known record of annual visitation shows 1,835 visitors.

1940: Arches CCC camp established.

1943: Former Dalton Wells CCC camp becomes internment camp for a total of about fifty Japanese-born and Japanese Americans.

1946: Marvin Turnbow's widow Susie sells Wolfe cabin and homestead to Emmett Elizondo, Colorado sheepman.

1948: Emmett Elizondo sells land and Wolfe cabin to NPS, continues to graze until 1982.

1949: Bates Wilson arrives as superintendent of Arches.

July 6, 1952: Charles Steen makes "Mi Vida" uranium strike in Lisbon Valley.

1953: Josef Muench makes photograph of Delicate Arch; featured on the cover of *Life* magazine.

Summers 1956–57: Edward Abbey works as seasonal ranger.

1956: Charles Steen and partners open Uranium Reduction Company's Moab mill (later the Atlas Uranium Mill) on bank of Colorado River, just south of Arches.

Lloyd M. Pierson arrives as Supervisory Ranger.

August 1958: First roads in Arches are paved, new entrance dedicated.

1959: Arches Visitor Center opens. Roads and visitor center are part of NPS's "Mission 66."

July 22, 1960: President Dwight D. Eisenhower issues proclamation reducing Monument by 4,240 acres for a total of 34,010 acres.

1962: Annual visitation tops one hundred thousand for the first time.

1964: Canyonlands National Park is created; Bates Wilson promoted to Superintendent of Canyonlands, Arches, and Natural Bridges.

Mitch Williams founds Tag-a-Long Tours, one of Moab's first "adventure tourism" companies.

1968: Edward Abbey's *Desert Solitaire: A Season in the Wilderness* is published.

1969: President Lyndon Johnson expands Arches by 48,943 acres for a total of 82,953 acres, including more of the Salt Valley.

November 12, 1971: President Richard Nixon signs law establishing Arches National Park, subtracting 9,574 acres.

1972: Bates Wilson retires to ranch in Professor Valley.

1973: Annual visitation exceeds two hundred and fifty thousand for the first time.

1975: Wolfe Ranch and surrounding complex listed as "historic district" on the National Register of Historic Places.

April 1980: Vandals badly damage "Moab Panel," petroglyphs and pictographs believed to have been created by Ancestral Puebloan, Fremont, and Barrier Canyon peoples.

1982: Grazing phased out in Arches; some trespass continues.

1983: Bill and Robin Groff open Rim Cyclery; first mountain bikes begin to appear in Moab.

1984: Atlas Mill closes.

1986: Desert Bighorn sheep transplanted from Canyonlands to Arches.

1988: Annual visitation tops five hundred thousand for the first time.

March 14, 1989: Jim Stiles, former Arches National Park ranger, publishes first *Canyon Country Zephyr.* On the same day, Edward Abbey dies in Tucson.

1994: Beginning of permit system for Fiery Furnace visitors.

1995: Twenty-foot slab falls from Landscape Arch.

October 30, 1998: President Bill Clinton signs bill enlarging Arches National Park by 3,140 acres, including the drainages of Lost Spring Canyon, Fish Seep Draw, and parts of upper Salt Wash.

December 3, 1998: gas pipeline explodes one-half mile north of Visitor Center; four injured.

August 4, 2008: Wall Arch collapses.

2009: Moab Uranium Mill Tailings Remedial Action (UMTRA) project begins to move tailings from the former Atlas Mill to a site near Crescent Junction.

2010: Annual visitation tops one million for the first time.

2013: Utah Office of Tourism begins "Mighty 5" campaign, advertising Arches, Bryce Canyon, Canyonlands, Capitol Reef, and Zion National Parks nationally and internationally.

2016: Annual visitation tops 1.5 million for the first time.

2021: Annual visitation sets a record: 1,806,865.

2022: Arches begins pilot timed entry for peak hours and season.

FURTHER READING

Abbey, Edward. *Confessions of a Barbarian: Selections from the Journals of Edward Abbey.* Edited by David Petersen. Boston: Little, Brown, 1994.

Amundson, Michael A. *Yellowcake Towns: Uranium Mining Communities in the American West.* Boulder: University Press of Colorado, 2004.

Barnes, F. A. *Geology of the Moab Area.* Moab: Canyon Country Publications, 1993.

Cahalan, James M. *Edward Abbey: A Life.* Tucson: University of Arizona Press, 2001.

Childs, Craig. *Tracing Time: Seasons of Rock Art on the Colorado Plateau.* Salt Lake City and Torrey: Torrey House Press, 2022.

Cuch, Forrest S. *A History of Utah's American Indians.* Logan: Utah State Division of Indian Affairs, 2003.

Firmage, Richard A. *A History of Grand County.* Salt Lake City: Utah State Historical Society, 1996.

Fradkin, Philip L. *Fallout: An American Nuclear Tragedy.* Tucson: University of Arizona Press, 1989.

Gómez, Arthur R. *Quest for the Golden Circle: The Four Corners and the Metropolitan West, 1945–1970.* Lawrence: University Press of Kansas, 2000.

Grand Memories. Grand County, Utah: Daughters of Utah Pioneers, 1972.

Hoffman, John F. *Arches National Park: An Illustrated Guide and History.* San Diego: Western Recreational Publications, 1981.

Jones, Kevin T. *A Quick Trip to Moab: Insurrection in the Wilderness.* Kevin T. Jones, 2022.

Knighton, José. *Coyote's History of Moab.* Moab: Compost Press, 1994.

Lincoln, M. L., and Diane Sward Rapaport, eds. *Wrenched from the Land: Activists Inspired by Edward Abbey.* Albuquerque: University of New Mexico Press, 2020.

Lohman, S. W. *The Geologic Story of Arches National Park.* United States Geological Survey Bulletin 1393. Washington, DC: U.S. Government Printing Office, 1975.

McCourt, Tom. *The Moab Story: From Cowpokes to Bike Spokes.* Boulder, CO: Johnson Books, 2007.

Nabhan, Gary Paul, and Caroline Wilson. *Canyons of Color: Utah's Slickrock Wildlands.* New York: Tehabi Books, 1995.

Newell, Maxine. *A Story of Life at Wolfe Ranch.* Moab, UT: Canyonlands Natural History Association, 1980.

Peck, Steven L. *The Scholar of Moab.* Torrey: Torrey House Press, 2011.

Quintano, Jen Jackson. *Blow Sand in His Soul: Bates Wilson, the Heart of Canyonlands.* Friends of Arches and Canyonlands Parks, Bates Wilson Legacy Fund, 2014.

Schaafsma, Polly. *Indian Rock Art of the Southwest.* Santa Fe: School of American Research, 1980.

The Southwest of Josef Muench: The Photography of Josef Muench, from the pages of Arizona Highways. Phoenix: Arizona Highways, 1974.

Tanner, Faun McConkie. *The Far Country: A Regional History of Moab and LaSal, Utah.* Salt Lake City: Olympus Publishing Company: 1976.

Till, Tom. *In the Land of Moab: Photographs of a Canyon Wilderness.* Moab, UT: Fable Valley Publishers, 2001.

SOURCES AND PERMISSIONS

Abbey, Edward. "Cliffrose and Bayonets." In *Desert Solitaire: A Season in the Wilderness*, 22–38. New York: Simon and Schuster, 1968. Reprinted by permission of Don Congdon Associates, Inc. © 1968 by Edward Abbey, renewed 1996 by Clarke C. Abbey.

Abbey, Edward. "The First Morning." In *Desert Solitaire: A Season in the Wilderness*, 1–7. New York: Simon and Schuster, 1968. Reprinted by permission of Don Congdon Associates, Inc. © 1968 by Edward Abbey, renewed 1996 by Clarke C. Abbey.

Allred, B. W. *The Life of a Horse and Buggy Stage Line Operator*. Falls Church, Virginia: The Potomac Corral of the Westerners, 1972. Reprinted by permission of Allred family.

Anderson, Joseph C. "Geological Reconnaissance in the Arches National Monument." Office of the Chief Scientist. Department of Interior. National Park Service, 1934. Accession no. 01-ARCH-34A-01059, ARCH 3324. Southeast Utah Group Archives, National Park Service.

Bailey, Rebecca. "Wall Arch." Reprinted by permission of the author.

Beck, D. Elden. "Arches National Monument Natural History Survey," 1947. Southeast Utah Group Archives, National Park Service.

Beckwith, Frank A. "17-Year-Old Youth Finds Dinosaur Bones While Herding Cows: Further Rich Paleontological Deposits Discovered in Arches National Monument Area." Moab *Times-Independent.* February 1, 1934. Reprinted by permission of Moab *Times-Independent.*

Beckwith, Frank A. "Arches National Monument Scrapbook," 1933, 1934. J. Willard Marriott Digital Library. The University of Utah. https://collections.lib.utah.edu/ark:/87278/s6b884bj. Reprinted by permission of Jane Beckwith.

Breed, Jack. "Utah's Arches of Stone." *National Geographic Magazine* (August 1947): 173–192.

Callahan, Gerald N. "Almost Like Dancing." In *River Odyssey: A Story of the Colorado Plateau*, 45–55. Niwot: University Press of Colorado, 1998. Reprinted by permission of the author.

Correspondent Todd. "Arched Entrance Arches Eyebrows." *Stinking Desert Gazette.* vol. 1, No. 6. January 1987.

Feela, David. "A Picture is Worth, Maybe, 25 Cents." In *How Delicate These Arches: Footnotes from the Four Corners.* Durango, CO: Raven's Eye Press, 2011. Reprinted by permission of the author.

Hamilton, Bruce. "Edward Abbey: Druid of the Arches." *High Country News.* March 27, 1989. https://www.hcn.org/issues/21.6/edward-abbey-druid-of-the-arches. Reprinted by permission of *High Country News.*

Hoffman, John F. "Devil's Garden: The Case of the Perambulating Place-Name or, How Arches Became Part of the National Park System." In *Arches National Park: An Illustrated Guide and History*, 63. San Diego: Western Recreational Publications, 1981.

Irvine, Amy. "The First Morning." In *Desert Cabal: A New Season in the Wilderness*, 4–10. Salt Lake City, Torrey, and Moab: Torrey House Press and Back of Beyond Books, 2018. Reprinted by permission of Torrey House Press.

Knighton, José. "Near Delicate Arch." In *Sandstone.* Salt Lake City: Compost Press, 1979. Reprinted by permission of the author.

Langworthy, Mary. "William Grandstaff, African-American Frontiersman." Adapted from "Tracing the History of Black Frontiersman William Grandstaff, " Moab Museum blog, March 31, 2021. https://moabmuseum.org/william-grandstaff/. Reprinted by permission of the author.

McCourt, Tom, and Wade Allinson. "Quit-Sub-Soc-Its." In *The Elk Mountain Mission: A History of Moab, Mormons, The Old Spanish Trail and the Sheberetch Utes, 1854–1855*, 91–96. Price, UT: Southpaw Publications, 2017. Reprinted by permission of the authors.

National Park Service. "Arches National Park Superintendents' Reports," 1941, 1945, 1947, 1950, 1954. ARCH 1860, Series 1, folders 2, 6, 8, 11, 15. Southeast Utah Group Archives, National Park Service.

National Park Service. "Commendations and Complaints." Accession no. ARCH 1860, A3415/3615, Box 1, Folder 43 (1978); Accession no. ARCH 1860, A3415/A36, Box 1, Folder 49 (1987). Southeast Utah Group Archives. National Park Service.

National Park Service. "Elephant Butte trail registry," 2009–2011. Southeast Utah Group Archives, National Park Service.

National Park Service. Memorandum, Acting Superintendent, Canyonlands, to Regional Director, Southwest Region. "Town meeting on extension of Arches boundary—February 10, 1969." Southeast Utah Group Archives, National Park Service.

Olsen, Erica. "Adventure Highway." In *Recapture and Other Stories*, 5–16. Torrey, UT: Torrey House Press, 2012. Reprinted by permission of Torrey House Press.

Poe, Noel. "Dealing with Cremains." Reprinted by permission of the author.

Ringhoffer, Alexander. "To Department of Interior, January 28, 1928." Accession no. ARCH 1860, Box 6, Folder 4. Southeast Utah Group Archives, National Park Service.

Ringholz, Raye. "Bonanza at Big Indian." In *Uranium Frenzy: Saga of the Nuclear West*, 57–70. Logan, UT: Utah State University Press, 2002. Reprinted by permission of the author.

Rison, Esther Stanley. "Wolfe Ranch Memories." *Wolfe Ranch Historic District Collection*. Accession no. ARCH 1800, Series 1. Southeast Utah Group Archives, National Park Service.

Sajé, Natasha. "a meeting." Reprinted by permission of the author.

Sanders, Ken. "The Pasty White Shellfish Comes to Arches National Park." Reprinted by permission of the author.

Sloan, Tom. "New Arches Opposed (?)." *San Juan Record.* April 14, 1977. Reprinted by permission of *San Juan Record.*

Stiles, Jim. "Ken Sleight Remembers: Arches." February 1, 2016. *Canyon Country Zephyr.* February/March 2016. Reprinted by permission of the author.

Stiles, Jim. "Quiet Times at Arches National Monument." October 1, 2013. *Canyon Country Zephyr,* October/November 2013. Reprinted by permission of the author.

Stiles, Jim. "The 'Stabilization' of Delicate Arch." December 1, 2015. *Canyon Country Zephyr.* December/January 2016. Reprinted by permission of the author.

Stiles, Jim. "Tourists in the Vortex." In *Brave New West: Morphing Moab at the Speed of Greed,* 137-50. Tucson: University of Arizona Press, 2007. Reprinted by permission of the author.

Stoffle, Richard, Evelyn Pickering, Katherine Brooks, Christopher Sittler, and Kathleen Van Vlack. "Arches National Park Ethnographic Overview and Assessment." Tucson: Bureau of Applied Research in Anthropology. University of Arizona, 2016. Southeast Utah Group Archives, National Park Service.

Swensen, James. "*Life* Comes to Arches: Josef Muench's 1954 Photograph of Delicate Arch, Utah." Reprinted by permission of the author.

Till, Tom. "Tom Till's Arches." Reprinted by permission of the author.

Travers, Doug. To Superintendent Arches National Monument, September 23, 1969. Accession no. ARCH 1860. Southeast Utah Group Archives, National Park Service.

Webster, Jim. "Where There's a Will, There's a Way." Reprinted by permission of the author.

Webster, Sam. "Mountain Lion." Reprinted by permission of the author.

Williams, Brooke. "The Colorado: Archetypal River." In Hal Crimmel, ed., *Desert Water: The Future of Utah's Water Resources,* 203–217. Salt Lake City: University of Utah Press, 2014. Reprinted by permission of the author.

Williams, Mitchell M. "Mitchell M. 'Mitch' Williams Oral History." Dan O'Laurie Museum of Moab/Grand County Historical Preservation Committee, 2004. Reprinted courtesy of Moab Museum. Southeastern Utah Society of Arts and Sciences.

Williams, Terry Tempest. "The Coyote Clan." © 1989 by Terry Tempest Williams. In *Red: Passion and Patience in the Desert,* 23–26. Vintage, 2002. © 2001, 2002 by Terry Tempest Williams. Originally published in slightly different form by Peregrine Smith, Layton, Utah. Used by permission of Brandt & Hochman Literary Agents, Inc. All rights reserved.

Williams, Terry Tempest. "Winter Solstice at the Moab Slough." © 1993 by Terry Tempest Williams. In *An Unspoken Hunger: Stories from the Field,* 61–65. Vintage, 1995. Originally appeared in *Three Essays: Bill McKibben, Terry Tempest Williams, William Least Heat Moon.* Nature Conservancy, 1993. Used by permission of Brandt & Hochman Literary Agents, Inc. All rights reserved.

Wilson, Alan "Tug." Video Oral History Interview by Chris Goetze. August 5–6, 2012. Transcribed by Brittney Phetchamphone. Southeast Utah Group Archives, National Park Service.

Wilson, Caroline. Video Oral History Interview by Joette Langaniese. 2012. Southeast Utah Group Archives, National Park Service.

Winslow, Arthur. "A Natural Bridge in Utah." *Science*. New Series, vol. 7 no. 173 (April 22, 1898), 557–558.